THE PHENOMENOLOGY OF RELIGION

BOOKS BY EDWARD J. JURJI

Published by The Westminster Press®

The Phenomenology of Religion
The Middle East: Its Religion and Culture

THE PHENOMENOLOGY OF RELIGION

by

Edward J. Jurji

THE WESTMINSTER PRESS

PHILADELPHIA

LIBRARY OF CONGRESS CATALOG CARD NO. 63-12594

PUBLISHED BY THE WESTMINSTER PRESS®
PHILADELPHIA 7, PENNSYLVANIA

PRINTED IN THE UNITED STATES OF AMERICA

CONTENTS

PREFACE

THE HISTORY of man is inseparable from the history of religion. That dictum of Mr. Justice Hugo L. Black of the Supreme Court challenges our concern with man's religions. This book on the phenomenology of religion is a modest attempt to meet such a challenge. In contrast to much wrestling in the field, the present inquiry takes the essence of religion for its point of departure.

Briefly, the phenomenology of religion, conceived here, is the objective descriptive analysis of religious essence as it displays itself on the world stage. Although the volume springs from this central motif, certain peripheral matters unavoidably insinuate themselves into the presentation. With the inclusion of illustrative data no claims to finality should be read into the book's organizational design. Suffice it if the methodology succeeds in awakening more perceptive vigor and more mature perspective in the reader.

In keeping with the above format, the question of truth and validity is never far removed from one's consciousness. Preference for cherished beliefs will inevitably assert itself. In particular, the extraordinary character of Christianity, along with a certain irreducible core of other religious types, tends to demand wholehearted allegiance. Yet primary and ultimate as these issues may be, they are not raised here along the lines of an intransigent apologetic. In a prior work, the author devoted serious thought to the problem of a Christian interpretation of religion.

What the present phenomenology seeks to discover is precisely how a given religion exhibits itself in authentic records, historic settings, and career of founder, saint, and philosopher. Further disclosures are sought in sacred text, symbol, and doctrine, in piety, in social structure, and, above all, in religion's idea of the holy and its expression of faith. The treatment relies upon extensive scholarly research supplemented by on-the-spot observation. Living folkways, mythology, and popular epic, no less than festival and sociopolitical pattern, have been examined in their Western, Near Eastern, and other environments. For the benefit of the general reader, foreign words in this text follow familiar American usage rather than the more technical systems of transliteration.

In India investigation of ritual and cult and the study of devotional manifestations at holy city and in temple worship have been undertaken. There, before the illusion of friendship with China collapsed, the author prosecuted in 1960, a project broadly designated as " Comparative Religion and Modern Thought." A Fulbright Award enabled him to carry out research in association with the Department of Philosophy, University of Madras, to which he was accredited as a Senior Research Scholar. He owes a heavy debt to colleagues in Asia and Africa, Europe and the Americas, whose writings have opened up the scope of religious phenomenology in its national, social, and theological dimensions as well as its relevance to the history of religions.

I am especially grateful, moreover, to President James I. McCord, of Princeton Theological Seminary, and to the Board of Trustees, for a sabbatical leave, which offered an opportunity for an around-the-world exploration of religious phenomenology at close range.

Hosts of students across the years furthered knowledge of alternative cultures and other religions. Noteworthy among these were the contributions of Dr. Robert Burns Davidson, Beirut, Lebanon; Dr. Richard Min-jui Chen, formerly of China; and Dr. Walter Bonar Sidjabat, of Indonesia. Inestimable, too, was assistance rendered by Dr. Joseph Harry Haines, Malaya, now of the World Council of Churches, Geneva, Switzerland; Dr. Solomon Era Quila, the Philippine Islands; Bhikku N. X. Bao, An Quang Buddhist Institute, Saigon, Vietnam; Prof. John H. Watson, Victoria, Australia; and Prof. Alfred A. Schlorholtz, Forman Christian College, Lahore, West Pakistan.

In preparation of the manuscript, the reading of proof, and the compilation of the footnotes and index I am most thankful to my wife, Ruth, for competent criticism and sound judgment. Dr. Willard G. Oxtoby, Faculty of Divinity, McGill University, offered expert advice and greatly facilitated textual revision.

To all these, as well as the officers and staff of The Westminster Press, deep appreciation is hereby recorded.

E. J. J.

Princeton, N.J.

INTRODUCTION: THE SCOPE AND RELEVANCE OF RELIGIOUS PHENOMENOLOGY

THE WORD " phenomenon " has acquired a meaning distinctively historical and empirical in import. It conjures up the facts disclosed through appearance and manifestation. Yet the precise connotation of the term will vary in line with the particular science or philosophy involved.

In the realm of religion, phenomenology denotes an order of attested spiritual manifestations as well as a body of verifiable doctrines and persuasions. Its standards include an objective description of realities and a systematic evaluation in keeping with what primary sources reveal.

As regards symbols and rites, phenomenology invokes the affirmations of engaged believers. Meticulously, it endeavors to formulate judgments that correspond with a devotee's conception of the truth. Its object is to arrive at a solid understanding of the facts, valid inasmuch as it represents an approximation of that which displays itself. In other words, it seeks to depict with fidelity and accuracy the essence of a given religion under study. In the normal course of critical research, due cognizance is taken of whatever seems meaningful regarding all religions on the world stage.

This scientific method which views religion as a phenomenon bids fair to open up new vistas of comprehension. Its approach to the spiritual life relies on the assumption that all meaning owes its source to an intent of consciousness. It further implies that intimations of the spirit are just gestures if severed from such motives as impel them.

Conceived as a scientific discipline, the phenomenology understood here is by no means an unconditional surrender to alien doctrines. Where we no longer desire to restrain profound convictions, these may be conveniently introduced in parentheses. The integrity of one's own commitment is thus upheld. Although it may figuratively stand in suspended animation, our personal involvement in religious essence is thereby established beyond any shadow of doubt. Deep insights in the pilgrimage of others call for sympathetic evaluation even where outright approval is held in abeyance.

Equation of truth with meaning is not in any sense contemplated. To describe a phenomenon dispassionately is not a token of endorsement. Amid a variety of settings, one begins to discover the contours of incisive meaning in many structures of faith. The task is not unlike that of a trustworthy and deft translator.

In a passion to reproduce with adroit precision the thought and spirit of a particular author, a competent translator will be exacting yet judicious. There is even more need for being so where he is least disposed to credit the viewpoint expressed. At some subsequent stage, he might emerge as judge qualified perhaps to advance an opinion on the merits of the case. For the moment, however, the loyalty of a true friend must be maintained.

But the task of the phenomenologist is never easy. His is a scholarly assignment, self-imposed and beset by insuperable obstacles. What stance should a scholar assume in a world where men are moved by a seemingly infinite variety of religious experience and motivation? Surely indifference under such circumstances will profit him little.

An intolerant individual comprehends only what he has in advance embraced. Instead of such narrow provincialism, there is a path of comprehensive sympathy. It inspires a willingness to be a genuine participant in the agonizing quests of others. It is a free and open determination to be so involved before any serious thought of conversion is entertained. Be it religious or humanist, all dialogue tends nonetheless toward conversion. Prior understanding, however, is an unalterable requirement.

In what follows, this chapter will try to implement the above theoretical design along four principal lines. In the first place, a central thesis will be introduced in terms of a basic religious phenomenology. Secondly, the idea of the holy will be set in proper perspective. In turn this will stress the scope of phenomenology, laying bare the broad dimensions of the work. Thirdly, attention will be drawn to the relevance of phenomenology to the history of religions. Fourthly, such relevance is made more vivid in its applicability to the exposition of the great religions forming the core of Part Two in the text.

I

A thesis undergirds the investigation that the book presents. Steeped in nature, molded by culture, and sharpened by intuition as well as environment, the phenomenon of religion manifests a transcendent, existential significance. Religion is simply irreducible to what are merely functional and traditional attributes of society.

Religious essence is technically known as the numinous. Such an essence is geared to the idea of the holy. Stripped of this essence, religion is little more than sounding brass. How common, however, is reduction of the holy to some sacred category. Its dissipation in worldly instrumentalities and secular concerns follows in neat order.

Implicit in this central thesis is the school of phenomenology of which Edmund Husserl (1859–1938) is the chief expositor. Phenomenology, in his view, was the rigid descriptive analysis of "that which displays itself." We see the object as "essence" or *eidos.*[1] Husserl's method was applied to religion by Rudolf Otto (1869–1937) in his well-known *Idea of the Holy.*[2] The present work is an attempt to develop further Otto's thesis of the holy or numinous in all religions. It will also seek to relate this to the many manifestations of religious faith in the world today.

Such a concern with religion is not merely an endeavor to isolate and catalog man's multiple outlooks on mystery. On the one hand, religion is inherent in human behavior at its ordinary and sublime levels. On the other, it is ultimate to the deep thirsts and longings of spirit and mind. Real religion is not just an expression of society, a symptom of sickness in the soul. Religion is hardly ever at its best as adjunct to national stature, worldly power, or glory of culture.

[1] Edmund Husserl, *Cartesian Meditations: An Introduction to Phenomenology,* tr. by Dorion Cairns (Martinus Nijhoff, The Hague, 1960), pp. 69–72. See Herbert Spiegelberg, in Marvin Farber, ed., *Philosophical Essays in Memory of Edmund Husserl* (Harvard University Press, 1940), pp. 86 ff.; Marvin Farber, *The Foundations of Phenomenology* (Harvard University Press, 1943), pp. 203, *passim.*

[2] *Das Heilige* (C. H. Beck, München, 1936), Eng. tr. by John W. Harvey (Humphrey Milford: Oxford University Press, London, 1933).

This numinous is in all religions. It manifests itself to man in a unique way that he can apprehend by his religious faculty or consciousness. It is quite different from what the sacred is usually interpreted to be. This general religious consciousness, or intuition, manifests itself in many different ways, in history and in contemporary forms, individual and social. To find the essence of religion beneath various religions is to further mutual understanding and appreciation. What is even more important, it is to further knowledge of the truth.

Religious phenomenology demonstrates that primitive, folk, and world religions live through the stress and strain of interaction with law and ethics. They are quickened through ritual, social change, and historical interpenetrations.

The idea of God is represented in this text through documentation in several religious traditions. Inspired by its own idea of God, each tradition develops its characteristic attitude toward other faiths. These attitudes might in certain cases crystallize in methodologies for structuring the history of religions. Such a methodology might also serve in correlation of data drawn from the original and classical sources.

Investigation and analysis make it abundantly clear that this phenomenology serves admirably well for treatment of the great religions of the world. It affords direct and intimate encounter with religions reared in India. With extraordinary depth and clarity it discloses the caliber of religion that arose in the Near East. Those two ancient cradles of religion and civilization indeed shed light on the problem of genesis. Such a contact with the history of religion at the core proves decisive. It illumines our awareness of stages traversed by primitivism. How vividly it captures, moreover, the image of high religion.

Rivals of such living faith are carefully identified and squarely confronted. They include secularism, scientism, and humanism, as well as such variants as nationalism, historicism, and communism. Yet no responsible scholar seriously lays claim to mastery over the entire terrain of religious phenomena and their antithetical rivals. Instances of what really matters are, however, cited. An openness to whatever yields deeper understanding should govern and integrate research. Religious essence, social change, and dynamism are the subjects of study whereas historical criticism and anthropology are disciplinary methods. Upon these subjects and methods the norms of religious phenomenology are based.

The ideal espoused is not necessarily that of a generalist. It is, rather, an ideal in close rapport with the specialist. A sober specialist must soon realize, however, that to spell out everything is to obscure history's message. Rarely does one discharge an obligation adequately if he chooses to divulge all there is to say. This is particularly true in the history of religions. For there is a given essence here that defies our mortal preoccupation with finality.

The primary aim is to elucidate the phenomena of religion in a manner conducive to communication and coordination. Concentration on major problems and criteria is an attempt the more effectively to achieve that aim.

II

The reality of the holy, we surmised earlier, is paramount in our confrontation with religious phenomenology. Such a reality all too often is reduced, however, to some notion of the sacred. Man is prone to recognize in an experience of the holy perhaps the illusory character of his own frailty. Or he might conversely exult in an experience of ecstasy. Perchance he will imagine himself lifted up on the wings of faith.

In response to confession of sin and guilt, an assurance of pardon is received. Power to forget past foibles and wrongs is instilled within. The sinner is thus set free. From forebodings of doom and disaster, the conscience is delivered. High religion thus tends to isolate the individual. He is set face to face with the ultimate ground of being. Such an ultimate may be a god he learns to adore. Adoration is not primarily a corollary of ritual. It is, rather, an outpouring of the creature before the creator.

Hence the holy being is inwardly perceived. This constitutes a challenge to the self. From the outset, the holy is hardly ever manifest as visible in form. It is seen with the eye of faith. Less is it perceived through ceremonial, more in a serene orientation of personality. Not uncommonly therefore the holy is squeezed into the dimension of the sacred. It may in fact denote such objects of deep longing as are external to religion. That which sums up life's ambition comes to be esteemed as sacred. Held sacred, too, might be whatever is construed as vital to total existence. Supreme values, venerable persons, memorial objects, symbols of eternity, the goals for which one will hazard dear life, all these occasionally assume prerogatives of the sacred.

A singular touchstone enables the believer to draw a line of demarcation between the sacred and mundane. Sacred is that thing, idea, or person to which one defers in all matters of ethics and principle. It is that which defies all attempts at probing. Doubt and sheer criticism scarcely ever succeed in annihilating the sacred in man's conscience. Nor is it in this sense vulnerable either to repudiation or to betrayal.

Contemporary Western civilization is to a bewildering degree engaged in a radical transvaluation of the sacred. Supplanting the traditional sacred of religion are secular, lay, and humanist norms. This is generally a transaction of massive proportions. It is not at all clear whether such improvised norms are real and viable. For even where radical standards and norms prevail, a stubborn religious judgment on life persists. The gods may well disappear. But temple arches remain. Longings that once erected the temples have not deserted the soul of man.

What maximal aspirations mark the religious conscience? Is it not to relate itself to its principal source in union and communion? Such is not a mere affinity through observance of ethical standards and revealed verities. Nor can it be a unity merely corroborated through proof and judgment. It is a nearness to the divine implicit in more than outward expressions of faith. Religious union and communion with ultimate reality are governed by an act of utmost complexity: an infinitely ennobling experience for which the expression " love of God " serves as symbol.

Definition of such love along conventional lines is never worthy. Genuine love is not an outcome of success, nor equivalent to it. There can be a practical and disciplined life, as in proverbial Pharisaism, without this kind of love. In one odd moment, however, the order of love under discussion redeems what a whole lifetime squandered. In other words, genuine love transcends the dimension of both wisdom and empiricism. Yet in personality, love reaches a depth that the self never quite knows how to fathom. Nor is self ever quite certain whether it initiates or merely annexes such love.

Hence this definition of religious essence: love and faith toward the holy, the two in the state of conjugal interaction. So inextricably related are these two, no one knows which precedes. Faith is initiated by the love it instigates. An intellectual inquiry is in order. Is the religious conscience, to which the above essence is applied, an illusion? Are Feuerbach and Marx right in the assumption that the religious conscience in the last analysis projects nothing save itself?

A perfectly human self-adoration stands unmistakable. A more apt expression of man's obsession with himself and his handiwork is hard to seek. How he revels in projecting himself to fanciful heights and realms of splendor! Even when man adores Deity, more often than not he tends to esteem his own creatureliness. Such anthropocentrism indeed earns the approval of psychology. It does not stand well, however, with a religious conscience it tends to mute. It renders growth in grace null and void. Flagrant in our era, it relies all too heavily on the one-sided data of anthropology.

Apart from religious conscience, however, intercourse with the source of being is inconceivable. The irony of it all comes to the forefront when the religious conscience strikes a compromise with imperfection. Ambiguity is glossed over as guilt is covered up. The conscience might even flatter itself on having resolved standing problems. Such deviation erodes the dynamic quality of religion, vitiating its purificatory character.

Before us arises a religious phenomenology wherein theory and practice are paired together. On the one hand, concern with the numinous, the idea of the holy, and religious essence, and, on the other, impressive evidence derived from historical settings, those are two orders that prove complementary the one to the other. Illustrative of such scope are the three immediately following chapters. These are intended to shed some light on the vast implications of the subject.

Thus Chapter 1 helps fix the gaze on the American, Western scene; under the rubric " Religion and the Stature of Nations," heeding a well-known advice, the effort is made to start where we are. Chapter 2 turns to the origins, history, and continuity of things religious; under the title " How Religions Live " answers are sought to questions that primitive and advanced religions pose. In Chapter 3, " The Idea of God and the History of Religions," thought moves within a strictly theological frame of reference. Such is the primary thrust of Part One in a book that sets out to depict religious phenomenology in essence and in its concrete manifestations.

III

In sketching the chief problem broached in the volume, we must move on from the scope of religious phenomenology to the method it proposes as relevant for exploration of the history of religions.

The history of religions has rather tardily attained scientific stature. It did not come to age till about the turn of the century. Few will contest today its right to exist. Its long strides and remarkable advance prove it more than vindicates a capacity to fill a void. Controversy attending its coming to maturity centered in two dissimilar camps: agnosticism and theology. As a rule creedal conflicts did not figure as burning issues.

If the history of religions declines the role of handmaiden to theology, it is not because the latter is regarded as adversary. The existence of boundary lines must be conceded. However, encouragement of cross-fertilization between two fields of study is not the signal for domination of one over the other. This is a delicate matter that involves the systematic theologian more than it does the historian of religions. The latter happens to embrace the history of theology, Christian and otherwise, within the scope of his own cardinal areas.

The historian of religions arrogates no authority to brief the theologian on conclusions to be reached. In return he expects that theological correlation of research shall not take for granted findings in the history of religions. What is even more crucial, he trusts such findings no longer will be subject to a priori judgment.

Like any other science in the formative stage, the history of religions is constrained to abide by a clear-cut methodology. It must steer its course and define terms in relation to collateral fields. Indeed the study of the world's religions may be entered through different gates. An eminent contemporary master in this field of knowledge, Raffaele Pettazzoni,[3] of the University of Rome, has defined

[3] See his *Essays on the History of Religions* (E. J. Brill, Leiden, 1954); and *The All-Knowing God* (Methuen & Co., Ltd., London, 1956).

the approaches with magnificent probity and aptness.

One of these approaches consists in analysis of particular phases from a purely external point of vantage: that of philology, archaeology, ethnology, and sociology. Without trespassing beyond their domains, these disciplines are inevitably involved in religious subject matter. With little or no interest in essence, such religious matter is coordinated subject to the perspectives of the science concerned.

Whereas the history of religions is by no means dependent upon these correlations, without them it must remain proportionately poorer. Eventually, the scholar intent upon the study of the religions must choose one or the other of two methods: the history of religions per se, or religious phenomenology.

An investigator will thus devote research in the history of individual religions, envisaged in their historical settings and chronological order. This is the history of religions par excellence.[4] Alternately, an investigator will cut across frontiers of diverse religions. Out of a cumulative diversity, he distills a basic rationale. He might succeed in the isolation of rudimentary types. Forms characteristic of the several religions will probably emerge under persistent inquiry. The implications of such study carefully appraised and interpreted enhance the quality of observed verifiable knowledge. Such a technical approach informs the already mentioned second chapter headlined "How Religions Live."

Under such a phenomenology, the scholar studies, for instance, the notion of the sacred and the idea of God, as well as pivotal topics such as myth, rite, sacred text, and cult. His analysis of religious themes is effected within a cultural setting somewhat apart from consideration of time and space. A vision of universality is achieved. This is a welcome new horizon to the historian purely concerned with the annals of all religions. The relevance of such a phenomenology is self-explanatory.[5]

The range and essential merits of religious phenomenology leave little doubt as to its solid contribution to human knowledge in this

[4] A classic example of this methodology is the manual of Chantepie de La Saussaye, *Lehrbuch der Religionsgeschichte,* 4th edition by Bertholet and Lehmann (J. C. B. Mohr, Tübingen, 1925).

[5] A pioneer thereof was the Dutch G. Van der Leeuw. His *Phänomenologie der Religion* (J. C. B. Mohr [Paul Siebeck], Tübingen, 1956) first appeared in 1933. See also Mircea Eliade, *Traité d'histoire des religions* (Payot, Paris, 1949).

critical field. One readily agrees with Pettazzoni.[6] "Phenomenology," he writes, "represents the most important innovation which has come about in the realm of our studies during the last half century." This is far from saying, however, that phenomenology supplants the science of religion conceived as a historical discipline.

This is equally far from saying that the field ought to be partitioned into two departments: phenomenology and history of religions. The two are virtually indivisible. It would be better to think of them as two distinct components. They represent an interpenetration of knowledge. Together they strengthen the fiber of the science of religion. A historical approach is absolutely indispensable.

It is the history of religions that imparts cogency to phenomenology. Apart from sound historical data religious phenomenology incurs the risk of falling into arbitrary systematization. The pages of the book which treat Hinduism and Buddhism, Judaism, Christianity, and Islam, as well as primitivism, and other faiths, should spell utter futility were they not grounded in historical criticism.

Phenomenology delivers the scholar from the deluge of fragmentation, outcome of excessive specialization. There are actually few authorities who merit the title "historian of religions." Such historians are for the most part engaged in study of one or several related religions. Philological reconnaissance in itself, for example, taxes the faculties of most first-rate minds. Yet, how does anyone study a religion save through the medium of its linguistic self-expression? But where are the scholars competent in both Arabic and Chinese, Sanskrit and Egyptian hieroglyphics?

Such unavoidable factors partition and splinter the field. We owe it to religious phenomenology that a modicum of coherence has been assured. Thanks to it, a vision of an ensemble has been kept alive. An integrating principle gave promise of more fruitful research. Thus unity was accomplished in the face of stratifying obsession with specialization. Since specialities are required for scholarly depth and scientific precision, here as elsewhere cooperative research seems of the essence.

[6] *Essays on the History of Religions,* p. 217.

IV

Where does one begin and under what presuppositions is a relevant approach to another faith made? Our inquiry itself is scarcely free of presuppositions. Each direct preoccupation with religion, its external form and essence, sets a chain reaction: an inward confrontation with reality, a call for empathy, self-criticism, and reappraisal. Such a sequence need not be an exercise of futility. It can culminate in reform.

Mischief is inevitable, however, where empathy, rethinking, and reform — joint heirs of inward confrontation — prove abortive. It is the sort of mischief manifest in empty interfaith relations. Where they are not summarily dismissed the symbols of a strange faith are ingeniously cataloged and classified on purely detached rational grounds. The logical outcome of such an approach can hardly be anything save continued ignorance trailed by intolerance.

There was an intellectual epoch when the science of religion, child of the Enlightenment, tended to cultivate precisely that sort of cold rationalism in its outlook upon the great religions and those not so great. It bequeathed little better than a caricature of religion. Modern criticism endeavors to set the record straight. It seeks to right serious defects in former studies and deformed images.

Two impulses seem to emanate from this area of the science of religion. They are comparative religion and an order of values. In a sharpened order of values, a possible starting point is this. Faiths are to be explored and assessed on the basis of their meanings to their respective constituencies.

As conceived in this work comparative religion is on guard against two dangers: hasty identification of religious manifestations and the temptation to condemn them. Condemnation of the arbitrary sort is too obnoxious to require further comment. As for hasty identification it has exacted a heavy toll on the scholarly attainments of many a former generation of students in the field. Those were days when Western scholars were amazed at discovery of parallels among Oriental religions deemed to fall under the law of universal sameness.

A case in point is the idea of God in Christianity and the Buddhist idea of multiple deities. The two orders of belief are neither homologous nor analogous. If Buddhism contains anything at all analogous to the Christian idea of God, it must be recognized as the concept of Nirvana, an impersonal yet absolute reality.

As for Buddhism's accretion of many gods, they are themselves depicted as in desperate need of salvation. Like unto men, animals, and ravaged souls, they are victims of unending rebirth. The comparative study of religions will inevitably pose the question: What lies behind the preconceived phenomena of religious history manifest in corporate and personal behavior?

In keeping with the precepts of modern research comparative religion has not merely dropped an unrealistic condemnatory attitude. Its explications reflect a quiet reserve. Parallel religious phenomena no longer of necessity suggest the impact of one culture upon another. Some such parallels are explainable on the basis of causality—like causes yielding identical results. Parallel cultural and spiritual phenomena may be the outcome of similar environments. Correspondence may likewise occur in response to humanity's incurably religious nature.

Linguistic science fulfills an extraordinary purpose. Conversely, not too much zest is left for so-called "comparative mythology," product of romanticism. It saw similarity in the names of Indo-European deities. Soon it fell for the notion that a religious identity of some sort lay behind widely dispersed cultures. Indo-European philology does unreservedly qualify, however, for a conspicuous place of honor if only for such findings as those of Prof. Georges Dumézil, of the Collège de France.

Triads of deities, bearing distinctive highly differentiated attributes, occur among certain religions of Indo-European vintage; for instance, Jupiter, Mars, and Quirinus in the sunrise phase of Roman religion. To Dumézil, these seemed to reflect a tripartite functionalism: priest, warrior, and peasant, incidentally confirmed in Hindu caste.[7] Linguistic science thus opens new doors. It offers a clue, whereas sociology determines the shape of religious phenomenology.

Rendered more definite through linguistic science, and structured in reliance upon social research, the phenomenology of religion sharpens perspective on existence, its form and substance. Perceived in relation to the stature of nations, religion acquires a more chal-

[7] Georges Dumézil, *Jupiter, Mars, Quirinus IV, Explications des textes indiens et latins* (Presses Universitaires de France, Paris, 1948), pp. 25–30.

lenging significance. This is the hinge whereon Chapter 1 rests. Other themes will thereafter lay claim upon our attention. Those constitute a narrative conceived within the twin spheres, alluded to already, of scope and relevance.

Part Two of the book exemplifies the relevance of religious phenomenology to the study of the major religions. The applicability and validity of our central thesis are hammered out on the anvils of world faiths. In Chapter 4, "The Phenomenon of Hinduism," and in Chapter 5, "The Phenomenon of Buddhism," India's two foremost contributions of faith are examined. Such relevance is likewise actualized in Chapter 6, an expository descriptive analysis of the three great theistic faiths that owe their inception to what took place in the religious witness of Hither Asia.

By way of rounding out the inquiry, mention of relevance evokes an obligation to reckon with an ostensible irrelevance of religion. This leads us where secularism, historicism, and the rest presumably tend to immunize the soul against any such thing as living faith. This is the cardinal problem wherewith Chapter 7 wrestles.

Lastly, a brief chapter has "Postscript" for its heading. In a spirit and manner little pressed before in the volume, the claims of religious phenomenology are set forth in a new light, that is, as a means of revealing massive interest in all genuine religious enterprise as vital and illuminating. Sound and critical knowledge of today's religions is proposed as an indispensable aid to more meaningful relations among peoples and cultures. Such pursuit of knowledge under scholarly standards is a vital form of creative dialogue making for the strength of men and nations.

[Part One]

NATIONAL, SOCIAL, AND THEOLOGICAL SCOPE

CHAPTER

1

RELIGION
AND THE STATURE OF NATIONS

A CLEAR-CUT distinction must be drawn early in this chapter between, on the one hand, phenomenology as a discipline and, on the other, its subject matter, the phenomena of religion. In the American and Western tradition, the phenomena of religion are disclosed in manifold ways. Within a given nation, these are discernible in ideas and persons, in institutions, in social dynamism, and in cultural movements. Through these factors the scope of religious phenomenology is broadened to encompass areas that determine the character of populations.

Authoritative faith and political power, despite collusion, back-and-forth encroachment, and control of one by the other, do stand in a kind of juxtaposition. All too often, contemporary faith, religion, and ethics betray shaky structures and obsolete techniques scarcely adequate to prime the nature of man for action, let alone mold the stature of nations. Yet the fact remains that within society the phenomena of religion are generally a source of order and stability. The place of religion in national life may be discussed under four main propositions.

The first proposition is that psychologically an encounter with a holy Reality indeed tends to vivify personality. Such an encounter renews the spirit, engenders an inward glow of goodness, and converts the individual. It transforms anxiety and pain into a joyful, albeit dangerous, adventure.

The second proposition is of a philosophical order of meaning. It is based on a rigorous standard of research. It affirms that the thrust of the religious phenomena in the structure of a nation displays itself in a certain interpenetrability of faith and reason.

The third proposition is that the phenomenon of religion has manifested itself historically in freedom, democracy, and enlightened institutions. This is the kind of practical wisdom, for instance, which obviates the necessity to deprecate such cardinal historical eras as those of Renaissance, of Enlightenment, and of our more recent technology. Admitting the obvious spiritual hazards that such developments incur, a true wisdom born of faith will duly recognize, their magnificent contributions to human welfare and knowledge.

The fourth proposition is that in the realm of politics and sociology, the phenomenon of religion manifests a faith that stimulates action. It seeks to acknowledge all that moves men to give, without counting the cost, of themselves and their substance for the common causes of community, nation, and humanity. Nevertheless, it is a faith that ever stops short of equating divine will and purpose with any form of patriotism, no matter how elevating.

Before launching formal discussion of these four propositions, some preparation of the mind for what lies in store might be in order. A beginning is accordingly attempted in the next few pages through a concise statement touching upon three pertinent facets of the subject.

These are Santayana's reflections on liberty and society; Emerson's reaction from organized Christianity along with his spiritual and moral robustfulness; and lastly a word on the importance of the Magna Charta. The latter happens to manifest a deep consciousness of freedom. It also forms a background for subsequent separation of church and state in America.

With inimitable discernment, George Santayana, that daring Spanish-born American philosopher, rejected organized religion while retaining a profound sense of religion. To him faith in the unknown was symbolized in the doctrine of essences. The reader will recall that he resigned from Harvard after a long and distinguished professorship in philosophy. In Italy, where he retired, he lived in a convent, detached from the social pursuits of the twentieth century and in seclusion from direct contact with either people or events.

Santayana conveyed his last will and testament in *Dominations and Powers,*[1] a book consisting of reflections on liberty, society, and government. The title was drawn from a New Testament passage that speaks of " all things created, that are in heaven, and that are in earth, visible and invisible, whether they be thrones, or dominations, or principalities, or powers " (Col. 1:16).

Dominations and powers are not the same, according to Santayana, since the former are distinct and more complicated. All dominations involve the exercise of power, but not all powers are dominations. Nor does the difference lie in the strength or prevalence of the influence exerted so that any irresistible power could be called domination simply because it was irresistible.

On the contrary, if a power prevailed pervasively like the atmosphere or the force of gravity at the surface of the earth, so that life had arisen and taken shape under that constant influence, this power would not exercise any domination. It would, rather, be a prerequisite for the development of every sort of free life in the world.

In other words, the distinction between dominations and powers is moral, not physical. It does not hang on the degree of force exerted by an agent but only on its relation to the spontaneous life of some being that it effects. The same government that is a benign and useful power for one class or one province may exercise a cruel domination over another province or another class.

The distinction between dominations and powers, therefore, arises from the viewpoint of a given person or society, having initial interests of its own, but surrounded by uncontrollable circumstances. Such circumstances will at once be divided by the person or society into two classes: one, things favorable or neutral; the other, things fatal, frustrating, or inconvenient; and all the latter, when they cannot be escaped, tend to become dominations.

To pursue this poetical language of Santayana's a step farther, there are in addition to powers and dominations, virtues. Virtues have been described as an order of angels. They signify something presupposed by both power and domination. But the fundamental difference that sets virtues apart from powers and dominations is that virtues might be primarily conceived as spirits, having only a lyrical life. Perfect in themselves, they are not addressed to the exercise of any influence upon other beings. In mankind, the corresponding

[1] Charles Scribner's Sons, 1951, pp. 1–3.

virtues would be such gifts as health, wit, or poetic inspiration. They might even include pure intelligence and kindness. Yet in merely mentioning kindness and intelligence, we may notice how close virtues come to being, by accident, powers.

Life itself is intrinsically a virtue in the body that possesses it. A great store of virtues is hence presupposed in any capacity to exercise power, not to speak of exercising domination. Human society may be said to owe all its warmth and vitality to the intrinsic virtue of its members. Yet how blind we are in the realm of politics and naked power to the physical or spiritual life of the individual. How eloquently does this use of the word "virtue" as a metaphor serve in Santayana's prose to depict, unwittingly to be sure, the scope of religious phenomenology. Amazingly enough, he described the recession of religious vitality in society as loss of the art to wield virtue.

A creative response to the morbid religious forms of his time was executed by a noteworthy American figure of the nineteenth century. Out of an unpromising New England Puritanism, Ralph Waldo Emerson (1803–1882), essayist, poet, and philosopher, wrought a meaningful way of life for himself and for others who sat at his feet. An undistinguished scholar at Harvard, Emerson, nonetheless, achieved excellence and enduring fame.

Long friendship with Carlyle; a meeting with Coleridge and Wordsworth; readings in Plato, the Neoplatonists, the Sacred Books of the East, Swedenborg, and Montaigne, turned him toward German idealism. Belief in individual worth marks his *Lectures* (1836), particularly an address, "The American Scholar," wherein he advised independence from European cultural tutelage.

At bottom, Emerson had no doctrine at all. The deeper he went and the more he tried to grapple with fundamental conceptions, the vaguer and more elusive they became in his hands. Did he know what he meant by Spirit or Over-Soul? Could he say what he understood by the terms, so constantly on his lips, Nature, Law, God, Benefit, or Beauty? "He could not, and the consciousness of that incapacity was so lively within him that he never attempted to give articulation to his philosophy. His finer instinct kept him from doing that violence to his inspiration."[2]

[2] George Santayana, *Interpretations of Poetry and Religion* (Harper & Brothers, 1957), pp. 218, 221, 228–233.

The source of Emerson's power, we are told, lay less in his doctrine, more in his temperament. The rare quality of his wisdom was due not so much to his reason as to his imagination. In every sphere he traced the same spiritual laws of experience. These were compensation, continuity, the self-expression of the soul in the forms of nature and of society. The soul will thus finally recognize itself in its own work and see its beneficence and beauty.

To be sure, the contradictions of life and the shocks of experience often bring us face to face with an alien and overwhelming power. Reflection, however, is an ever-present help in trouble. It can humanize and rationalize that power. It will do this by helping us conceive the laws of power and by ever holding before us a sense of beauty and order in these very laws.

Two forces gave Emerson an uplift where formalized religion seemed to fail him. One was the freedom of imagination, and the other, a habit of worship inherited from his clerical ancestors and enforced by his religious education. The spirit of conformity, the unction, loyalty unto death, and acceptance of divine grace, were inspired by the Christian faith in which he was bred. These were the attributes of a disposition acquired by long discipline and rooted in too many forms of speech, of thought, and of worship for a man like Emerson ever to be able to lose.

Calvinism was in Emerson's blood and it knew how to combine an awestruck devotion to the Eternal with a not very optimistic picture of the nature and destiny of man. For over two hundred years Calvinism had been breeding in the stock from which he came, a willingness, as the phrase had it, " to be damned for the glory of God."

Emerson inherited the problems and preoccupations of the theology from which he sprang. In one sense he was like the German idealists. With all their pretense of absolute metaphysics, they were in reality only giving elusive and abstract forms to traditional theology. As has been observed, the religious tradition in which he was reared was that of Puritanism. His was a Puritanism, however, which while retaining its moral intensity and metaphysical abstraction had minimized its doctrinal expression and become phenomenally free.

A Puritan whose religion was all poetry, a poet whose only pleasure was thought, Emerson showed in his life and personality a fully ethical behavior. It was a behavior reminiscent of his clerical forebears with their characteristic meagerness, constraint, as well as frigid yet conscious consideration. A literal belief in Christian doctrine repelled him. In his view, such an approach to faith and religion manifested no understanding of the meaning which as allegories these doctrines might have to a philosophic and poetic spirit.

"We say the old forms of religion decay," wrote Emerson [3] in the essay on "Worship," "and that a skepticism devastates the community." He did not think it could be cured or stayed by any modification of theological creeds, less by theological disciplines. "The cure for false theology is mother-wit. Forget your books and traditions, and obey your moral perceptions at this hour. That which is liquefied by the words *moral* and *spiritual* is a lasting essence, and, with whatever illusions we have loaded them will certainly bring back the words, age after age, to their ancient meaning. I know no words that mean so much. In our definitions we grope after the *spiritual* by describing it as invisible. The true meaning of spiritual is *real* — that law which executes itself, which works without means, and which cannot be conceived as not existing."

The measure of this spiritual and moral vigor is a humility that Emerson [4] employed a story to demonstrate. There was a man known to the church as St. Philip Neri. Of his discernment and benevolence many stories were told at Naples and Rome. Now in a convent not far from Rome, a nun appeared who laid claim to certain rare gifts. The Holy Father at Rome was duly informed by the abbess of the wonderful powers shown by her novice.

The pope consulted St. Philip, who undertook to visit the nun and ascertain her character. Philip hastened through mud and mire to the convent. As soon as he met the nun, he stretched out his leg, and desired her to draw off his boot. The young woman drew back in anger and refused the office. Philip immediately ran out of doors, mounted his mule, and returned to the pope. "Give yourself no uneasiness, Holy Father, any longer," he said. "Here is no miracle, for here is no humility."

What, then, are the sources of order and strength within society? What role, if any, do religions perform in determining the character of populations? For one thing, authoritative faith and naked power do stand in proximate and interpersonal juxtaposition. For another,

[3] *Works* (Walter J. Black, Inc., n.d.), pp. 383 ff. [4] *Ibid.*, p. 388.

there are certain definable glories beyond the decadence and atrophy of religious structures.

Behind our American theory of church and state, there is an eventful English background. The record involves the foundations of individual rights, political security, and personal liberty. June 15, 1215, is a stirring date especially if coupled with the place name Runnymede.[5] We must look at the Bible, when authoritatively understood and rightly interpreted, as the great charter of the human soul, as the Magna Charta of the spirit.

How unforgettable was that moving scene enacted upon the heath at Runnymede. How crucial the circumstances that gave rise to the Magna Charta. Everyone knows how the barons of England, representing the people, met upon that historic spot and parleyed with John, the King. They said, " We will come to terms with you here." They said: " There are certain inalienable rights of English-speaking men which you must observe. They are not given by you, they cannot be taken away by you. Sign your name here to this parchment upon which these rights are written and we are your subjects. Refuse to put your name to this document and we are your sworn enemies. Here are our words to prove it."

That memorable episode in the struggle for freedom is closely related to the principle of separation between church and state. An expression of religious and civil liberty, that separation is relatively incomplete even in the land that bore it.[6] The fight for separation began with the Virginia Constitutional Convention of 1776. The outcome was the Act for Religious Freedom, more explicit in some aspects than the First Amendment to the Constitution which simply declared " Congress shall make no law respecting an establishment of religion or prohibiting the free exercise thereof."

Thomas Jefferson, who wrote the Virginia Act of Religious Freedom, thought of the First Amendment in very uncompromising terms. When he became President he refused to proclaim fast or thanksgiving days on grounds of unconstitutionality as well as of principle. " I consider the Government of the United States as inter-

[5] Cf. Woodrow Wilson, *College and State* (Harper & Brothers, 1925), Vol. II, p. 295.

[6] Loren P. Beth, *The American Theory of Church and State* (University of Florida Press, 1958), p. 61.

dicted by the Constitution from meddling with religious institutions, their doctrines, discipline, or exercises." [7]

To speak of a proximate and intimate juxtaposition of church with state is to refer to this peculiarly American tradition of partial separation. One must at the same time bear in mind the realities of social change at home and abroad. Within those contexts, the " church " becomes a variety of religious communities and beliefs in an essentially pluralistic society. Ideally, the church as such elicits respect not as a tool of state policy but rather in view of its special character and position. Such confidence in the cause of religion is fully justified. Even where institutional and structural patterns are inadequate, there remain a number of glories which the churches may rightly claim.

With these ideas in mind, we proceed with discussion of the four propositions.

I

[A] Psychologically, as we noted, religion vivifies personality and renews the human spirit. In an address delivered about fifty years ago, Woodrow Wilson [8] drew attention to the importance with which Christianity endows the individual: " You know what the distinguishing characteristic of modern society is, that it has submerged the individual as much as that is possible," he prophetically declared. " In economic society," he went on, " particularly we see men organized in great societies and corporations and organic groups in which each individual member feels that his own conscience is pooled and subordinated, and in cooperating with which men, as you know, constantly excuse themselves from the exercise of their own independent judgment in matters of conscience.

" The great danger of our day," as it seemed to Wilson, " is that men will compound their conscientious scruples on the ground that they are not free to move independently, that they are simply parts of a great whole, and that they must move with that whole, whether they wish to or not." All of which was supported by Wilson from personal experience: " I have had men tell me who were in the pro-

[7] Thomas Jefferson, *Writings,* ed. by H. A. Washington, 9 vols. (Taylor & Maury, 1853–1854), Vol. 5, p. 236.
[8] Wilson, *op. cit.,* p. 179.

fession of law to which I was originally bred . . . that it is extremely difficult to thread their way amidst a thousand complicated difficulties in giving advice to the great bodies of men whom they are called upon to advise, and to discriminate between what is legally safe and what is morally justifiable."

Our world has become so much more organized since Wilson made the above critical observations. Religion must find the individual and help him find himself. To that end, religion must understand and thread the intricacies of modern society. There are daily choices to be made, and the individual must make them at the risk of the integrity of his own soul. He must understand, as Wilson rightly insisted, that he cannot shift the responsibility upon the organization.

Every great age of the world, Wilson reminded his audiences, was an age not characterized chiefly by cooperative efforts but characterized chiefly by the initiative of the indomitable individual. You cannot give any age distinction by the things that everybody does. Each age derives its glory from the achievement that individuals perform by their own choice. Every turning point in the history of mankind has been pivoted upon the choice of an individual.

Religion, faith, and ethics have at their best stood by the individual. When some great spirit who would not be dominated took a firm position, it was faith and religious perseverance that proved his blessed companions. Where else shall we look for the moral fiber of great personality?

[B] How far popular religion in America has gone, how soundly it has operated in reclaiming the individual and in vivifying personality, the reader will determine for himself. Social science has rendered a valuable service in unveiling the role of faith mediated for mass consumption. Taking inspirational literature as a specific area, subject to scientific study, the result is indeed revealing. This will bring to mind the popular writings of such men of eminence as Norman Vincent Peale, Bishop Fulton J. Sheen, Harry Emerson Fosdick, and Joshua L. Liebman.

In 1932, Emmet Fox [9] counseled the reader, " If only you will find out the thing God intends you to do, and will do it, you will find that all doors will open to you; all obstacles in your path will melt away;

[9] *Power Through Constructive Thinking* (Harper & Brothers, 1932), p. 23.

you will be acclaimed a brilliant success; you will be most liberally rewarded from the monetary point of view; and you will be gloriously happy."

In the same decade, Mary Pickford[10] promised that "God is a twenty-four-hour station. All you need to do is to plug in. You plug in with your thinking. Good thinking. Kind thinking. Unselfish thinking. And you can have and use all the Love, all the Power, all the Courage, all the Energy, all the Cheerfulness, all the Activity, and all the Kindliness of God."

In 1950, Norman Vincent Peale and Smiley Blanton,[11] using the first-person singular, offered the kind of therapy that no sufferer from anxiety could take lightly. "I am going to give you what I call a prescription to drive out the fear that lies in your mind like a poison. Here is a text from the Scriptures. Take it. Repeat it to yourself over and over again, until your mind is completely possessed with it. Conceive of it as a medicine dropping into your mind, and it will spread a healing influence that will give you an immunity from fear."

The foregoing are but brief cullings from a luxuriant literature.[12] Inspiration literature is represented in the United States by a flood of books, pamphlets, magazines, and newspapers. It is conveyed through the great media of television and radio.

Scientific investigation of best sellers in the field during the period 1875–1955 netted forty-six volumes. All these publications satisfied three criteria.[13] First, they assumed the general validity of the Judeo-Christian religious tradition. Second, the authors sought to inspire with the hope of salvation, a salvation now or in the hereafter. This-worldly salvation tended to carry with it an emphasis either on peace of mind or on financial and business success. Third, certain "techniques" were recommended. These had a broad range. One technique might consist in withdrawal from business associates for a few minutes during the day to find spiritual refreshment in a private room; it might involve deliberately constructing a vivid image of God. Such an image implied God's strong personal interest in one's welfare. Finally, in each of the forty-six books there was an attempt to wrestle

10 *Why Not Try God?* (H. C. Kinsey & Company, Inc., 1934), p. 21.

11 *The Art of Real Happiness* (Prentice-Hall, Inc., 1950), p. 16.

12 Louis Schneider and Sanford M. Dornbusch, *Popular Religion* (The University of Chicago Press, 1958), p. 1.

13 *Ibid.*, pp. 3–4.

with the everyday problems of real people. Down-to-earth, common life situations were singled out for special treatment.

Constant analysis of this popular religious literature disclosed a set of recurring themes and trends. It thus shed light on the function of faith among vast segments of the population.[14] The notion, for instance, that religion gives life meaning in the sense of providing a justification for existence became significant in the years just before and immediately after World War I.

Another theme is that religion will make a better world by leading toward peace, brotherly love, and removal of poverty. Although it is found to some extent in the pre-1936 period, this is a theme that gains greater ascendancy in the wake of 1940.

There is also more discussion, from 1936 onward, of the idea that religion binds one to one's fellowman and makes the individual more fully a member of a well-knit community. Intersecting with the two themes of meaning and solidarity is the view that religion will bring "our nation" leadership or victory over our enemies. This last conviction comes to the fore during World War II and in the period of the postwar anticommunist crusade.

Certain reservations emerge from a careful analysis of best-selling religious literature. Relatively weak is the linkage of riches with evil and of poverty with virtue. Reinhold Niebuhr once remarked that the hero of the Judeo Christian culture is a poor man. The investigation does not, however, bear him out. Nor is the appeal overwhelming now that religion will bring prestige and recognition in the world.

Since the mid-thirties, the idea that possession of wealth symbolizes religious or moral rectitude has declined. The fact is, however, that authors such as Peale and Blanton [15] are not writing for lower-class society. When they list goals, they say, "We want to be successful in business, to write a book, to climb a mountain . . . to become a doctor, to make a speech." The inference must be that this is a largely middle-class literary development in our country.

[14] *Ibid.*, pp. 148–155. [15] Peale and Blanton, *op. cit.*, p. 82.

II

Philosophically, the scope of religious phenomena is seen in an interpenetrability of faith and reason, of law and truth. In that capacity, religion acquires a formative, constitutive role upholding the stature of a nation.

Religion does promote a philosophical spirit. Quite apart from the fetters of systems and the shackles of dogma, it fosters research and quest of the truth. For many thinkers, philosophy can never be a matter of setting up a system. It is, rather, a disengagement from all systems in order to grasp the truth, be it spiritual or material, in all its purity.

It has been well said that a philosopher is one who perceives difficulties where others see nothing.[16] Indeed he is one who is ever in search of verities that lie beneath the surface of admissible truth. He excels in freedom of thought. Essentially he is antidogmatic. Only in that sense does the philosophical spirit stand in apparent contradiction to the religious.

Where the religion of maturity prevails, an interpenetrability of faith and reason, truth and law, supervenes. In that event, there arise side by side an obedience to dogma and a morality, on the one hand, and, on the other, a welling forth in the soul of prophet and mystic of such knowledge and wisdom as would transcend rule and order.

Any well-informed Roman Catholic will assure us neither the Index nor the Inquisition is more religious than Paul's affirmation concerning the "glorious liberty of the children of God" (Rom. 8:21). Nor would he be likely to belittle Augustine's admonition "to love God and do as you please." Greater guarantees of the interpenetrability in question can scarcely be cited.

Were conflict to occur between religion and philosophy, but one thing would be required: a spirit of serene acquiescence where we cannot prove. In a word, what is thereby conceded is the fact that there are limits beyond which reason cannot go. And that is the kind of spiritual and intellectual honesty that cannot be gainsaid.

To posit such an interpenetrability is to defend a modern concept, that of the freedom of research. Where the conflict between religion

[16] Joseph Wilbois, in *Histoire des religions,* ed. by Maurice Brillant and René Aigrain (Bloud et Gay, Paris, 1953), Vol. I, pp. 54–56.

and philosophy happens to choke us, and to drive us to the point of violating religious sanctities, we must remember the age in which we live. Our world and time are marked by a spirit of free inquiry. Research is so highly developed in certain fields and phases of investigation that it evokes the admiration of all. But free inquiry and scientific research are not equally diffused in all countries and departments of learning. How strikingly accidental and ultramodern in certain instances it is anyone can see.

There are populations that inhabit isolated areas, nomads living in desert or steppeland. Others belong to remote forest regions; the heavy demands of an industrialized age have set armies of workers apart. Labor battalions and farm laborers form unique collective societies. Meanwhile, populations that enjoy a modicum of culture participate in a variety of mass organizations centered upon job, trade, or business. There are collectivities besides built on the foundations of class, caste, position, status, or dependent upon party, province, economic school, or artistic affiliation. To excel in too much originality would amount to a countercurrent course for those who live under the generality of collective orders.

Indeed anyone living under homogeneous and compact group requirements might soon forget all about the excitement of fresh and disturbing ideas. His best bet is to leave to the chieftain responsibility for mental operations that for the most part are at any rate inspired by tradition.

If a primitive genius should by chance appear, he would by the very sin of nonconformity incur the penalty of excommunication. Ostracized and hounded out of the community, he has nowhere but the wilderness to turn to. There destruction awaits all rebels, either from hunger or by tooth and claw. In sum, under such conditions, originality of thought does not pay.

It is obvious, moreover, why in societies of limited horizon, even in more differentiated communities, the mental faculties rarely have an opportunity of free exercise. Should a novel occurrence take place which calls for an explanation, it is indeed easy to bypass that intangible something called logic. The word " logic " itself might not have been invented or discovered yet. Under the circumstances, who would not wish for some authority who might disclose the truth about novel and phenomenal aspects of existence?

" The master said " might not necessarily be the mark of intellectual cowardice or laziness under those conditions. It could very well be a legitimate assurance against error. When Descartes wrote that evidence is the criterion of the truth, he was involved in the difficulties of a public opinion embarrassed with the implications of free thought. His was an attempt to tackle public opinion as one does a newly enfranchised slave unpracticed in the art of freedom.

Essentially, belief in revelation ought not conflict with the proper norms of thought. If objectivity and detachment are basic requirements for the establishment of standards in secular life, that is all the more reason why it is necessary to formulate for the religious life special positions of faith under the designation of doctrine. Doctrines were first declared revealed in the Vedas, the Bible, and the Koran. Hence the immutability of first principles in matters of religious faith. Insofar as form and detail are concerned, however, such first principles are surely subject to evolutionary change. Evolution in this area has not been uniform. It is less observable in modern Islam, more evident in the classical Christian traditions.

Christianity unfolded in a world saturated with Hellenistic ideas, a world where thought was highly prized. Its primitive revelation was not unexpectedly couched in the form of dogmas. Aimed at the masses of believers, these dogmas were not in the nature of iron collars but, to change the metaphor, more comparable to beachheads chosen for the transfer of religious truth. Nor were such dogmas intended for imposition from the outside. Formulated by councils which presumably spoke for the whole church, they were an expression of common belief.

We need not see only an authoritarian mood in Christian dogma. What needs to be seen is a consensus of the believers. This last sentence paraphrases what happens to be the view of a Roman Catholic scholar.[17] He goes on to add that while it may seem odd to a Roman Catholic who is more papist than the pope, this view of dogma might well commend itself to others. He cites among those others Christians of the Greco-Slav heritage, whose communal perspective, by reason of ethos and culture, draws them closer to the genuine spirit of the primitive church.

Hardly any major religion today really forbids thinkers to think.

[17] Wilbois, *loc. cit.*, p. 56.

Surely thought abounds in Hinduism and its daughter Buddhism. Islam has come by a rich medieval heritage of thought, science, and letters. As for Judaism and Christianity, in every age their thinkers have been legion. Where thinkers went astray, authority at least among Christians served the purpose of holding them in line.

When judiciously exercised such an authority gave effect to the kind of curb that followed violation. A dogmatist rarely attained stature save at the close of a career marked by luminous contribution. A prophetic personality was, on the contrary, readily recognized and invariably honored without delay. Mystics, too, were enthusiastically acclaimed and held in popular esteem among churchmen. Christian philosophers tended to admire both the prophet and the mystic. Not only did the Christian religion leave them free to think and to cultivate their talents as seers, it went one step farther in placing at their disposal the vast resources of the Christian tradition; it called them to a partnership in shaping the fortunes of society by molding the believers' faith.

Would it sound too trite to reiterate that pursuit of the sacred domain, and of the worldly simultaneously, tends to perfect the whole man? This is what religious authority deplores most in the experience of a thinker: that he should be more attached to the letter than to the spirit. That was the self-inflicted damage of certain religionists such as the Islamic commentators. Their shortness of breath was partly due to a failure to attain the gift of interpenetrability, a lack of nerve when faith and freedom came together. Given the wager of an Isaiah or a Theresa, however, the inspired words of Augustine might ring true when read, " Love God and think as you please."

III

Historically, there is in religion a wisdom renouncing futilities, while acclaiming insights, of such transformations as those of Renaissance and Enlightenment, of modern science and technology. Lord Acton (1834–1902) rendered valuable contributions elucidating our present theme under the headings of freedom, modern history, and political power. Noted for his genuine and liberal Roman Catholic views, he was admittedly one of the most brilliant and influential scholars of his age.

Lord Acton's articles, essays, and lectures were brought together after his death. They bring out three things about their great author. First, that he was truly committed to his faith. In spite of his religious liberalism and reservations, he regarded "communion with Rome as dearer than life." Second, he was a devoted adherent and admirer of Gladstone. In fact, the two men had the very highest regard for each other. Matthew Arnold used to say that "Gladstone influences all around him but Acton; it is Acton who influences Gladstone." Third, at Munich, Acton had studied under a famous Roman Catholic theologian, Johann Joseph Ignaz von Döllinger (1799–1890). Döllinger fought for reconciliation of the church with the principles of modern society.

Acton was inspired by Döllinger with a deep love of historical research and a profound conception of its function as a critical instrument. In the great crisis that rocked the Roman Catholic world in 1870 over promulgation by Pius IX of the dogma of papal infallibility, Döllinger opposed the dogma. And Lord Acton was in complete agreement with his teacher on this issue. In 1895, Lord Acton was appointed to the Regius Professorship of Modern History at Cambridge. It will be recalled that that university had denied Acton admission as a student. It was then impossible for a Roman Catholic to be accepted.

Acton had assembled a magnificent historical library with the object, never in fact realized, of writing a monumental history of liberty. In politics, he was always an ardent liberal. He spent much time in the chief intellectual centers of Europe and the United States. He counted among his friends Montalembert, De Tocqueville, von Sybel, and von Ranke. Though he left little published work, he was one of the most deeply learned men of his time.

Lord Acton is remembered today for his influence on others. Through him, it may be said that religion in its historical treatment became a force in the stature of nations. His extensive library, consisting largely of books full of his own annotations, was purchased immediately after his death by Andrew Carnegie and presented to John Morley. The latter forthwith gave it to the University of Cambridge.

Acton's is the voice of informed religion and wisdom heard from above the merciless and warring extremists of a sorely perplexed time.[18] The greatness of his soul is measurable by the duration of its moral force. Acton's perennial appeal is due, above all, to moral integrity. We are brought back again and again to his vindication of the supreme human truths as they shine forth in the course of history: religion, veracity, justice, the hatred of lies and cruelty.

Here was a historian who wrote of men's greatest concerns earnestly and scrupulously, with brilliant illumination, following the discoverable evidence. He was a powerful, indefatigable explorer of human nature and human events, rich in ideas, deep in thought, highly practiced in reflection. Historical exploration was to him the true demonstration and sovereign guidance of private and public conscience. Acton must have read some twenty thousand books, as a competent critic has computed. Yet he never succeeded in writing that history of liberty as he fully intended to do. Greater integrity hath no man than this, says an acute biographer, than that a man should abandon his unwritten book when intellect declares the materials inadequate.

Rated as a modern oracle, Acton holds that honor because he is a universal historian, a thinker of immense range and perspective. To him, history has meaning. The meaning is spiritual. It offers lessons on the nature, capacities, and destiny of man; the relationship of individual conscience to the movement of society; and the rights of man to the power of government. It promises to enable us to make political science and political judgments effective. The standing attraction of this kind of history is its assured offer of something like the full formula of human nature in politics.

Acton's history vindicates human freedom which he sets above any other human interest. " Liberty," he says, " is not a means to a higher political end. It is itself the highest political end." Now everybody is a devotee of freedom. Motivation is another matter. Whether one can bestow it on all, without denying a proportion of it to each, is also another matter.

Yet the prayer for liberty must find eager admirers in an age chastised by total war, diabolically ingenious torture, economic and social perplexities. How relevant all this is to our own time in which

[18] Herman Finer in Preface to Lord Acton's *Essays on Freedom and Power,* selected by Gertrude Himmelforb (Beacon Press, Inc., 1948), pp. vii–xii.

developing democratic conscience is at odds with almighty economic entrepreneurs and hereditary vested interests. How pertinent it is in an era of conscious and extensive state economic planning, and intransigent, despotic, and murderous politicians of extreme left and right, who have contemptuously discarded charity and banished truth, virtue, and mercy.

People seek a broad, sweeping historical induction that shall be the truth, the whole truth, and nothing but the truth, utterly convincing in its finish and definition. But such a definition cannot be won, once and for all, at any one time by a single man, or a sect, church, or nation, or even by an international body of scholars, less by a body of jurists or United Nations representatives.

Acton deplored the imperfection of historical materials. His efforts furnish a grand practical dual lesson in history: what we must add to historical induction to reach valid social conclusions, and with what qualifying spirit the historians' conclusions must be read if their account of human nature is to be helpful to those who are governed and those who govern. How foolish it would be not to listen to so earnest, learned, and wise a man, speaking on the grandest of human concerns, simply because it is given to no man to be capable of uttering any more than a broad hint or warning.

His conception of the role of history was provocative. "The inexplicable integrity of the moral code is, to me, the secret of authority, the dignity and the utility of history. If we may debase the currency for the sake of genius, or success, or rank, or reputation, we may debase it for the sake of a man's influence, of his religion, of his disgrace. Then history ceases to be a science, an arbiter of controversy, a guide to the wanderer, the upholder of that moral standard which the powers of the earth and religion itself tend constantly to depress."

Acton's value to the student of history, and still more to the student of politics and society, is his perennial concern with the grand themes of Power, Democracy, Equality, Liberty, Nationality, and Religion. People are less interested in mere narration than in social judgment. All of Acton's teaching is conditioned by his disavowal of Power. "Power tends to corrupt and absolute power corrupts absolutely. Great men are almost always bad men, even when they exercise influence and authority." Another of his sayings is: "The greatest crime is Homicide. The accomplice is no better than the assassin; the theorist is worse." [19]

It is this which puts a limiting perimeter on his admiration for Democracy, Liberty, and Equality, and even, it must be said, for Religion, for he certainly and abundantly recorded it of his own church. He appreciated the values in the various liberties. He gladly acknowledged that they constituted human progress. He joyously applauded the movements in history that overthrew the various varieties of despotism.

Acton welcomed the men and doctrines that established the principles and institutions of triumphant, liberal, and representative states. He saw also that if any single untempered idea should attain the exclusive dominion over the mind of man, however good it was, the power needed to establish its victory and cement its reign — thus Equality, or Democracy, or Nationality — must limit and debase liberty. Though he did not quote Charles de Montesquieu (1689–1755), the French jurist and philosopher, their minds moved together: "Virtue itself hath need of limits," for freedom and tranquility lie in self-restraint. To demand all is to lose all by very excess.

Yet, though these are indispensable truths, they ought not obscure an equally indispensable truth, namely, that power is beneficent. Blaise Pascal spoke concerning this, once and for all: "Without Power, Justice is unavailing." [20] For the kingdom of politics is of this world. Power, as the biographies [21] of so many statesmen reveal, heightens sensitiveness, stimulates the imagination of purposes and expedients, generates invention, develops compassion when it places men where they confront the sorrows that government exists to assuage and the trials that must be visited on some in order that others may have a more abundant life. Power also develops humility and fortitude. These are precious qualities in the service of mankind and inseverable from power. Together they will one day enable humanity to progress, as Acton recommended, from nationalism to an embracing state that shall include the whole world.

[19] *Ibid.*, p. x.

[20] Cf. Blaise Pascal, *Pensées* (J. M. Dent & Sons, Ltd., London, 1931), p. 85.

[21] For example, that of Sir Thomas More (1478–1535), English philosopher and statesman, author of *Utopia*, a classical picture of ideal state, canonized, 1935.

IV

Finally, in the realm of political science, religion provides a strong, sacrificial motivation to serve the causes of community, nation, and humanity. Religious faith must constantly stop short, however, of equating divine will with any form of patriotism, no matter how elevated!

[A] Toynbee's *A Study of History* is scarcely a history of liberty. Insofar, however, as it is a significant history of civilization, Toynbee's work is bound to be invaluable for the study of liberty. It is just barely conceivable that Acton did not succeed, where Toynbee did, for the simple reason that he was prophetic enough to realize that success meant failure. Toynbee's success, which he did not purpose, consists in almost completely revealing gaps in a full and final account of man in society. And not only this, but the dreadful inevitability of gaps, the fatality of the necessary escape of facts and understanding which the historian tries to domesticate.

What religion has to say about security and world peace may be construed as novel and unique even where it is revolting to the secular mind. One of the most vivid pictures of World War II was that of a poilu sitting in a rocking chair, bundled up for maximum comfort. The time was 1940 and the place the Maginot Line. Behind those defenses, France had an army of a million and a half men, a crack European fighting force. How the magnificent French Army melted like snow before the fury of the blitzkrieg!

The Maginot Line was a symbol of security for French military leaders who thought in terms of World War I trench warfare. Their security was rudely shattered by a new war of movement and lightning velocity. World War II was ended by exploding an atom bomb. A stockpile of these bombs promptly became a new Maginot Line behind which the United States retreated. There we stayed until one Klaus Fuchs betrayed our secret to the Russians. A book published then, entitled *No Place to Hide,*[22] showed how utterly futile protective measures would be if a bomb were to explode in our immediate vicinity.

Religious faith maintains the human race is in dire straits indeed

[22] David John Bladley (Little, Brown and Company, 1948).

when it makes security a primary end and goal. Toynbee [23] reminds us that Greece declined because of its creed. " Not happiness and not progress, but stability is the Alpha and Omega of the Athenian philosophers' social creed." He chose the " insect mind " to illustrate the flair for stability. " Instinct predominates in the insect mind: intelligence in the mind of man." Arrested development in a civilization, the beginning of decline, " may be explained in psychological terms as a mental reversion from the human toward the insect type of mental rhythm: from blundering but progressive mobility of reason, to the infallible but inflexible rigidity of instinct."

[B] The bearing of religion on the problem of world peace is even more perplexing. Is it the function of religion to bring men together in a universal enterprise for secular well-being and world peace? [24] Society has a right to use religion for secular purposes because religion is an element in the secular structure of human life. But religion must be wary of the way secular society employs it. Society is not concerned with the authenticity of the religious purpose and configuration, but religion itself is. As the Christian sees it, there are two dimensions to the Christian: one dimension belongs to Caesar and the other belongs to God.

This general situation affects Christianity no more than other faiths. The primary fact that we must recognize is that the different religions of mankind do not say the same thing. They have indeed elements in common. Yet these very elements have a different value in the different systems because each system is a homogeneous unity of its own. Unless all men are willing to enter into a completely new religion that will be the only one of mankind, we must expect from our religions, in spite of all their good intentions, a divisive influence on the world.

If the religions of the world cannot produce a unified impact on man, there is still much they can do. They cannot form a religious solidarity. Each can, however, individually stress those elements in its own tradition which will make for peace. If we cannot form one re-

[23] Arnold J. Toynbee, *A Study of History* (Oxford University Press, London, 1939), Vol. III, pp. 93, 96, 110.

[24] Cf. Gustave Weigel, S.J., " Christian Ethics and International Relations," p. 16 (a paper presented in connection with an autumn consultation of The Church Peace Union held at Princeton, New Jersey, in 1959, and used with the author's permission).

ligion from all those extant in the world, we can bring the religions together to hold conversation together in a meeting of minds and dialogue in favor of an end that is not in conflict with the vision of any religion that we know. This end is peace on earth, a real peace, giving to all men the opportunity to enjoy freedom and secular well-being.

The purpose of this coming together would not be to harness religion to the secular chariot. The finality of religion is not secular. Rather, it would be to make each religion aware of its own inner and consistent responsibility toward its proper action with reference to the proper concerns of others. The purpose of congress would not be to make religion a secular project. It would rather be an exhortation to the religions to be themselves. The more they are themselves — since each without exception stands for righteousness — the more they will contribute to world peace. What a mighty formative influence of religion that would be on the stature of nations!

This chapter tried to cite evidence on the scope of religious phenomena in American and Western culture. We were incidentally bound to cover aspects in a worldwide perspective. In all logic, we ought now to consider this phenomenology itself, its standards, and its discoveries with regard to the way religions live and develop.

CHAPTER

2

HOW RELIGIONS LIVE

IN SETTING FORTH the scope and range of religious phenomenology, this chapter moves one step farther. Presently our investigation will be extended to take up certain outward manifestations of religious phenomena. Recorded evidence will be sifted and examined, allowing for the possibility of new discoveries. In other words, we are about to be brought face to face with the fact of religion, particularly its interaction with secular society. The quest is essentially for more satisfying knowledge of how religions live, how they manage to persist in a world of change and decay.

There are four distinct areas that promise to shed light on the subject. First, there is the area of interaction between religion and law on the frontiers of history as well as on those of the modern world. Such interaction might well account for that characteristic situation where spiritual perspective generally arises. Only scientific analysis determines the exact distinctions between law and religion and the degree to which religion lives through the law it inspires.[1] Evidence in support of our basic assumption is sought from primitivism as well as from the advanced cultures of China and Iran, of India, the ancient Orient and Greece.

Furthermore, this link between religion and law is detectable in the nascent societies of Asia, Africa, and the Middle East. These are societies currently passing from colonial to self-governing status. Where else does law acquire authenticity and validity if not in living contact with a dynamic society? Apparently what vitality law acquires it will draw from interaction with human personality.

[1] Pierre Martin, "Droit et coutume," in *Le monde non-chrétien* (Paris, 1956), Vol. 37, pp. 38–39.

Let it be said, in the second place, that religions tend to live today by the doctrines setting them apart. In this respect, religious phenomenology underscores the so-called theory and logic of phenomena. Whereas theory, as here understood, is scarcely a matter for debate, logic of the phenomena is a subject open to scrutiny and analysis. Through such direct confrontation with the structure of historic faiths, certain eye-opening and illuminating generalizations are formulated.

Thirdly, although to a casual observer the classical religions at times seem doomed to atrophy, the truth is more likely than not that they tend to pass from stage to stage of metamorphosis. Patently, in the fourth place, religions live not just through a given interaction with law and by virtue of some doctrine or measurable metamorphosis; they also thrive on ethics since their growth seems validated in ethical programs.

I

When Pascal coined that trenchant phrase "a meridian decides what is the truth," he had law, not religion, in mind.[2] What he implied was that juridically plausible truth on one side of the Pyrenees could rate as error on the other. That dictum holds true on a worldwide scale. On six diverse frontiers, interaction of law and religion sheds fresh light upon the way faiths live.

[A] There is the frontier of primitivism. Here an initial impression gained is that neither individuality nor personality counts for much. The individual primitive has been justly regarded as a forgotten creature almost fully abandoned to absorption into the group. Not so in a civilized community where law obtains. Law here is recognized and constitutes one of the mechanisms of social coordination. What a contrast to primitive existence which suffers the individual to fade into the mass.

The sociology and anthropology of law are therefore intimately bound up with our theme. As such, they seem to serve as explorations into the nature of evolution from primitivism to civilization. As for ethics and primitive mentality, Lucien Lévy-Bruhl (1857–1939), the French ethnologist, established a distinct incompatibility between

[2] Arnold Toynbee, *Christianity Among the Religions of the World* (Charles Scribner's Sons, 1957), p. 31.

primitive and civilized modes of thought. It was the British-Polish sociologist, Bronislaw Malinowski (1884–1942), however, who demonstrated that there are facets and degrees, a scale of rules, within the context of nonjuridical, primitive society.

Law is a historical phenomenon, a product of the evolution of culture. Power is a determining factor that distinguishes law from ethics. Ethics and power might exist side by side, the one independent of the other. Circumstances might conspire to unify the two. As for individuality, its rise is ordinarily within the scope of a mythical harmony between law and religion, a socio-religious ensemble. Normally the ego is not confined to any given spot but is conceived in terms of a network of relations.

Totemism is largely a phenomenon of primitive Australia, Melanesia, and North America. One of a class of living or inanimate objects, a totem is regarded by primitive people as having a blood relationship to a specific family or clan. It thus offers a necessary base for the development of the personal " I." With the help of a totem, such a development is conditioned by collective beliefs particularly through such identity with the cosmos as is forcefully experienced among the Melanesians.

Upon this kind of basis rests individual initiative to pry oneself loose from those group participations which confine the person to totemic practices. Émile Durkheim (1858–1917), French sociologist and thinker, believed it was the detachment of the physical organism from community participation that furthered individuality and set it in a surefooted posture. Through its mythology, primitive mentality had laid hold on extra-empirical realities. It had fed its own predilections, created its own rules.

However, such predilections and rules lacked the effectiveness of law. They were merely acts and attitudes engendered in a spree of spiritual excitement when a worshiper was imbued with excessive emotion as participant in a mythological rite or ceremony. Only divested from the myth did the juridical pattern reveal an independent character. The first exhibition of such rules and predilections was religious and it discharged a moving, transforming role. The second was juridical and to it attached a permanence and a stability inherent in the exercise of power.

[B] On a more advanced level, Chinese history is a second frontier where interaction between law and religion threatened or advanced the cause of faith. The scholarly works of Koo Yen-wu (1632–1682) [3] reveal a facet of the more typically Chinese mentality traits. These varied, he assumed, according to whether an individual Chinese happened to come from the North or South. Between the two major sections of the land, the Yellow River was evidently the chief boundary line. The "tough-minded" Northerners and the "tender-minded" Southerners represented two alternative responses to an inexorable challenge set by a rugged topography.

Integration of multiple national traits was furthered by the advent of Confucianist ethics in the sixth and fifth pre-Christian centuries. A brilliant philosophical era was to follow. Maturity in ethics and morality, ever in touch with ritual and religion, was paralleled by a trend in favor of law. The two came together as the cultural effervescence outlasted the fourth century. A century or so later authoritative law was vigorously upheld. Under the leadership of the Northwestern state of Ch'in (221–207 B.C.), the unification of China was achieved.

For many centuries, thereafter, the isolation of China was a foregone conclusion. Largely due to the vastness of the territory, the country received little or no stimulation from the outside world. Its immediate neighbors, moreover, were for the most part backward or nomadic. This state of affairs was gradually altered as during the third to the eighth centuries foreign influence increased. Contact with India in that epoch was marked by the introduction of Buddhist religion and ethics. China provided an amazingly fertile soil for the dissemination of Mahayana Buddhist ideas. In the course of events, an already rich culture caught the vision of new horizons, and the relation between law and religion was correspondingly modified.

This situation did not materially change until contact with Europe began. Western influence, dating, though intermittently, from the seventeenth century, was impressive. The passing of old China, the founding of the Republic, and the rise of the Communist political power are but end results in a checkered era of internal evolution and external pressures. Throughout, two influences, Indian and Western, had a bearing on Chinese law and religion. These, as well as ethics

[3] Sarvepalli Radhakrishnan, ed., *History of Philosophy Eastern and Western* (George Allen & Unwin, Ltd., London, 1952), Vol. I, p. 549.

and doctrine, have not been the same since.

[C] A third frontier where law and religion vitalized each other was ancient Iran. The importance of that ancient frontier derives from a simple account it gave the problem of evil and from its peculiarly eschatological perspective. That was indeed a timely message addressed to a society deeply preoccupied with issues of peace and immortality. Mazdaism[4] is the religion of ancient Iran, a religion that inspired action, struggle for freedom, and was admirably adjusted to the deep longings and spiritual desires of the common man.

As elsewhere, faith and political power, law and ritual, had a historic record of challenge and response. Asceticism and fanaticism were at first conspicuously absent. In its later stages, however, such as under the Sassanid Empire (A.D. 226–641), Mazdaism departed from tradition. It betrayed intolerance against Christianity. But from that form of absolutism state religions are rarely free.

Strangely enough, an almost identical naturalism, compounded with elementary morality, among the Aryans of Asia produced opposite results on the two sides of the Indus Valley. Starting from similar origins, Indian and Iranian religion took two divergent pathways. Indian thought soon turned toward mysticism. It pushed asceticism to excessive limits. Religion thus crystallized in philosophy or theosophy and culminated in pantheism.

What a contrast did Iranian religion provide. Here a dynamic morality of a practical nature prevailed. For its expression it had an ethic based on dualism. Exaggerated in general, this was a morality closely knit to human psychology.

Zoroaster himself did not originate this system. He did, nevertheless, cultivate it and contributed immensely to its realization. This he achieved through proclaiming a doctrine that was as socially valid as it was religiously attractive. Whereas his ideal was that of the " honest " man, India's was the " saintly " man. Iran acknowledged a revelation and a doctrine. India espoused a tradition that looked to the Vedas as its highest authority, an authority immutable across the ages.

Due to their strictly sociological nature, neither Mazdaism nor Brahmanism achieved universality. That role was left to their respective offshoots, Manichaeism and Buddhism. The first won marked success in the Occident, where its ideas long survived among

[4] A more accurate term than Zoroastrianism.

the Cathari and the Albigenses. The second made extensive conquests in the Far East, where it currently ranks as a supranational faith.

Despite much clarity and restraint, neither Mazdaism nor Manichaeism was destined to inspire a great literature. The chiefly religious Pahlevi texts [5] are for the most part stilted, repetitious. India's sacred text suffered from the very opposite drawback. Its enormous copiousness proved fantastic, immoderate in style. As a rule, it failed to capture an international audience. In the Western world it did not strike a responsive chord.

While the West stood relatively aloof to Indian religious thought, it came under striking Iranian influence. Next to Judaism and Greek philosophy, it was surely Iran that contributed most to the making of Christian ideas. A concrete form was thus bestowed upon many a concept already known to the church in seminal essence. It has been said quite often that had the Western world missed conversion to the Christian religion, it might have turned perhaps to Mithraism or Manichaeism, the two descendants of Mazdaism.[6]

[D] The interplay of law and religion proceeded along a fourth significant frontier, that of India. Geographically this frontier centered upon the middle reaches of the Ganges River in the Province of Bihar. Situated there are the holy places of Buddhism where Gautama the Buddha (563?–?483 B.C.) received enlightenment at Bodhgaya. There, too, lies Benares, Hinduism's sacred city par excellence. Within this Indian orbit of vivid religious memories, it is Hinduism today that holds court, claiming the allegiance of a Hindu majority. Buddhism did not establish permanent foothold in the land that gave it birth.

The exit of Buddhism from its cradle land was compensated for by extraordinary expansion abroad. As the so-called Greater Vehicle (Mahayana) of the truth, it overran Tibet, China, Japan, and other neighboring lands. As the Lesser Vehicle (Hinayana), it thrives in Ceylon, Burma, Thailand, Indo-China, and adjacent parts. It had once penetrated central Asia as far as Afghanistan, where extinct today it nevertheless is represented by a number of imposing monuments.

[5] Third to ninth century A.D.

[6] A. Carnoy, "La religion de l'Iran," in *Histoire des religions,* ed. by Brillant and Aigrain, Vol. II, pp. 262–263.

In its classical expression Hinduism was anchored in an inward intuitiveness. This marked off the domain of dharma, religious law, as the law and destiny which shapes the believer's end. Corresponding with the six classes of sacred texts, there appeared a cluster of religious concepts and cults. These represented the impact of Hinduism upon India and the world of religion. Included among these was caste, a peculiarly Hindu phenomenon inherent in the system of social stratification. Nor was caste unrelated to the significance attached to color, *varna,* and birth, *jati.*

The defects of the Hindu structure did not elude the Brahmans themselves. They were quite conscious of the fact that their own power and prestige had left the gods in a state of eclipse. Consequently they sought a Supreme Being who would be worthy of contemplation and adoration. In the view of many thoughtful people, salvation came to signify release from the dreadful necessity of returning to this seemingly purposeless and futile tragedy of existence. Existence and the tragic sense of living were crystallized in *ḳarma,* law of the deed, an eternal chain of cause and effect.

Since the succession of births was a bleak and endless story, the Buddha undertook to find release in a new domain of religious experience. For seven years he experimented with fasting and mortification of the flesh only to set these aside in the end as utterly inadequate. One day as he sat under a tree, he experienced an absorption wherein the redeeming knowledge of deliverance from rebirth unfolded to him.

In his teaching the Buddha emerges as a compassionate rationalist. He was a reformer whom Albert Schweitzer recognized as the Martin Luther of Hinduism. His most revolutionary theme was denial of the existence of both universal and individual souls, thus emphasizing his complete break with the Brahmanical doctrine of redemption.

According to the Buddha, the spirit should be concerned only with what was direct and practical meaning — that is, only with results wrung directly from evidence. From this central theme, two deductions were drawn. First, that in terrestrial joy there is no real joy, for all life is suffering. Unlike Brahman philosophy, he did not explain deliverance from karma and reincarnation on the basis of liberating the soul from the world of senses. Rather did he stress the need for drastic suppression of desire by curtailment of life through disavowal of the will to live and all human longings. Secondly, he breathed into Hinduism a new breath of life conveyed in his ethics. Though not limited to theory, this ethics was essentially psychological and hence incomplete even if compassionate.

The Buddha was probably the first teacher to express the idea, a fundamental law in the history of religions, that the ethical spirit in itself implies energy, the release of which produces an incalculable impact upon mankind. Thus, to endure enmity, and to forgive evil, not only leads to moral perfection but sets forth a new and lofty standard for the world. India and Hinduism took pause, and for centuries awaited uncertain as to the true meaning and intent of the Buddha. In the end, India cast off his life-suppressing theme, retaining only the ethics.

Edwin Arnold's *Light of Asia* is a partial exposition of Buddhism which interpreted the life of the Buddha as savior. Indeed his qualities of gentleness and compassion, his message of virtue and deliverance from sorrow, gave the masses of Asia a light they hoped for. Buddhism brought Asia under heavy debt by its spiritualization of life and work.

[E] A fifth frontier where crucial battles between law and religion raged is the Near East. Both Judaism and Christianity look to Palestine as a holy land. Equally committed is Islam although its specific shrines are Mecca and Medina in the province of al-Hijaz under the Saudi Arabian flag.

Throughout this Bible world, Islam, a religion that claims the allegiance of a worldwide community transcending race and geography, holds sway. Where Christianity has not been literally supplanted by Islam, it has shrunk, save in the Republic of Lebanon, to minority status. After centuries of dispersion unto the far corners of the earth, Judaism has recaptured a sizable portion of Palestine to which it has applied the ancient and hallowed name of Israel.

Christians, too, have been uprooted or chose to push out on their own. They have moved in four different directions.[7]

The Assyrian-Nestorians were driven eastward into Kurdistan and Southern India. Monophysite Christians were forced southward into Ethiopia. The Eastern Orthodox moved northward into the Balkan

[7] Toynbee, *op. cit.,* pp. 32 ff.

countries and Russia. As for Roman Catholic and Protestant Christians, their trek was first into Western Europe. Thence they crossed the Atlantic into the New World.

It may be a parable of this entire frontier that in an inaccessible fastness of Ethiopia, a Jewish community should survive today. This Jewish island is surrounded by an inner ring of Christians who themselves are encircled by an outer ring of Muslims.

In all this process of transformation, displacement, dislocation, and spasmodic revival, a heavy price has been paid. It was the price of fierce intercreedal conflict, involving the substance of national, international, and divine law.

[F] Ever since Greek philosophy and Roman law made their mark, the West tends to assume the role of moderator, expositor, and analyst-catalyst of religion, law, doctrine, ritual, and ethics. During the whole Hellenistic age, writes the historian of science, George Sarton,[8] there flourished in close rivalry three kinds of popular religion. There was, first, the old Greek paganism; second, Judaism; and, third, various Oriental mystery cults, such as those of Mithras, Cybele, and Attis, of Isis and Osiris. " The appearance of a new incomprehensible mystery, that of Jesus Christ," Sarton added, " and its gradual triumph characterized an entirely new period."

The towering personalities of Alexander the Great (+323 B.C.) and Aristotle (+322 B.C.) foreshadowed the role of the West as arbiter and disseminator of civilization. That role persisted in the Christian era. In the modern upsurge of science, it has attained hitherto unprecedented heights.

The Hellenistic world was somewhat cosmopolitan, polyglot, and molded by many religious faiths. Greek held primacy as a language. But with the success of Roman arms, Latin steadily gained in prominence. Under Greek tutelage, a fantastic mixture was allowed to brew. This involved, in the first instance, Hellenistic and Roman materials; also, Egyptian, Jewish, Iranian, Syrian, Anatolian, and other ingredients. Under those circumstances, the polarized traditions of the West, ancient Oriental and Occidental Greek, were bound to act and interact.

The encounter of European, Asian, and African ideas proved crea-

[8] *A History of Science, Hellenistic Science and Culture in the Last Three Centuries,* B.C. (Harvard University Press, 1959), p. 527.

tive. Original work might be done in many places — in Western Asia, North Africa, or Europe — yet invariably the leaven was Greek. In the closing centuries before Christ, geometry, astronomy, anatomy, and grammar were established forever. Technology and medicine began to blossom.

Where law and religion were concerned, note must be taken of a triple struggle that took shape.

This comprised, first, a rivalry between Greek ideas, on the one hand, and those of Western Asia and Egypt, on the other. Constituting a second conflict was the rude impact of Rome upon the aforenamed two sides. The third was a tension between Greek philosophy and the rising Christian religion; eventually this tension was resolved by an alliance between the two. Such an alliance shed much light upon the subsequent role of the West and its expanding religious vitality.

Greek philosophy had emanated from four principal Athenian schools. These were the Academy, founded by Plato, the Lyceum of Aristotle, the Garden of Epicurus, and the Porch or Stoa, most influential of all. As regards ethics and politics, the significance of Stoicism can hardly be exaggerated. Zeno (+264 B.C.), first teacher of the Porch, was of probable Phoenician background. In a chaotic and immoral age, Stoicism stood as a citadel of personal and civic virtues.

Stoicism stands as the noblest ethical doctrine of the ancient world. Until the collapse of paganism, it continued to quicken and sustain the best minds in state and culture. By laying stress on conscience and duty and by emphasis on belief in Providence, it encouraged acquiescence in one's destiny, stood for a harmonization of personal life with the universe or nature. It gave rise to obedience before the Eternal. It urged equal participation and fellowship among men. It fostered justice and a spirit of brotherhood.

Yet on the side of ethical doctrine Stoicism left much to be desired. It was abstract and left the heart cold. Hence the ultimate victory of Christianity. That victory was secured through New Testament love, mercy, and peace. These were a counterpoise to, and a fulfillment of, the power of law.

[G] That religions live by, and in tension with, law may be illustrated from the contemporary religious scene.

In the emergence of Asia, Africa, and the Middle East, religion and law march side by side, or in diametric opposition. This indeed is an age of longing for most of the world's peoples. Hitherto dominated races are not only beginning to live under new constitutions and to enjoy the liberty of self-determination. They are also eager to share in shaping human destiny. In one country after another, this is a revolutionary period as well as a time of awakening.

In Asia alone a billion and a half souls are involved. Of these no more than forty million are Christians. In the Middle East are some hundred and ten million people. Of these around seven million profess Christianity. It has been suggested that Asia, Africa, and the Middle East confront modern Christianity with a predicament not unlike that faced by the New Testament churches in their conflict with Greco-Roman civilization.

There is an almost analogous, if not more devastating, danger of collision with the gnosis of rival cults and philosophies. Classical Confucianism and Taoism, Hinduism and Buddhism, Zoroastrianism, Shinto, not to mention Judaism and Islam, along with countless superseding cults, are out to thwart what news the gospel calls good. The thrust of dynamic faiths is met at different levels. Inevitably, a crucial question is evoked whether or not the church has sufficient stamina to transform inherited superstition and reactionary social traits.

The analogy with Greco-Roman antiquity breaks down in the political sphere. Not just one but three integrating superpowers currently hold sway in Asia. Russia controls the north from the Caucasus to the Bering Strait. China, with an area twice that of India, stretches across the central land mass of Asia. The United States of America, although sovereign over no Asian territory, exerts tremendous authority, nonetheless, through treaties and alliances. To say that the Communists have drained Western reserve strength in Indo-China and seized Tibet is to voice an understatement. They are in fact intent upon the same objective throughout the non-Occidental world.

Suspicion of the West and opposition to Christianity in this vast resurgent domain requires a word of explication. It will be recalled that for four centuries — ever since Europe's age of discovery, exploration, and colonization began — these countries have barely existed in areas neglected as the world's backwaters. Only recently have they shaken off lethargy and acquired a voice in current affairs. It is quite obvious that resurgent movements in the ancient faiths of the non-Christian world represent efforts on the part of long-suppressed societies to achieve a correlation between creed and culture, religion and law.

The modern prophets of this non-Western world recognize that the destiny of their homelands is unavoidably linked to that of humanity as a whole. There is hardly anything they covet more for their own nations than partnership with the West in shaping the historical drama. It is of the essence that we grasp the potency of that determination whether in the domain of religion or international law.

This age of longing springs into being on three different levels. First, it is the longing of awakened peoples, intoxicated with the heady wine of revolution, a revolution transcending every aspect of existence. Second, the longing surges where ancient faiths have long catered to the hunger of famished souls, the nostalgia and homesickness of a prodigal for his father's home. Third, and on the deepest level, the longing, regardless of form or content, is the response of men in Asia, Africa, and the Middle East to the call of the Eternal.

What we describe as response to the call of the Eternal translates itself in social change, new institutions, and the uplift of society through liberalized education and recodified law as well as reformed government and religion. Such a dynamic motivation lies behind much neutralism in the so-called uncommitted world. Recalcitrance and isolation on the part of an erstwhile colonial world often comes under the same verdict. The long-range perspectives of a meaningful coexistence consist, among other things, in interfaith dialogue, international exchange of scientific and research personnel, as well as extensive economic cooperation.

Law and social change are meanwhile pivotal points testing the vitality of religion and the implementation of ideas. Malinowski, to whom earlier reference has been made, underscored " functionalism " in social anthropology. His study of the primitives of Trobriand Islands, off New Guinea, led to a distinct contribution in the evaluation of law. He vigorously insisted that law was an aspect of society and culture generally.

How well aware Malinowski was of the gaps that occur between the ideal and the actual norms of law.[9] It was perhaps his personal experience as a Pole under Austrian rule that taught him at first hand something about the situation of ethnic minorities in Europe. At any rate, that problem was never very far from his mind, particularly so when he considered cultural and social changes imposed from the outside.

In his Europe the imposition essentially consisted in the suppression of the modes of behavior. Such a suppression appears in the enumeration of cultural traits. These might include distinctive ritual, public celebrations, and the use of a language other than that of the ruling group. As a student of social phenomena, however, he never thought of cultural traits as separate from the persons in whose behavior they were manifest.[10] His primary concern was with social relations. He insisted on the primary significance of the institution. This he defined sometimes as a system of activities and sometimes as a group of persons. Cultural change is therefore social and consists less in the diffusion of traits and more in the encouragement of institutional change.

Application of the above principle to the contemporary resurgence of the non-Western world and to the way religions live might prove revealing. Where legal systems operate as an expression of living religion the units of transformation apparently are not traits or trait complexes. Transformation occurs instead through organization and institutions. Even when the wholeness of a culture justifies discussion in terms of a pattern, the pattern needs to be seen in art forms, in ceremonies, and in the type of personality that is admired. Yet with all the flaws of such a functionalism as a yardstick of social change, there seems to be a virtue to the assumption that an institution as such is a qualified agency of coherence and perpetuity in a changing society.

Such an interpretation of resurgence vitalized and stimulated by religion and law seems plausible. The guiding thought is that social change as an end result takes place basically through institutions and by organization. This leads to a reopening of the subject in reference

[9] I. Schapira, "Malinowski's Theories of Law," in *Man and Culture,* ed. by Raymond Firth (Humanities Press, Inc., 1957), p. 155.

[10] Lucy Mair, "Malinowski and the Study of Social Change," Firth, *loc. cit.,* pp. 232–235.

to the impact of industrialization on a peasant society. Involved is not only Africa but the entire underdeveloped world.

It was Malinowski's contention that culture change in Africa does not fundamentally differ from that which is at present transforming the rural and backward countries of Europe from peasant communities into a new type closely akin to the working classes found in the industrial districts of the United States of America, Great Britain, and France. Indeed, methods originally based on work done among primitive peoples have been applied within the last decade or two to village communities in France, Spain, Turkey, and the New World, even to selected localities in advanced metropolitan areas such as London and New York City.

In sum, a resurgent religion lives as it focuses on social change and institutional development.

II

Religions are alive today in the doctrines they hold, defend, and by which they set themselves apart. Christianity is a case in point. Its unceasing scrutiny of religion and the religions is prodigious. There is here revaluation reflected in the history of religions; in missionary ecumenical motivation and strategy that are ever under review; as well as the regrouping and reorganization of communions and denominations. There is the new interest in sociological and psychological research. A progressive doctrinal movement makes itself felt in withdrawal from isolation and controversy, on the one hand, and advance toward appreciation and conversation, on the other.

There are scholars, of course, who act as though they considered the history of religion a history of the gradual dissolution and disappearance of religion. Behind their investigations and discoveries is an attempt to reduce religion to psychological and sociological factors. Religion defies reduction, however, to nonreligious categories and formulations.[11] That religions are alive today may be partly due to their doctrinal tenets validated in meaningful experience.

Study of religious phenomena has aided immensely in such validation. It is a painstaking examination of religious essences. An endeavor is thus made to comprehend religious phenomena in religious

[11] C. J. Bleeker, "La structure de la religion," in *Revue d'histoire et de philosophie religieuse* (Presses Universitaires de France, Paris, 1951), Vol. XXXI, p. 407.

terms, that is, from the viewpoint of the religious person.[12] One does not conclude such an inquiry without raising a sobering question: Why does a certain phenomenon convey meaning to certain groups or individuals whereas it fails altogether in leaving a lasting impression on a modern mentality?

Two things are implied in the phenomenology of religion: theory and logic. The theory of religion involves doctrine, revelation, vision, essence. The logic of phenomena is entirely different. It lends itself to objective study, scientific verification, and research. Such a logic endows religion with a structure wherewith theory acquires dynamism, becomes an active, concrete reality. In this sense, religion ceases to be solely subjective, an inscrutable mystery of the soul. It takes on instead the aspect of an objective reality, reliant upon strictly religious laws yet maintaining a structure of its own. The logic of any such religious structure will of necessity come to light only along general lines. Ambiguity and irrational detail indubitably will conspire to offset clarity.

Such a logic will concern itself at once both with religion as such in the abstract and with the plurality of religions taking them individually one by one, and collectively. To ponder religion in the abstract is to concede that every religion offers its own way of self-realization. As for the plurality of faiths, the problem may be stated schematically: Religion is founded upon some idea of God. From that idea arise particular practices of cult and ritual. Thence a conception is derived, pointing the way to salvation and what has been called peace of mind, body, or soul.

The structure of religion therefore may be described in simple language.[13] There is a holy vision, a holy action, and a holy pathway. Although this scheme is strikingly formal, it is highly significant. Indeed, it applies to all the religions without exception. If in a sketch of a particular religion, one of the above three elements is lacking, a conclusion would be in order that the sketch is defective no matter how expertly drawn up.

Insofar as the structure of the historic religions is concerned, four [14]

[12] Van der Leeuw, *Phänomenologie der Religion,* pp. 768–798.

[13] Cf. Gustave Mensching, *Die Religionen und die Welt* (L. Röhrscheid, Bonn, 1949), pp. 20–24.

[14] See Bleeker, *op. cit.,* pp. 409–416.

generalizations may be in order. In each instance an understanding is afforded of the manner whereby religions live by doctrine.

[A] For one thing, comparative religion long ago discovered a variety of resemblances, constant forms, among the world's different faiths. To say that the religions have certain features in common is by no means to confirm their similarity. No matter how striking resemblances may seem, each religion has an originality of its own and an utterly distinctive character. Analogies and parallels do suggest, however, a highly illuminating line of interpretation. As regards the nature of constant forms that religions manifest, these too shed highly instructive light.

Scientific study of the religions dispels the notion that in expressing themselves the religions had recourse to an inexhaustible abundance of forms. To entertain any such idea is to fall victim to a deceptive illusion that has misled many an otherwise reliable scholar. Accurate investigation of the problems involved leads to a directly contrary conclusion. The fact dawns that religious forms are numerically few, the faiths relatively short on possibilities for self-expression. An apparently infinite variety of colors and designs observed among religious phenomena ought not distract attention from the truth of the matter. The truth is that forms wherewith religions express themselves are surprisingly fewer than ordinarily surmised.

Identical metaphors, for example, serve to describe the relation between the human soul and God. These happen to be four. The relation between God and man is construed as analogous to that between master and servant,[15] father and child, friend and friend, lover and beloved. Each of these images acquires a special connotation in the believer's heart. Let it be reiterated that conclusive evidence shows these metaphors to be operative among adepts of religion in a worldwide distribution. How strange it is that the religious imagination, deemed exceedingly prolific, has really produced no other anthropomorphic[16] images than those cited to depict the relation between God and man.

A similar approach is possible to the structure of the cult. The

[15] The servant image applied to God in Christianity is not a reversal of this relationship. Whereas the Eternal takes the form of a servant, the human soul does not thereby become master.

[16] Spiritism, mysticism, and primitivism have, of course, produced other, though not anthropological, images.

sacred act is performed in keeping with certain established norms and procedures. These recur in diverse religions. Here again appearances prove deceptive when an immense multiplicity of cultic forms is supposed to exist. Taken in a purely formal and detached fashion, however, the structure of cults presents a fairly homogeneous and essentially simple order for all faiths.

When he comes to articulate his faith, man across the entire world fulfills his relationship with the Eternal through sacrifice and prayer. Each of these two, sacrifice and prayer, has its own inner logic and rhythmic character. Cultic observances indeed vary, and divergent traditions do appear in response to cultural traits and creedal disposition. Yet everywhere Deity is approached at shrine and on holy days through sacrifice and prayer.

How unmistakable, moreover, is the uniformity that prevails in the domain of ethics. Norms and standards in this field may at first seem incomputable. Yet nothing could be more inexact. A historian of religions must readily concede that the list of commandments and prohibitions is strictly limited. Taking a vast number of religions into account will indicate a fairly regular frequency of commandments and injunctions.

In short, it must be allowed that religious ecstasy borrows freely along channels of restricted scope. Verification thereof is available in the field of mysticism. The Godward ascent of the spirit is effected along a uniform plan corroborated in the works of many mystics in widely dispersed traditions. Three stations assure the soul supreme felicity, namely, purification, illumination, and union with the divine.

[B] For another thing, despite these striking traits of similarity, the religions bear the stamp of individuality and of a particularly irreducible character. Some forty years ago, comparative religion devoted much time and energy to the subject of parallels. Behind those attempts was a hidden desire to prove the religions avid borrowers the one from the other. What they borrowed ostensibly were concepts, metaphors, and motifs. The outcome was to weaken, perhaps obliterate, the likelihood of any real originality in the history of a given faith.

The phenomenology of religion assumed responsibility to set these irreducible factors in proper perspective. It has reminded us that its scientific procedures will radically differ from those of natural science. The latter represents a search for such laws and general theories as govern nature. Phenomenology is a historical science and hence concerned with the meaning of individual acts. It claims possession of an antenna, so to speak, permitting detection and valuation of the contingent, that is, acts and events explicable under any law whatever.

Precisely at this point did phenomenology score its major victories. Those were victories won in commitment to the task of characterizing specific religious traits by an allusion to their essential meaning. Only extensive and positive knowledge of the facts could effect such an accomplishment. But mere knowledge was not enough. Beyond it was the need to explore religious phenomena by an intuitive penetration of essence.

Phenomenological research, while empirical, in a sense, bears a close affinity to that of art. One is hardly ever in a position to prove a phenomenological sketch absolutely true. One can only trust, in such a field, that ultimately truth will vindicate itself. Granted an open mind and a resolute faith, irreducible factors in the vast arena of religious experiences will eventually gain in clarity.

To a primary truth in this connection reference has been made already. It rests on the assumption that genuine religion cannot be reduced to nonreligious factors. Space does not permit a full discussion of this theme. It more appropriately belongs to the philosophy of religion. Suffice it at this juncture to say that a repudiation of the above view will not advance understanding of religion. Religion is *sui generis;* its domain is the sacred.

The first religious thinker to declare the sacred as the core of religion was a distinguished specialist in the history of religion, the Archbishop of Sweden, Nathan Söderblom (1866–1931). His precise observations on this theme anticipated the contribution of Rudolf Otto, the celebrated Marburg professor to whom earlier reference was made. Otto conceived of holiness as the thread of meaning in religion upon which everything else was strung. Even a critic of Otto who denies that everywhere the essence of religion is the idea of the holy might concede that under the rubric of the sacred we find an irreducible element of religion.

What we are trying to affirm is that religion manifests itself as a unique phenomenon. Equally clear it is that the several historic religions uphold structures of their own. To each an individuality attaches which cannot be rightly comprehended save from the inside. Each religion tackles the problem of existence in its own way.

The great scandal of life is that all pass away, that nothing under the sun is perfect and that here whatever is is defective. Religious intellectuals have all had to wrestle with the problem of imperfection. Suffering, guilt, sin, and anxiety have kept them bowed down. If only they could find relief from such fetters. They fight so ardently for freedom and happiness.

This problem of life's tragedy has received treatment in diverse ways. Thus Christianity counsels the faithful to bear life's burdens with patience and humility. Sin is the chief adversary to be overcome. Granted, suffering and the cross are inexplicable, the mind can cite no reason for them. They must be victoriously endured, in the same manner Jesus endured his agony with power, as an unshakable faith in God.

What if the tragedy of existence seems altogether insufferable? Abolition of the entire fabric of being is in that event the only practical way to liberation. Is that not the message of Buddhism and of Greek tragedy? Buddhism takes the position that man is enchained by ignorance to a round of existences, a cycle of birth and rebirth, with all the sufferings in between. Only as he acquires a liberating knowledge of his untenable state does he develop fitness for self-release. Escape from the grip of the transitory will lead to the blessedness of Nirvana.

As for the Greek understanding of tragedy, it followed a somewhat different course. Under a dramatic format, man's utter enslavement to sin and suffering was noted. Evil was there and man could see no way out. Finally, the issue was removed. Only by his own destruction and death was man able to expiate a guilt for which he was hardly to blame.

Each of the above treatments of evil and suffering — Christian, Buddhist, and Greek — represents a different and unique approach and is therefore an irreducible phenomenon.

[C] In the third place, phenomenology seeks to uncover core elements among constant religious forms and unique irreducible structures. The trained eye of the scholar early discovered that religious phenomena tended to gravitate around certain focal points. In order the better to comprehend these core elements and focal points, a religion under investigation had to be carefully studied.

At some risk of self-contradiction religion may be tentatively defined as a response or attitude. Each time a religious man expresses faith in a supernatural power, he does take a position and assumes a responsibility. Such a position, attitude, or responsibility becomes a core element, a pivotal point, and may be assigned a technical name. The word "habitus"[17] has been suggested. A habitus indicates precisely that point of reference which serves as an agent of crystallization.

An agent, or habitus, of crystallization naturally will engender a specific concept of divinity, a doctrine of salvation, a cult, and a moral code. When derived from a given habitus such religious essentials prove relatively homogeneous and mutually congenial. A shaft of light is thus shed upon the formal elements that constitute the structures of religion. It will be recalled that the schema of religion noted above included the three formal elements of holy vision, holy action, and a holy pathway. The assumption here is that differing types of habitus give rise to variations in the schema of religion and thus explain diversity in pattern and content.

Different habiti may be directed in different directions. Upon the nature of such orientation rests the structure of a given religion. An orientation of this kind is generally directed toward an aspect of reality wherewith the nature of divinity breaks through. Two orders of revealing reality have been detected, and each may be said to serve as medium for manifestations of the divine. These two orders are nature and spirit. It is vital from the outset to distinguish, therefore, between a habitus that looks to nature for the disclosure of religious truth and another that finds such a disclosure in the realm of the spirit.

There are religions, then, for which the principal, if not sole, source for the knowledge of God consists in nature. It would be grossly inadequate to call such religions naturalistic. The truth of the matter is that they discern the spirit in nature. Around the central motif of nature, three varieties of religion arise.

Primitive religion ranks first in this nature group. Although

[17] In anthropology, the term "habitus" refers to the body build and is generally used in connection with constitutional types.

creator of a complex civilization, primitive man lives literally too close to nature to disentangle himself from his environment. He must constantly measure himself up with natural forces over which he has hardly any control. To this same group another variety belongs — the great religions of antiquity. The religions of Egypt, Mesopotamia, Greece, and Rome, to be sure, had each its own peculiar character. Their common ground, however, consisted in an identical habitus. This was comprised in a cult of cosmic life whereby divine initiative revealed itself primarily in a power of periodic victory over death.

A third religion of nature moved farther along in regarding the universe as a veil concealing the sacred. India is the foremost pioneer contributing to the formation of such a doctrine. All major religious systems of Hinduism base themselves on the painful experience that life is vanity and travail. He who possesses right knowledge may lift the veil. He may resist the seductive power of this world and discover the Absolute.

Such are the three types of religion centered in nature.

As we turn to the religions focused upon the spirit, we likewise are confronted with a variety of types. The first of these is mysticism. Multiple and variegated, the vast forms of mysticism are all related to a single pattern of habitus. Essentially this is an orientation toward the expansive and void. Enraptured with limitless infinitude, the mystic endeavors to divest himself of human obstructions. His notions are normally romantic, ethereal, negative, and allegorical. The metaphors of mysticism are frequently drawn from contemplation in desert solitude or other haunts of withdrawal and seclusion. Like a lark, a mystic must fly. He mounts up with wings, soars in infinite spaces, and sings to the fullness of divine love.

Attention shifts from mysticism with its ascetic and intuitive impulses to other religions centered also in the invisible world of the spirit. Peculiar to these other religions, however, is discovery of the knowledge of God in history. To this group belongs the religion of Zoroaster, as does Judaism, as well as Christianity and Islam. It is an undergirding affirmation of these religions that they have received a revelation from God within sacred history.

There is, besides, a habitus that tends to reflect upon itself in the vain attempt to find a superior spirit therein. When nature proves incomprehensible and historical traditions of the spirit lose authority, man is constrained in sheer desperation to explore his inward spirit. Such is the hallmark of some contemporary religious phenomena.

[D] A fourth thing brought out by phenomenology is that religions in each case enshrine a typical set of traits. What is typical about a given religion obviously merits sober classification. It also requires initial definition. Of a variety of religious traits, let us recall, a religion tends to single out one trait in particular to serve as object of exploitation and as ideal form. Such a trait or idea may be encountered elsewhere, but only in an incidental, subordinate role. Nowhere may it be recorded as typical except in the one religion involved.

This is not the place to consider typical traits in the whole gamut of religion. Certain examples easily come to mind and may help clarify the principle in question. What do scholars mean when they speak of ancient Egypt and its strong attachment to the mystery of death? Is it not that every phase of that ancient civilization was somehow influenced by an intense preoccupation with a life surging from the dead?

Other religious traits beckon for attention almost everywhere we look. There was the Greek concern with the relation between form and creative reality. The Greeks were thus led to cultivate an approach, now beautiful, now severe, in art, conduct, and philosophy. They did make allowance, however, for inspiration, a sacred folly transcending forms and leading to involved and complicated patterns.

The Romans in turn held law in highest esteem. A consummate regard for the numina, moreover, bore specific determinations for cult, social practice, and personal relations. The ancient wisdom of China was to live in harmony with an order of the universe, the great Tao. Judaism was stamped with sacred terror before the God of Holiness. Such was the typical trait that animated the cult, ethics, and faith of Old Testament religion. Islam drew its very name from a word denoting submission of the faithful to the sovereign will of God.

That the religions come alive in doctrinal structures is therefore indicated. This is amply elucidated in Islam. As is generally recognized, Islam presents numerous parallels with the two other religions of Near Eastern rootage, Judaism and Christianity. It is not simply a matter of external appearances. Internal evidence, as well, gives force to this view. A cardinal example is the striking analogy between Islamic belief in predestination and its counterpart in Calvinist theology. Both bow before God's absolute sovereignty.

Yet certain competent scholars persist in maintaining that Islam is an inferior religion lacking originality. A serious historian of religion will scarcely share such a verdict. He will, on the contrary, detect in Islam, that woefully misunderstood faith, an energy and a resolution, as well as a capacity to organize votaries in a most compact brotherhood. If so, Islam would seem to possess not only such constant forms as are familiar to other faiths but, what is more, a core factor, the secret center of power in the realm of faith.

If one looks for an agent of crystallization in Islam, it should be clear its internal habitus can be none other than an attitude of the soul that confronts God in history. He is the God who revealed his will and nature through the instrumentality of Mohammed. As regards Islam's typical trait, the hallmark of the faith, what else can it be if not an absolute obedience before God, the merciful and compassionate Lord?

III

Although sometimes in atrophy, the classical religions are frequently in a state of metamorphosis, their potentialities and capabilities far from exhausted. Confucianism and Taoism are relatively quiescent. Hinduism and Buddhism are in the throes of an extraordinary renaissance. All but defunct, Zoroastrianism persists on a small yet vibrant scale in and around the city of Bombay. Shinto fluctuates with the ups and downs of Japanese self-consciousness. Islam, Judaism, and certainly Christianity are on the march.

Experience indicates the religions do not die easily. Even embalmed and interred, they spring back to life. At any rate, man's thirst for spiritual refreshment seems quite insatiable. Consider, for instance, the Roman Catholic revival in the wake of eighteenth-century French political cataclysm. Or the rehabilitation of Eastern Othodoxy in the U.S.S.R. after a persecution more crippling than anything known to church history since the Roman Emperor Diocletian (284–305). Across an urban civilization proliferation of sect, cult, and sanctuary proceeds. These and similar manifestations punctuate the vitalities of twentieth-century faith.

The religious problems of this era obviously are not those of Renan, Reinach, Frazer, Durkheim, or Nietzsche, nor of their adversaries who were constrained to meet them on suitable ground. We have reached a juncture marked by more and less skepticism; more, where illusion is concerned, less because of a newfound objectivity. Sound learning forbids the premature interment of any religion. It warns against a too far-reaching synthesis, farfetched comparison, and fragmentation of religious truth. The accumulation of precise data, as well as newly available information, is a spur to prudence and reserve in this field. How often we discover an incompetence to pose basic questions regarding the birth, death, and resurrection of religions. Whether believers or not, Christians or non-Christians, we cannot escape the stare of the sphinx and his probing of conscience.

To the Christian, faith provides the key answer. It is an answer that before non-Christians must be qualified by reason. It was not too long ago that the history of religions assigned a priority to apologetics and was consequently bogged down in the morass of self-defense. More recently, a source of inestimable strength was found which proved an asset to Christians and others. It consists in the espousal of a methodology grounded in objectivity, understanding, and explication. The common ground is rational research. A sign of maturity, this new approach is a call to reserve and serenity where explication of divine grace is not immediately clear.

Despite atrophy and metamorphosis, the religions demonstrate continuity of certain elements that outlast the death of particular faiths. Indeed, the birth and death of religions, as well as their renaissance and resurgence, disclose much of the vitality they live by. A historical and sociological apprehension of religious phenomena is therefore of the essence.[18]

Are religions really born and do they wither away and die? To give a reasonable answer one must recall that religious life in its stark reality and originality does not exist save under given conditions. There must be a common faith validated through beings and spiritual powers distinct from man. As a rule, these beings and spirit-

[18] Joseph Folliet, "Naissance et mort des religions," in *Histoire des religions*, ed. by Brillant and Aigrain, Vol. II, pp. 305–337.

ual powers are external to man at least in some respects. They are altogether mightier and more worthy. In their power, they stand absolute.

A corollary of such a faith is that man recognizes himself inferior to these powers. He depends on them, drawn by reverence, devotion, and obedience. A distinction between religion and magic is obvious. Under the first, unlike the second, man divests himself of the desire to impose his will or law upon the spiritual powers he worships.

There must consequently be adoration of the divine in a spirit of devotion and communion. Such a constituent of religion is lacking in some profane rituals of antiquity. In a religion, rightly so-called, ordinarily there are collective observances with a graded system of myths and dogmas. These range all the way from theogony to abstract dogma. Collective practices are conceived as obligations. These are a necessary implementation of the belief in an absolute, a conscious expression of the sacred in life.

Lastly, a minimal institutional organization, a vital center of community life and spirit, is essential. This is commonly exteriorized in assemblies and expressed in moralistic utterances and pious gestures. Such a religion will almost invariably crystallize in ritual. It will culminate in some form of interpersonal and social intercourse and corporate fellowship.

Despite innumerable works in ethnology, what do we precisely know about religion in prehistory and protohistory? That is to say, what do we really know about the relation of these to the gradual separation between religion and magic? By such separation we mean differentiation between priest and sorcerer (or shaman), between impure ritual and the interior life. Where does the human person emerge in closed societies and communities collectively determined?

Were religious attitudes first formulated in Babylonian psalms or in certain texts of ancient Egypt such as the ritual for the dead? Was the flowering of personality contingent upon the dawn of conscience, a revolutionary development, social, religious, historical? In this assumed dawn, one concedes the individual shared an immortality originally reserved for the Pharaoh, the community's incarnation. Was the breakthrough of religion dependent upon mythologies that projected personages, situations, and histories, corresponding with historical memories? Or, was it, as Freud and Jung have conjectured, an essential situation of mankind depicted in individual complex, universal archetype, and dynamic symbol? [19]

The birth of religion is hardly ever a start from scratch. Again, a case in point is the matter of originality in Islam. Along with that originality, the synthesis the Prophet proposed and the Koran enunciated is inescapable. It is a synthesis embracing diverse elements borrowed from the Arab culture of the day, Judaism, and Eastern Christianity. It included important other ingredients such as the cult of the Kaaba, the pilgrimage, and circumcision, as well as sundry borrowings from pre-Islamic folklore and Arab paganism. To realize all this is by no means to minimize the role of Mohammed but to discern what great synthesis was behind his faith.

A more recent example is the Theosophical Society organized in India by the Russian Elena Petrovna Blavatsky (1831–1891) and the English Annie Besant (1847–1933). Theosophy began as a protest against any exotic religion, should have ended as a "church," but did not quite make it. Despite its slogan "There is no religion higher than the truth," it was short on originality. It brought together elements of occultism, spiritism, and Christianity. It also employed current scientific ideologies as well as such Buddhist and Hindu ideas as were deemed alluring to Westerners.

Unique and challenging as Christianity is, even from a simple human standpoint, and setting aside for the moment explications of the supernatural, it certainly depended upon forerunners. We know it came after a long period of preparation — a pedagogy, one might call it. The Hebrew prophets, Isaiah in particular, prefigured the Evangelists. The more we know about the Israelite environment of Jesus' time, the greater our awareness of a maturity that Christ brought when he proclaimed the good news. The Dead Sea scrolls have deepened such an awareness. The birth of a religion is the birth of an organic being. It is a commencement, but not absolutely. There is at once a rupture with the past and a witness to continuity.

As to the atrophy and death of a religion, they too are fluid and mobile frontiers. Perfectly in order is the question whether a religion ever passes out completely. Do not the religions enjoy almost indefinite survival? The answer seems to be affirmative if we consider

[19] Jolande Jacobi, *Complex/Archetype/Symbol* (Bollingen Series LVII, Pantheon Books, Inc., 1959).

folklore and tradition; also, if we recall the continuing influence of a faith in the structure of another by which it is dethroned.

It is a banality to note in a religion as ecumenical as Christianity that the cult of saints reproduces in certain phases Latin cults of nymphs and dryads which themselves had succeeded older cults of trees and fountains. Islam, of no less exacting standards, did not escape the same kind of borrowing. It has allowed analogous survival. Shrines of Muslim hermit saints, such as the North African Marabouts, as well as sacred trees and fountains, are widely recognizable in the Maghrib, the Far West of the Arab world.

But to return to Christianity, the cult of St. Michael stands on the identical site of high places where Mercury was once worshiped in Latin paganism. The latter itself had replaced the worship of a Celtic divinity, a successor to a more ancient cult in primordial mythology. In the majority of cases, barring physical cataclysms and social catastrophes, the religions died slowly, imperceptibly, and somehow managed to survive at least in part.

Between birth and death religions exhibit the properties of their living organisms. Such properties include growth, expansion, struggle for existence, slow evolution, abrupt mutations, periods of equilibrium as well as of health, birth-giving, sickness, retractions, languor, critical and climactic stages such as decadence, senility, and mortality. Once a body " ecclesiastic " has been formed, events follow a generally uniform order. The style may differ, the sequence may vary, but the logic is everywhere the same.

Heresy is separation from a doctrinal standard such as the breakup of Buddhism into Mahayana, Hinayana, and tantric ritual vehicles. Schism is separation because of conflicting authorities such as the initial breakup of Islam into Sunnite and Shiite branches; although, here, too, strong shades of heresy are from the outset apparent. The truth is that disciplinary ruptures in time acquire an emotional and therefore increasingly doctrinal character.

The sect marks the secession of a small " perfectionist " group, sure of its doctrinal integrity in contrast with a parent body it regards as corrupt. In the United States of America, sects have discovered a fertile soil. Even the Roman Catholic faith was not immune to sectarianism. Not forgotten is that band of Boston educators who broke off with the Catholic Church. Their withdrawal was sparked by an unsatisfied desire to fasten an absolute connotation on the formula that there is no salvation outside the church.

Vitality also asserts itself at the center of ecclesiastical organization. There intellectual activity will thrive and grow vibrant in theological debate, in a reconstructed theology, or in a religiophilosophical synthesis. By these activities, the longing for unity might be fulfilled. Classification of theologians and labeled protagonists and antagonists arise. Today there are religious jurists, scribes, doctors of law, canonical authorities, whose function it is to strike a synthesis between religion, morality, and changing philosophies of life.

Religious ferment in thought and ritual, doctrine and personnel, often matures in internal reforms on both the moral and spiritual levels. The rule generally is return to original simplicity and the pristine quality of the faith. In this connection, modern Islam offers the striking examples of Wahhabism, the Sanusi movement, and diverse activities of contemporary ulama (theologians). New life is also engendered through the establishment of specialized organizations, that is, societies consisting of those who seek to perfect and promote religious solidarity and strength.

In monasticism, there is the cenobite cloister pattern, common to Christianity in its Catholic, Protestant, and Orthodox traditions. It is also common to Islam and Buddhism. Congregations, fraternities, or fellowships are thus created. They inject life-giving energy into the bloodstream of a given religion.

Revival is furthered through an experience of piety, verging on mysticism, that is, on the expectation of union with spiritual powers. Some kind of piety has been fostered by each major religion. Doctrinal formulations governing ascetic and mystical practice follow.

One last phenomenon of growth is of frequent occurrence. Around the great religions, a number of parasitic bodies tend to gravitate. These are ordinarily set up by esoteric, occultist, or initiation masters. In most of these instances, there is detectable beneath the surface, whether they be Christian or non-Christian, Jewish or pagan, a modern variety of "gnosis."

To this order belongs the tantric Buddhism of Tibet as well as Japanese Zen. In Islam the Sufi brotherhoods formerly exercised a formidable role in cultural, literary, and moral life. In certain parts of the Muslim world, they still retain a measure of their medieval glory by stimulating thought and faith. Nor is it irrelevant here to mention that anthroposophy founded by Rudolf Steiner (1861–1925). His was an attempt to develop the faculty of spiritual cogitation inherent in ordinary people though denied by modern materialism. He sought to explain the world in terms of the nature of man.

IV

We have seen that religions live by law, doctrine, and metamorphosis. There is a fourth order, that of ethics. Interfaith cooperation is an expression of ethical vitality in our time. This is an applied ethics imparting form and meaning to faith on the concrete level of behavior. Who will deny that such an ethics makes real the meaning of theological abstraction in the annals of history, if only because it conditions economic and political action?

Unless religions agree to the extent of generating overt deterrence to massive, even partial, extinction, their ethical injunctions are bound to remain a dead letter. The fear of utter annihilation is a call to defrosting religion and loosing it for articulation. It is also a spur to action on the East-West frontier. A truly creative encounter can only result from spiritual fellowship. Scientific and literary universalities have been achieved. They are but an index of deeper human yearnings. Concerted effort born out of love, ideas, persons, movements, and knowledge will draw men and nations closer. In all that, the role of religion is both normative and luminous.

Every religion, primitive or developed, exceeds the purely anthropological study thereof. That is not the same as saying, however, that anthropology has little or nothing to contribute. Indeed, there is much for the history of religion to learn from an anthropological approach. Anthropology discerns the three aspects of religion: dogmatic, ritual, and ethical.[20]

The essential interrelation of these three is important. In the doctrinal or dogmatic sphere, man affirms that Providence or supernatural powers exist. In religious ritual, he worships this Being, or beings, and enters into relations with him or them. Revelation implies that such a relation is possible and necessary. An ethical system

[20] Bronislaw Malinowski, *The Foundations of Faith and Morals* (Oxford University Press, London, 1936), p. 2.

is inherent in all religious activities because of the common concerns of the community.

Anthropology may brush aside the theological view that ethics and doctrine are associated and that they have been vouchsafed to mankind through revelation. Yet in confronting the enigma of ethics, anthropology carries the discussion to a meaningful stage. It is in the sociological unfolding of religion that the meaning of ethics is discovered.

Every organized belief implies a congregation. How slow, however, is science to incorporate the findings of simple and sound reason. Two distinguished scholars did not manage to go beyond treatment of religious systems as if they were philosophical or literary productions. These two eminent men are none other than Edward Burnett Tylor (1832–1917), the English anthropologist and specialist in primitive culture, and Friedrich Max Müller (1823–1900), Anglo-German Sanskritist and comparative religionist. It was left to William Robertson Smith (1846–1894), the Scottish Biblical scholar, to set the study of religion in proper sociological perspective. That was the task taken up by the French sociologist and thinker, Émile Durkheim, who made precise though exaggerated elaborations.

Anthropology regards worship as a response to the common concerns of the community.[21] And that is where the ethical element in all religions lies. Efforts, discipline, and submission on the part of the individual for the good of the community are thus required. Taboos, vigils, religious exercises, are moral because they express man's submission to spiritual powers; also, because they are a sacrifice of man's personal comfort for the common cause.

There is another ethical aspect that makes all religions moral at the core. Every cult is associated with a definite congregation. Ancestor worship is primarily based on the family, in certain instances on a wider group such as tribe or clan. It is not hard to perceive how ancestor worship becomes tribal when an ancestor spirit happens to be that of a former chieftain. Members of such a group of worshipers are naturally obligated by duty toward each other. The sense of a common responsibility, of a reciprocal charity, and goodwill flows from the same fundamental motivation and sentiment that moves clansmen, brothers, and tribesmen to common worship. The concep-

[21] *Ibid.*, pp. 6–7.

tion of the church as a larger family is not without rootage in nature.

Malinowski, to whom this study is deeply indebted, could generalize on the basis of anthropological research. Dogma, ritual, and ethics he considered three inseparable facets of the same essential phenomenon — a deep conviction about the existence of a spiritual reality. In superstition, man attempts to control this reality. By it he is controlled in true religion. There is a " sacred story," he concluded, at the heart of culture and ethics. Take away from the natives belief in the reality of sacred lore, destroy their sense of the spirit world, and you will undermine their whole moral outlook.[22]

There is, therefore, he insisted, an anatomy and a pathology of religion, confirmed by ethnology. Form and function are alternative explications. Every organized faith carries its specific apparatus by which its substance is expressed. There must be a doctrinal system backed by mythology or sacred tradition. There must be a developed ritual in which man acts on his belief and communes with the power or powers he believes are able. There must be an ethical code of rules binding the faithful and determining their behavior toward each other and toward the object of their worship. How close these forms and religious structures are to the reality of totemism, animism, and ancestor worship determines our understanding of primitive faith. How real they are in social change, juridical transformation, and political resurgence spells out the vitality of religion in the modern world.

The twin beliefs in Providence and immortality sum up the subject matter of every religion. Belief in Providence is a mystical conviction that there exist in the universe a Force or forces, a Person or persons, who guide man and are in sympathy with his destiny. Only superstition seeks to propitiate Providence.

This concept of Providence, the Christian believes, finds its sublime expression in faith in God, one and indivisible though present in Three Persons, who has created the world and guides it today. Deformations, yet nonetheless derivatives from the above, are such forms of polytheistic paganism as belief in ancestor ghosts and guardian spirits. Even so-called totemic religions are but a crude version of the belief in Providence. The heart of this crudity consists in the conviction that man's social and cultural order is duplicated in a

[22] *Ibid.*, pp. 25–26, 58–62.

spiritual dimension through which he can control the natural forces of fertility and environment.

Christianity teaches resurrection, not immortality. In its vestigial form, however, belief in immortality has a validity of some kind. It affirms that beyond the brief span of natural life there is a personal compensation in another existence. This is a far cry from the eternal life of Jesus Christ, rooted in knowledge of One who is the only true God, and that Other whom he did send.

Yet through belief in immortality man can act and calculate far beyond his own forces and limitations. The sufferings and efforts, the injustices and inequalities of this life, are fully righted. The spiritual force of this belief — especially if uncompromised by secularism — not only integrates man's own personality but is indispensable for the cohesion of the social fabric. Assuming the substance of religion to be given, its validation in experience must mean it is deeply rooted in human life and need. In a word, religion fulfills a very definite cultural function in every human society.

If indispensable to the proper integration of man and society, religion cannot be regarded as a trickery, an opiate, or an invention of priests, capitalists, or any other servants of vested interests. A scientific treatment of religion implies, above all, clear analysis of how it grows and of the needs of human life, and how it lives.

In the higher religions, man lives in order to enjoy communion with the Eternal. In the simpler forms, the ancestors worshiped are often mystically identified with environmental forces as in totemism. Religious development probably consists in the growing predominance of the ethical principle; also in an increasing fusion of two main factors of faith, namely, the aforenamed sense of Providence and hope for a hereafter.

Is such a religion obsolete in our modern world? Will it be supplanted by simpler creeds, less mysterious and mythological, more empirical and natural, creeds which for all their rationality might fail, however, to fill man's hunger for an Absolute? Is religion ready to lay down its armor of faith, ritual, and ethics? Will it surrender to crossbreeds between superstition and science, between credulity and economics, between nationalist hysteria and political power?

One thing seems inevitable. The abandonment of religious health for partisan and doctrinaire purposes will do us no good. It is one of those many phenomena in a pathology of culture which push society downward. And that is the way some religions have suffered eclipse, withered, and fallen by the wayside.

Religions live by commitment to eternal truths. These are the truths that guided man in his arduous journey upward: from barbarism and despair to culture and cooperative concern, from the disease of ignorance and confusion to the light of knowledge and love.

CHAPTER

3

THE IDEA OF GOD AND THE HISTORY OF RELIGIONS

IN THIS BOOK, the idea of God is seriously contemplated as identical with the truth. It is an order of truth that informs both reason and wisdom. Else there could have been no lamp unto man's feet as he trudged on a slow and trying evolutionary trail. As a fountain of staying power, this truth engenders vitality in the believer. As a ray of hope and a spark of courage, it ignites the noble and triumphs in the strains of the free and just. Both mind and spirit it fortifies with the precious will to live and outlive.

The idea of God is here to stay. It nerves intellect and spirit, moves the will, fires the imagination, and motivates behavior. And to the study of religion it brings clarity. To recognize it is an absolute mandate. Manifold ideas of God lie behind social actions; they are current in the varieties of religious experience. Tracing them enables us to make a fresh start in the history of religions. Along the avenues of social science this should impart both depth and authenticity to comparative religion.

The several religions of mankind disclose integral ideas of God wherein manifestations of religious essence are exhibited. Such manifestations provide an incisive, profoundly inward, yet direct and immediate expression of the religious phenomena. Thereby the scope of religious phenomenology is made more real, its frontiers of meaning pushed farther back.

In the present chapter, discussion will center in the so-called "five integrities," representing as many diverse ideas of God in a total panorama of these major religious phenomena: Hinduism and Judaism, Islam, Christianity, and Buddhism. In each living faith an attempt will be made to capture something, if only a glimpse, of special modes and emphases displayed.

The exposition will next introduce for study of the history of religions five independent " methodologies," drawn from attitudes and motifs engendered by the ideas of God encountered. Such methodologies indeed are implicit, moreover, in certain widely divergent orders of religious perception. They each seem identifiable with some intellectual giant in the realm of thought and erudition. The methodologies range all the way from near eclecticism to a relatively committed yet avowedly tolerant approach. They vary from a dogmatic theological position to what may be regarded as either that of a naturalist dynamism or, alternately, that of critical existentialism.

A third and final part of the chapter will seek to show that these deep-seated ideas of divinity are as potent in shaping the drama of history as they are in their influence upon the domain of sociology; over political institutions no less than ecclesiastical structures, they seem to exert considerable formative power.

I

Is it unreasonable to project, if only provisionally, a plan to isolate a few hard-core " integrities " where the idea of God shines through? Are there no clusters of human thought discernible on the subject of the Eternal? Are these not palpably instinct with insight, intuition, and faith? If there are such clusters, there let us enter at the holiest of all thresholds, the threshold of divine reality.

[A] In the first instance an intensely radiant and storied integrity arises within the ancient and contemporary scope of Hindu religion and society. Nowhere else did the " lure of the Infinite " take on a more colorful garb. There is an unmistakable distinctively Hindu concept of the Eternal. Absolute, incoherent, divine, unknowable, yet pervasive and immanent in all things, this is an adorable deity. Of it, the erudite Madras philosopher, Prof. T. M. P. Mahadevan.[1] writes: " One of the fundamental beliefs of Hinduism is that there is one all-pervading and all-transcending *Spirit* which is the basic reality, the source and grounds of all being. This is usually referred to as God (Ishvara); but the wise realize it as the impersonal Absolute (Brahman). The reality conceived of as God is the cause of the

[1] *Outlines of Hinduism* (Chetana Limited, Bombay, India, 1956), pp. 23–27.

universe. God does not create the world out of nothing, nor out of any stuff external to him. It is God that has taken, as it were, all the forms that we see. The Hindu mind is averse to assigning an unalterable or rigidly fixed form or name to the Deity. Hence it is that in Hinduism we have innumerable god-forms and countless divine names. And it is a truth that is recognized by all Hindus that obeisance offered to any one of these forms and names reaches the one supreme God."

Hindu literary history endorses such a concept of the divine. The full gamut of Vedic writings may be said to reflect both Hindu iconography and the oral tradition of wisdom. What it tends to sharpen is an image of ultimate reality inherent in India's worship and ritual congenial to its environment and manners. Shankara (A.D. 788–820) was the first consolidator, though not innovator, of this doctrine transmitted under the rubric of an *advaita* (nonduality) philosophy that denied the belief that the creator and creature are two.

In the speculations of other respected Hindu teachers, the doctrine of God received further elaboration. Among these, the name of Ramanuja (A.D. 1017–1127) readily comes to mind. He held that Brahman was *saguna*. By this he meant that the deity possessed knowable characteristics. A third figure, the sixteenth-century God-intoxicated Tulsi Das, also had something to say on the subject. Especially remembered is he for bringing *bhakti,* devotion, to the common man. Not unlike Ramanuja, Madhva (A.D. 1199–1278) identified God with Vishnu-Narayan. But unlike him, he advocated a frank *dvaita* (duality) which recognized the creator and creature as two, rejecting the notion that they are one.

Clearly, then, this Hindu idea of God in its manifold expressions lays claim to a nature of its own. It was perpetuated and purveyed through the sacred documents and multicolored arts and archaeological monuments of the country. Over an extensive Indian landscape, a plurality of gods and goddesses held sway. Yet treatise and law, discourse, ritual, and commentary corroborated an Absolute being. Even so, a central idea of God did not develop apart from ethnic tone and local color.

Above and beyond was Brahman. Together with Vishnu and Shiva, Brahman stood triune, Trimurti, impersonal and utterly incomprehensible. He was nonetheless real. The wise were wont to believe him ground of all things, an adorable All-in-All.

[B] A second imposing integrity is the hallmark of historic Hebrew faith. Divine being, one, holy, personal, God is understood as the Thou of history. The Old Testament acknowledges God as the object of worship and focus of individual commitment. He is Lord of national allegiance as well as security and destiny. In the Hebrew scriptures, Martin Buber discovers not only the God of power. The God of Israel, he notes, is equally the God of love. Like as a father, this Creator is immediately and directly accessible in divine-human wrestling and intercourse.

In the throes of conflict, anxiety, and adversity, the Divine Presence keeps vigil over man and is ever within reach. He is a spirit, invisible, and inscrutable, yet closer to man than breathing, nearer than hands and feet. Despite an immeasurable disparity between the infinite God of power and finite man in all his depravity, the Eternal reinforces his children with an abiding assurance and sustaining comfort. Every believer on his name is further assured there is no need for a mediator. So accessible is the Eternal that all who seek him may come unto the throne of grace provided their approach is made in proper consecration of heart, soul, and might.[2]

Buber details further what he deems the central Biblical teaching on man. Created in the divine image, man receives freedom to choose obedience or disobedience. As regards the absolute and eternal Thou before whom man stands accountable, Buber holds an illuminating view.

"In every sphere in its own way, through each process of becoming, that is present to us, we look out toward the fringe of the eternal Thou; in each we are aware of a breath from the eternal Thou; in each Thou we address the eternal Thou."[3]

On his own initiative this eternal Thou bestows upon man abundant grace and blessing. He reveals power and wisdom as maker and sustainer, as master and friend — a master, that is, of the total historic process. God is arbiter of ends, instigator of an eventful confronta-

[2] Malcolm L. Diamond, *Martin Buber: Jewish Existentialist* (Oxford University Press, London, 1960), p. 180.

[3] Martin Buber, *I and Thou,* tr. by Ronald Gregor Smith (T. & T. Clark, Edinburgh, 1937), p. 6.

tion and communion between himself and man.

Such an idea of God within the Hebraic frame of reference professes him as the one and only reality. He is both ultimate and creative. He is Lord of time and eternity. The course of civilization he endows with design and significance. To the march of historical events he gives a meaning that transcends tragedy.

By virtue of divine participation history takes on special importance. It emerges as a stage upon which the Eternal reveals glory. Even more, history acquires a dramatic character. It is the register of God's purpose, the scene of his abiding presence and articulate will. Whether conceived as a battleground fought over inch by inch, or as a theater where decisive action initiates new eras of artistic taste and psychological outlook, history's title role inevitably devolves upon God and to him all its secrets revert.

On the stage of time, God reveals himself as Chief Actor. In that essential role, he disposes of all things and reveals both promise and fulfillment. Apathy and disaster he transmutes into victory and success. The havoc of destruction and harassment he crowns with renewal and revival. Tragedy becomes a pedestal, looking to bright horizons of hope and retrieval or, conversely, meting out judgment in the disintegration and bafflement of the reprobate.

[C] There is thirdly, the closely related, though radically different idea of God in the Islamic religion. An essentially unique concept, it is enshrined in the Koran and transmitted through the message of the Arabian Prophet. Heavy accent falls upon the divine and absolute nature of God. In sovereignty, he is without equal; in power, peerless. "God is all that counts," said a West African of Senegal to a visitor from the West. "We ask a politician if he is a believer. If he has a God, he is good; if he does not, he is bad, no matter what he says or does." [4]

One comes to grips here with a veritable Islamic order of things and sequence of events. Man is brought face to face with a consciousness of the altogether transcendent Creator. The Allah of Koranic revelation and devotion is the compassionate no less than absolute sovereign of the universe.

In such an unequivocal idea of God, Islamic faith and theology

[4] "Islam Spreading in West Africa," in *The New York Times* (Feb. 5, 1961), p. 4.

have traditionally found their tower of strength. Peace of mind and a confident heart have been the portion of the believer who trusts in God. Allah is the name of One greater than all things imaginable, mightier than any power the intellect can conjure up. In the life and action of the elect community, the Ummah of Allah, God manifests his sovereign and solemn will. Within that brotherhood, he makes himself immanently known.

Proclaimed across the warmer latitudes of the earth's surface, Islam permeates the daily lives of countless tongues and breeds. A superbly dynamic, missionary, and civilizing force, Islam effectively penetrates myriad societies in Asia and Africa. No less is its vitality in its historic cradle in the Near East. Cairo has made efforts in recent years to penetrate Africa with a new Islamic determination to convert. Egyptian teachers have been commissioned to teach both Arabic and the Koran. In certain countries the United Arab Republic has added religious attachés to its diplomatic missions.

Islam weaves itself into the indigenous social pattern. It inspires a demonstrably articulate capacity for spiritual elevation and the conquest of fear. Among illiterate masses it engenders personal dignity and self-respect. Social stability through brotherly solidarity is thus accelerated. In the reorganization of Africa and the developing Asian world Islam is frequently able to build more firmly than the agents of Moscow.

Aristocratic strata of society have similarly rallied to the Koranic cause. Previously impervious to the advances of higher religion, primitive Africans respond to the call of the minaret. In some of the villages where most of the people were animists only a few years ago, up to 80 percent are Muslims now. In many a land, the elite, too, awakened to the call of freedom, find in the Islamic faith in Allah both an incentive and a sustenance.

A distinguished Shiite Muslim of Madras, India, graciously offered the author a printed copy of a prayer ostensibly narrated by one Kumail and ascribed to Caliph Ali (A.D. 656–661). The Arabic text and English rendition, reproduced side by side, convey deep longings and surrender to Allah:

" O Allah, I implore thee by thy mercy which has permeated all things; by thy power through which thou hast dominated all things, and to which all have submitted and surrendered. . . . O Allah, forgive my sins which taint my innocence . . . which bring down thy wrath upon me . . . which intercept my prayers. . . .

"O Allah, I approach thee through remembrance of thee and I seek thine intercession with thyself. . . . I beseech thee begging as one in utter need who in his agony presents his needs unto thee, and whose craving is great for things which are thine. O Allah, great is thy sovereignty, exalted is thine abode, and inscrutable are thy signs. Thy command is clear and thy might overwhelming. Thy power is ever controlling and escape from thy dominion is impossible."

Further excerpts from the same supplication leave little doubt as to the nature of Islam's idea of God.

"O Allah, there is no one to forgive my sins, or cover my blemishes, or change any of my misdeeds into virtue, but thou. There is no God but thou, glory and praise to thee . . . O Lord . . . Master of my freedom that holdest my fate in thy hand and knowest my misery and poverty and knowest my penury and starvation . . . strengthen my limbs for thy service and intensify my will in this determination. And grant me that I might endeavor to fear thee and remain forever occupied in thy service."

Equally revealing are the closing passages of the same contrite prayer.

"Therefore, in the name of thy honor accept my prayer, and cause me to reach my objective, and by thy favor do not cut short my hopes. But protect me amply from the malice of my foes, from among the jinn and men. . . . O Light that consoleth those that are bewildered in darkness . . . bless Mohammed and the descendants of Mohammed and do that unto me that befits thy position. Lo, Allah hath blessed Mohammed and the faithful leaders among his descendants, and hath given them peace and tranquility in abundant measure."

[D] There is, fourthly, a Christian idea of God. By virtue of historical associations, Christianity is akin to the last two integrities. Yet this faith, as will be presently seen, claims a conception of God which bears the marks of true novelty. Such a novelty sets the church apart both in essence and in consequence. What the Christian religion actually inculcates through its several classical traditions is a concept of God unlike any other. Such a concept consists less in a philosophical definition and formulation, more in a declaration of the divine will. It is a divine will intent upon the deliverance of man from death and fear, the salvation which means rescue from the fetters of the flesh and a peace of God passing all understanding.

Hence the irrevocable stress of Christianity upon its message as a proclamation. Briefly, the proclamation consists in a gospel. The idea of God is mediated as good news, namely, the good tidings of what God, whose other name is Love, has wrought. The object of such favor is recovery of man and society from a tragic sense of living, a false acceptance of what life is all about.

Salvation is this recovery of man and society. It is a salvation that involves release from captivity to sin and the anxiety engendered thereby. There is nothing particularly novel about the idea of a Deity who reveals himself as Redeemer. What is novel is the historicity of such a Redeemer.

Novel, too, is the conception of an Almighty who humbles himself, taking the form of a servant. The believer begins to fathom the depth of salvation as in company with the Servant of all men, Jesus called the Christ, death loses its dominion over him. Apart from the death and resurrection of Jesus such an experience has little if any meaning. Whoever speaks of the Christian answer to folly, insecurity, and shame needs to take seriously One who passed through the valley of the shadow and came out victor.

Lord of history in the exalted Hebraic sense, God to the Christian believer is both transcendent and immanent. A suffering Servant, Triune God, Father, Son, and Holy Spirit, he identifies himself with man's abject depravity. In the person of Jesus Christ, this God once for all invades time. As crucified and risen Lord, he abides among his people, an everlasting contemporary. Thus blessing and consoling, he furthers them in communion with him and with one another.

Whatever the Christian's idea of God, it must be grounded in the Scriptures. In church history, its outreach and fulfillment may be traced; also in tradition, dogmatics, and interpretative theology. A Biblical anthology on the idea of God would far outrun the limits of this essay. Suffice it to reproduce a few relevant passages even at the risk of arbitrary selectivity.

"The eternal God is thy refuge, and underneath are the everlasting arms. . . . The fool hath said in his heart, There is no God. . . .

In the beginning was the Word, and the Word was with God, and the Word was God. . . . And the Word was made flesh, and dwelt among us, (and we beheld his glory, the glory as of the only begotten of the Father,) full of grace and truth." (Deut. 33:27; Ps. 14:1; John 1:1, 14.)

"God is a Spirit: and they that worship him must worship him in spirit and in truth. . . . For ye know the grace of our Lord Jesus Christ, that, though he was rich, yet for your sakes he became poor, that ye through his poverty might be rich. . . . God is faithful, who will not suffer you to be tempted above that ye are able; but will with the temptation also make a way to escape, that ye may be able to bear it." (John 4:24; II Cor. 8:9; I Cor. 10:13.)

In its expository facet, modern Christian theology is seized by a judgment that it understands in the idea of God. In Europe and throughout the Protestant world, the Swiss theologian Karl Barth commands high esteem. The crisis theology of Barth finds the righteousness of man under condemnation by the judgment of God.

"This means not simply the pronouncement of judgment over atheism and humanism, over autonomous morality and human pride, over culture and other towers of Babel, but this judgment directs itself especially to man as via *religion* he seeks to make his way to God. It is *precisely in religion* that Barth detects the most refined and cunning human effort to reach beyond himself. Here even more than in other areas, man attempts to establish his own righteousness, and to secure himself against the divine judgment."[5]

In the United States, Reinhold Niebuhr relates the idea of God, as far as the divine sovereignty is concerned, to the unity of history. In his opinion, the Biblical idea of the sovereignty of God over historical destiny is not in itself unique, though it does possess a unique quality. Israel does not choose God. God out of sheer grace chooses Israel. God is not conceived as a projection of the nation's desires and values, nor as an extension of the nation's power.

On the contrary, God is the limit of the nation's power and the judge and enemy of all her pretensions. Out of this conception of the relation of God to historical destiny, two basic ideas of the Hebraic-

[5] G. C. Berkouwer, *The Triumph of Grace in the Theology of Karl Barth* (Wm. B. Eerdmans Publishing Company, 1956), pp. 26–27.

Christian interpretation arise — the idea of a universal history and the complexity of that history.[6]

"The scandal that the idea of universal history should be the fruit of a particular revelation of the divine to a particular people, and finally in a particular drama and person, ceases to be scandalous when it is recognized that the divine majesty apprehended in these divine revelations is less bound to the pride of civilizations and the hopes and ambitions of nations than the supposedly more universal concepts of life and history by which cultures seek to extricate themselves from the historical contingencies and to establish universally valid values." [7]

The Christian view of history, then, is that history has unity. All historical destiny is under the sovereignty of the one God. The unity of history is discerned by faith. It is not the product of empirical investigation. Believers, as well as skeptical historians, unite against the attempts of the philosophers of history to reduce the variety and complexity of historical phenomena to intelligible patterns.

As for the complexity of history, it stems from the fact, according to Niebuhr, that the historical drama is not so much a contest between good and evil forces in history. Rather is it between all men and God. History is the realm of both the providence of God and the confusion of men.[8]

The complexity of history is thus rooted in its moral ambiguity. Individuals and nations are destroyed not just because of pride and vanity. They fall because they are powerless. Yet the sovereignty of God is not pure mystery. The experiences of life in which egotism and self-worship are punished are in rough and inexact relation to an ultimate judgment upon the self, perceived by the self in the experience of repentance and faith.

Faith in the sovereignty of God over historical destiny illumines, as Niebuhr sees it, both the unity and the complexity of history. Here is the root distinction between the Biblical interpretation of history and both the classical and the modern views. "In contrast to historical cultures, Biblical faith affirms the potential meaning of life in

[6] Gordon Harland, *The Thought of Reinhold Niebuhr* (Oxford University Press, London, 1960), p. 111.

[7] Reinhold Niebuhr, *Faith and History: A Comparison of Christian and Modern Views of History* (Charles Scribner's Sons, 1949), pp. 113 ff.

[8] *Ibid.*, pp. 125–132. Harland, *op. cit.*, pp. 112–113 ff.

history. It is in history, and not in a flight from history, that the divine power which bears and completes history is revealed. In contrast to idolatrous historical cultures, the revelation of the divine, which manifests itself in history, casts down everything which exalteth itself against the knowledge of God." [9]

[E] A fifth integrity manifest throughout East Asia stems from the teaching and example of Gautama the Buddha (563–483 B.C.) and the doctrines advanced by his heirs and interpreters. Between Buddhist doctrines, on the one hand, and those of the Hindu, Hebraic, Islamic, and Christian faiths, on the other, certain undeniable similarities exist. Such similarities extend even to the view on ultimacy and the religious systems derived therefrom.

Yet equally irrefutable is the fact that Buddhism represents a new departure in the history of religions. It introduced the Eastern world to an ingenious religious format. The Buddhist tradition is stamped with an essentially Buddhist emphasis. Inherent therein is an incompatibility that all systematic and unsystematic ideas of God reflect.

A formidable spiritualizing and compassionate force, Buddhism struck a note to which masses of Asia's populations hearkened. Constituting a Buddhist family of flocks, these distinct expressions of the original religious stock held certain things in common. They all subscribed to a faith undergirded by two simple principles.

The first Buddhist principle consisted in a belief in psychological ethics, the rules of the earliest community as they were once outlined by the master. There was, secondly, the practice of a humanist faith centered in the idea of love. As for the strictly Buddhist understanding of Deity, the subject may be crystallized under the three major categories of nonbeing, being, and becoming.

Buddhist doctrine on ultimacy provides the nearest semblance of an idea of divinity. However, as reported in the *Parinibbana Sutta* [10] the farewell advice that the Buddha gave his disciple Ananda left scarcely an inkling of eternal reality. It was instead an affirmation of nonbeing, possibly of total extinction upon death:

"Therefore, Ananda, be a lamp and a refuge to yourselves. Seek

[9] Niebuhr, *op. cit.,* p. 114

[10] A. Thyagarajan, "The Tripitakas," in *The Great Scriptures,* ed. by T. M. P. Mahadevan (The G. S. Press, Madras, 1956), p. 96.

no other refuge. Let the Truth be your lamp and refuge. Seek no refuge elsewhere." The Master counseled further: "And they, Ananda, who now or when I am gone, shall be a lamp and a refuge to themselves, seeking no other refuge but taking the Truth as their lamp and refuge, these shall be my foremost disciples — those who are anxious to learn. Behold, I exhort you saying: The elements of being are transitory. Strive earnestly, work out your salvation with diligence."

Such was primitive Buddhism's stress on the transitory character of life. It fell to the Mahayana Buddhists to explore further aspects and possibilities. In their Trikaya doctrine, three ways for contemplating the Buddha were envisaged. Nirmana Kaya referred to the historical Buddha; Sambhoga Kaya had to do with a Buddha who enjoyed an ideal body and preached to the Bodhisattvas; whereas Dharma Kaya took a view of the Master which cast him in the role of a universal being, Lord of the whole world. Detectable by now was a marked trend toward belief in deity.

This shift in emphasis from nonbeing to being is symbolic of the faith's amazing potentiality for change. Dharma Kaya came to signify an inwardly enlightened and therefore real body of the Buddha. Identical with supreme Reality, the Buddha becomes an eternal Amida, a heavenly Deity of the Pure Land.[11]

Nor was the upward ascent of Buddhist thought satisfied to stop at this rung of the ladder. Buddhism's total outlook on ultimacy is not preempted by nonbeing and being. There was its concept of becoming, a pivotal doctrine deserving a careful analysis and precise documentation.

Treatment of the idea of God negatively, as has been intimated, was but a preliminary, initial stage in the evolution of the faith. A positive emphasis on being was soon to emerge; and this was carried a step farther and amplified in the Buddhist emphasis on becoming. Writing on the true significance of Karman-Samsara to a Buddhist intellectual, Prof. Yoshinari Takeuchi,[12] of the University of Kyoto, Japan, explains:

[11] M. B. Niyogi, "The Mahayana Scriptures," in *The Great Scriptures,* ed. by Mahadevan, pp. 107 ff.

[12] "Buddhism and Existentialism: The Dialogue Between Oriental and Occidental Thought," in *Religion and Culture: Essays in Honor of Paul Tillich,* ed. by Walter Leibrecht (Harper & Brothers, 1959), pp. 308 ff.

"When a mother says to her child who is crying in a nightmare, 'It is just a dream, dear,' it is a simple fact of waking up the child. In the same way, the concept of transmigration (*karman* and *samsara*) is not predictable as an objective judgment on the fact of being. The proposition that all mortals are subject to transmigration likewise simply calls for an awakening; for those who accept this call, this proposition is an unconditional imperative. Unfortunately, however, the doctrine of *karman-samsara* is not ordinarily understood in this way. Looked at merely objectively the doctrine may seem to emphasize a fatalistic and deterministic view of life. Looked at negatively, and existentially, which I believe is the proper way of understanding the doctrine, it is conducive to liberty and salvation."

In a qualifying passage, Professor Takeuchi spells out what "becoming" conveys to a modern Buddhist. Despite its philosophy of "central void" and "nothingness" at the core of existence, Buddhism leaves open a degree of knowledge and ultimate being:

"When something throws a dark shadow in bright sunshine, its contour becomes clearly distinct, making the bright side look brighter in the sunshine. So the shadow of *karman* and *samsara* suggests another aspect of the picture, radiating the effulgence of the joy of emancipation and deliverance from this world. The theory of *karman-samsara* in this sense is a springboard: our religious existence first takes a firm stand on this, in the assurance that, leaping from it, we may plunge into the bliss of salvation and emancipation."

At this juncture, a word of caution might be in order. The foregoing fivefold classification represents but so many orders of belief. In an inordinately more complex world setting, these are but a few of the baffling range of ideas about the nature and being of deity. The five major integrities are barely alluded to in the preceding account. They by no means preempt the plethora of man's outreach toward the eternal or his quest for certainty with regard to things real and ultimate.

These five distinctive varieties include nonetheless in their sweep important classical configurations. As such they may be said to occupy in the history of religions positions of extraordinary significance and influence. In fact, each of the above integrities may be seen to have evolved its own touchstone for comparative religion. In thus defining attitudes to other faiths, standards for varieties of comparative religion are set. Each new variety stands for a different relation to other faiths, and the relation, in turn, shapes a characteristic methodology.

Perusal of the five integrities is futile until and unless the accepted norms of religious phenomenology are reckoned with and absorbed. Admittedly, moreover, all ideas about the idea of God at best can be merely tentative. Above all else, a scholar who treats the idea of God in cultural history ever stands before the mystery of the Infinite. Doomed in advance is any attempt to reduce the Eternal to so-called propositional categories of truth, useful and rational as these may well be.

Yet a first step might well be in the direction of clearer understanding of issues at stake. If the only outcome were a more resilient self-examination of its own structures and finalities by each religion, the venture would be more than justified. The very challenge of conflicting views might of itself fulfill a higher purpose—freer intercultural, international, and interfaith dialogue and cooperation.

What one-world idea could ever really crystallize, much less mature, until more direct relations are cultivated among followers of the great religions? In our era, such relations cry out desperately for purification. This chapter refers to diverse integrities; and the fact that they are sharply ruptured is a common evil behind the agony of modern man. Yet all these integrities, each in its own way, affirm that ultimate truth, by some known as God. A self-authenticating truth, albeit along a variety of highways and through a diversity of channels, marks the religious pilgrimage of mankind.

II

Is there a methodology, practical and original, that provides for intelligent exploration across boundaries of outwardly discordant faiths? Such a methodology might be construed as normative if it offered an opportunity for research and verification, where divergent ideas of God prevailed.

One requirement for such a methodology is that it take cognizance of the above-named frontiers of classic integrities. Another is that it take seriously the existing network of resurgent religious communities and push back the frontiers of knowledge in that vital area of the modern world. Such methodologies may be largely attitudes, shaping the relation of one faith toward the others. Yet the assertion is here made that an attitude shapes a methodology. Imbued as such a methodology might be with the genius and passion of one or other of the living faiths, it ought, as a third requirement, to constitute an advance over what have hitherto been barren, if not decadent, procedures.

Of innumerable methodologies that suggest themselves, five deserve special notice. Of these some are geared to one or other of the integrities cited above. In that sense, they derive an impetus from, and are molded by, a particular outlook and orientation. In other instances, a methodology has been introduced because in it the horizons of several competing faiths and philosophies converge or merge.

[A] A primary methodology rests upon the central assumption of an *eclectic* ultimate reality. This happens, moreover, to harp on the formidable hypothesis that essentially coincides with the humanist quest for God. The underlying assumption is that all such quests deserve sympathetic consideration if not outright approval. They are valid, that is, to the extent that they emanate from a spiritual experience more adequate in a given society than in others.

Thus to accord validity to all man's endeavors to discover God is to honor the gropings of individuals and the longings of countless generations. It is also to foster their collective vision of intercultural solidarity, their foretaste of a global interracial kinship.

Whereas, according to this methodology, all religions may not agree, each conveys a sacred story of its own and perpetuates cherished memories of profound meaning. This explains the strikingly universalist, somewhat syncretist, nuances underlying such a subtle methodology. Steeped in the consensus of eminent men, this is a methodology that steadily gains momentum. Strategists of modern thought and architects of cosmopolitan society add their own prestige to its promulgation.

A position frequently defended by this methodology is as follows: The more religions one is able to comprehend, the stronger his grasp of the truth; the wider his embrace of other faiths, the better his feel for that reality beyond all being and in all being. No single religion is entitled therefore to a claim of absolute truth. No faith qualified for a place of superiority. The very concept of the superiority of a given faith is nothing short of a pretension. When all are seekers, and the truth infinitely beyond man's reach, the primacy of one's own creed over others must be out of the question. How utterly ill conceived is any single religion's aspiring to such a place of exclusive preeminence.

"All religions require us to look upon life as an opportunity for self-realization, *atmanatsu kamaya,*" declares Radhakrishnan.[13] "They call upon us to strive incessantly and wrest the immortal from the mortal. God is the universal reality, wisdom, and love, and we are his children irrespective of race or religious belief. Within each incarnate soul dwells the God-consciousness which all must seek out and awaken. When mankind awakens to the truth, universal brotherhood will follow, the at-one-ment with the great fountainhead of all creation. What gives Marxism its immense vitality is the vision of injustice made good, of the poor raised to power, and of the proud brought low."

To the foregoing, Radhakrishnan feels constrained to add: "Religion in this sense will be the binding force which will deepen the solidarity of human society. The encounter of the different religions has brought up the question whether they could live side by side or whether one of them could supersede the others. Mankind at each period of its history cherishes the illusion of the finality of its existing modes of knowledge."

Note further his unequivocal judgment that "[that] illusion breeds intolerance and fanaticism. The world has bled and suffered from the disease of dogmatism, of conformity. Those who are conscious of a mission to bring the rest of humanity to their own way of life have been aggressive toward other ways of life. This ambition to make disciples of all nations is not the invention of the Communists. If we look upon our formulations as approximations to the truth and not truth itself, then we must be prepared to modify them if we find other propositions which enter deeper into reality. Reality is larger than any system of theology however large."

[B] There is, secondly, what may be classified as a *theological* methodology. Within this methodology, the Eternal is the object of reverent contemplation. The medium is that of a reasoned faith. Con-

[13] In *The Great Scriptures,* ed. by Mahadevan, pp. 7 ff.

fessional, intellectual, and technical language is the order. Systematic study of the idea of God, and germane interests, takes on a highly specialized intrusive character. Such an interfering methodology makes a direct appeal to conservative, strictly critical opinion. In apologetic, dialectic, and polemic, it plays a primary role and among its adherents rates high as a vibrant dynamism.

Of course not all theology is frozen dogma. Nor do all doctrinal expositions of religious conviction consume themselves on the altar of fanaticism. Erection of an impregnable fortress for defense of faith is not the only goal of theology. Neither is it true that all apologetics need to be uniformly arid.

One thing is, nevertheless, true. Tomes of theological erudition do foster a certain idea of God. This in turn tends to shape an attitude to other faiths which engenders its own methodology for treatment of other religions. Such an attitude beckons thinkers to give the Lord of conscience the provisional consent of the mind. It is the kind of consent made captive to an a priori commitment. Two dedications, that of the mind and that of the heart, make strange bedfellows. The two are hard to hold together yet separately. They are frequently fitted into an unnatural marriage subject to arbitrary judgment.

What this methodology will do may be seen in the thought of the famed Dutch comparative religionist, Hendrik Kraemer. In two books, *The Christian Message in a Non-Christian World* (1938) and *Religion and the Christian Faith* (1956), Dr. Kraemer drew a sharp distinction between Biblical realism and Asia's " naturalist " religions of " transempirical realization." Such a distinction leaves scarcely any room for interfaith dialogue, let alone meeting of minds.

Attention was drawn above to Karl Barth's crisis theology. Barth's theology places all religions, even that of the church, under the judgment of God. Likewise in this methodology, there is a revival of the old dichotomy between a message from God and the various types of religion: between *Das Evangelium* and *Die Religionen*. Here then is a source for an attitude to other religions which gives support to a methodology professedly steeped in Biblical realism. Whereas Kraemer and his school claim abandonment of verbal inspiration, affirmations involving, for example, the above dichotomy suggest reversion to what cannot be too different.

In the former of his two volumes, Kraemer has some subtle insights on Asia's living faiths. In his more recent text he ranges over immense territory. Included is a whole section upon Indian religious thought. Far from irenic is the special treatment of Radhakrishnan and his philosophy of religion.

So far as the development of this methodology goes, one thing seems noteworthy. It is embedded in Kraemer's candid admission that his former volume showed little awareness of the consciousness of God to be found in non-Christian religions. This methodology springs from a further claim. It is to the effect that there are two levels of possible contact between Christianity and the other religions. These are reckoned as the level of practical evangelism and that of ordinary human contact. Insofar as human contact is concerned, Kraemer fully agrees it must be fostered.

As regards the level where exclusive concern for the truth operates, Kraemer holds strongly to a forthright thesis: There is really no way through from the non-Christian religions to the Christian faith; the former start from different assumptions, the latter is wholly given and does not work through the religions but independently of them. It is just at this central point that many Christian scholars take exception to the position that Kraemer maintains.[14]

[C] A third methodology takes *tolerance* as guide and from it derives its chief principles of arbitrament and correlation. In the study of coexistent religious phenomena, toleration serves a noble purpose in coordination and partnership. A specific point of departure is thus envisaged. It begins with the idea of a God who endows the creature with the right of choice. To all men the freedom is thus given to elect their varied ways with him in the light of conscience and circumstance. Yet everyone comes under divine judgment in keeping with divine righteousness and compassion as well as in accordance with the creaturely intuition and the purity of motive. A decisive factor must thus arise in connection with whatever man's confession possesses by way of an earnest and genuine character.

In his multivolume study of history, Arnold Toynbee finds in religion a key idea. His endorsement of tolerance as a principle comes very close to the point where it molds his outlook and determines the nature of his methodology. This is particularly true in his Gifford

[14] A. C. Bouquet, *The Christian Faith and Non-Christian Religions* (Harper & Brothers, 1958), p. 400.

Lectures, published under the title *An Historian's Approach to Religion.*[15]

" True spiritual freedom is attained when each member of society has learned to reconcile a sincere conviction of the truth of his own religious practices with a voluntary toleration of the different beliefs and practices of his neighbors. A toleration that is genuinely voluntary is the only kind that has any virtue in it; but the degree of the virtue depends on the motive, and the motives for toleration are various. They can be lower or higher, negative or positive."

The lowest negative motive for toleration, in Toynbee's view, is a belief that religion is of no practical importance; that, therefore, it does not much matter what religion one professes. The next lowest negative motive, in his opinion, is a belief that religion is an illusion; hence it is idle to inquire whether this or that form is true or false.

According to Toynbee, the next lowest motive is a prudential one. It arises from the observation that a resort to force is apt to provoke hostile resistance. However telling my own unprovoked first blow might be, I cannot be sure that the knockout blow might not spell my defeat. The neighbor whom I have surely antagonized by an unwanton assault might turn out to be an implacable foe.

The next negative motive in this catalog of undesirable tolerance traits arises from the observation that religious conflict is a public nuisance. It can easily grow into danger and trouble. Religious bodies are therefore advised to resign themselves to living and letting live. It is sheer folly for them to break the peace by an attempt at mutual liquidation.

Those negative motives for toleration, the same historian holds, seem prevalent in the Western world. That is why the West chose toleration in reaction against the evils of the Roman Catholic-Protestant wars. Current Western experience shows that toleration inspired by such negative motives is indeed precarious.

There is no guarantee that intolerance will not again erupt so long as men are not moved by any higher and more positive motives. Intolerance may not appear in religion as such. It may reassert itself in some psychological substitute. Such a substitute may take the form of secular ideology, nationalism, fascism, or communism.

Happily there are higher and more serene motives for men to espouse in the practice of tolerance. Some of these were manifest as

15 Oxford University Press, London, 1956, pp. 251–253.

far back as the seventeenth century. They then accompanied the upsurge of a profound and remarkable spiritual revolution. What are these motives which we need to confirm and strengthen in our hearts today? Upon the proper answer to this question hangs the distinctive methodology which tolerance will directly effect in the treatment of religions other than one's own.

This methodology discovers a fundamental positive motive for toleration. It consists in recognition of the truth that religious conflict is not merely a nuisance. In Toynbee's opinion, religious conflict is sin. Since it arouses the wild beast in human nature, what else can it be but sinful? Sinful, too, is religious persecution for the simple reason that no one has the right to interpose himself between another human soul and God. Every soul has the right to commune with the Almighty in the Almighty's and this soul's way. The particular way concerns no one but God and the particular soul. No other human has a right to intervene by the use of any means save nonviolent missionary proclamation and beseeching.

Violence in this field is both sinful and futile. Force is no way to promulgate faith. There is no such thing as belief that is not held voluntarily. A genuinely spontaneous inner conviction is nothing that an outsider may impose. Different people's convictions will differ. This is because Absolute Reality is a mystery of which no more than a fraction has ever yet been penetrated by, or been revealed to, any human mind. Even where fully revealed it can only be partially grasped and finitely understood.

"It is impossible that so great a mystery should be approached by one road only," said Quintus Aurelius Symmachus, spokesman of the Roman Senate, in a controversy with Saint Ambrose. The controversy was in the course of a campaign when the Christian Roman imperial government ordered the removal of the statue and altar of Victory which had been placed in the senate house by Julius Caesar.[16] However strong and confident may be a man's conviction that his own approach to the mystery of religion is right, he ought to be aware that his field of spiritual vision is relatively narrow. It is so narrow that he cannot know that there is no virtue in other approaches.

In theistic terms, the above verdict means that man cannot know, says Toynbee, that other people's visions may not also be revelations from God. Those may even be fuller and more illuminating revela-

16 Arnold Toynbee, *Christianity Among the Religions of the World,* pp. 111–112.

tions than the one that he believes he himself has received from the Eternal.

" Moreover, the fact that I and my neighbor are following different roads is something that divides us much less than we are drawn together by the other fact, that, in following our different roads, we are both trying to approach the same mystery. All human beings who are seeking to approach the mystery in order to direct their lives in accordance with the nature and spirit of Absolute Reality or, in theistic terms, with the will of God — all these fellow seekers are engaged in an identical quest. They should recognize that they are spiritually brethren and should feel toward one another, and treat one another as such. Toleration does not become perfect until it has been transfigured into love."

[D] A fourth methodology is a *naturalist dynamism* embedded in the thrust of certain universally acclaimed philosophies and philosophers. Of diverse inclinations and generations, these philosophers held one trait in common: theirs was essentially an appeal to the God of nature and of the intellect. Where such giants of the mind subscribed at all to the existence of a Providence, they tended to view him as one removed from the human scene. Remote and inscrutable, he was scarcely touched by any feeling for human infirmity. He had little to do with the petty details and agonies of human tragedy and the struggle that goes with civilization. Centered in history, such a methodology focused on the fortunes and debacles of movements, events, and the ever-unfolding drama of earthly vicissitudes.

A brilliant exponent of such a methodology might be discerned in the person of Karl Jaspers. A Swiss professor of Basel, Jaspers stresses what he calls an *Achsenperiode der Weltgeschichte,* an axial age of world history. In his work, *The Origins and Goals of History,* Jaspers conceives of such an axial age as extending from 800 to 200 B.C. The history of religion will therefore neatly fit into this pre-axial, axial, and post-axial sequence.

If the pre-axial phase is roughly construed to dovetail with primitive and early ancient times, scholars had already dealt with the subjects. To that phase, authorities of the stature of R. R. Marett and James Frazer had devoted valiant energies. More recently, E. O. James had rendered a solid contribution incorporating findings from archaeology and philology.

Transition to the axial age was marked by a radical change. This involved the appearance of stalwart individuals who laid traditional patterns under critical scrutiny. Simultaneously but quite independently, this radical break with the past was to entrench itself in the Fertile Crescent and Egypt, in India, and in China. Political no less than religious issues came under investigation. This presaged the dawn of a great new era in mankind's march toward intellectual and spiritual emancipation.

In the post-axial age this methodology recognizes a series of startling developments: the rise of Christianity and Islam, consolidation of Hindu and Buddhist influence. Spectacular effervescence is also noted in certain folk religions. Along with this went a continuing pre-axial deposit. Such was the order among the masses where primiitive religion retained a primitive taint. Even so, the advent of free institutions and democracy, industrialization, the machine age, technology, and Marxist philosophy add astounding color and deepen anxiety.

A methodology for comparative religion steeped in such a background proves exceedingly exciting. Associated, let us say, with the name of a philosopher like Jaspers, this methodology steers clear of involvement in the idea of a personal Deity. Preference seems to be for a God perceived through *Erdenken,* excogitation.

As a prodigious contributor to modern thought and the field of religion, Jaspers and his methodology arouse more than passing notice. His very discovery of a *Ziel der Geschichte,* a goal toward which history moves, is intriguing, to say the least. It provides an axis whereon not only history but this very ingenious methodology itself may be said to revolve.[17] Quite ironically, however, a methodology of this order tends to relate no specific idea of God to the naturalist philosophy that it propounds. It is bound therefore to leave many doors open and to content itself with a dazzling ambivalence, alternating between exposition and exhortation. Like Heidegger, Jaspers systematically ignores the intellectual development of the men with whom he deals.[18]

[E] A fifth methodology stems from an outlook and special orien-

[17] Cf. Bouquet, *op. cit.,* p. 405.

[18] Walter Kaufmann, *Critique of Religion and Philosophy* (Harper & Brothers, 1958), p. 22.

tation to religion which is essentially a *critical existentialism.* This methodology enters the field with due regard for the wisdom of the ages and without excessive prejudice against insights proclaimed elsewhere. It bases itself notably on faith in the God of Abraham, Isaac, and Jacob.

Central here is an idea of the God of peace, God of the living, not of the dead. Such a methodology could be utterly misjudged, its singular character lost sight of, if its basic universality were relinquished, ignored, or in any way minimized. As a highly generalized universality, this system begins and ends with the grace of God. How else do we comprehend the dynamic reality of his presence, his comforting Spirit, and his redemptive plan and purpose for man and society?

In justification by grace, through faith, this methodology is shaped by declaration of the love of God for all mankind. It rests everything in a massive gamble on that love. Its hope of a victorious life is nourished and illumined by none other than the Eternal. This is a methodology that may therefore be said to envisage truth and validity in all vital religion. However, this truth exists in all fullness and splendor nowhere save in what comes from the Creator. In the last analysis the Father of all spirits is the giver of every good and perfect gift.

As a contemporary philosopher of religion, Paul Tillich undoubtedly ranks as a man of stature. It is not suggested here that Tillich is author of this or any other methodology. Yet his ideas have long inspired both Christian and non-Christian thinkers. Even Buddhists find his *Systematic Theology* challenging. Its concern for being, nonbeing, and being itself, even where they do not find it admissible, is a treasure of provocative views and meaningful judgments.

To fathom Tillich's thought one must go back to the German classical philosophy of the early nineteenth century.[19] He wrote two books on Schelling, philosopher of romanticism. Schelling it was who proclaimed the presence of the infinite in the finite. The finite is not absorbed thereby in the infinite but rather fulfilled and enhanced. With the romanticists, Tillich shares a profound interest in myth, symbol, and sacrament.

Like Schelling and Hegel, Tillich interprets the symbols and

[19] See Walter Leibrecht in his own symposium, *Religion and Culture,* pp. 3–27.

myths of Christianity in a philosophical vein. For him myth is neither primitive science nor fantasy. It is, rather, an expression of the relationship of man's reason, ecstatic reason, to the power of being. Creative art is the key assumption underlying his concern with culture. In his lecture on "The Theology of Culture (1919)," which won him wide European fame, Tillich speaks of the artist as priest of the future church.

From poetry, art, and philosophy, Tillich's mind moves on to religion. His sermons offer a sharp diagnosis of human existence. They flash a vision of the holy, Ultimate Reality, God. His primary concern with the truth is the truth of man's being. What agitates his thought is not mere epistemology but the meaning of life. Hence the existential quality of his outlook. Is it permissible to build upon that outlook a methodology for the study of world religions?

Hence also the prominence in his thought of emphasis on *kairos,* the creative act in the moment of the invasion of the finite by the infinite. With Luther, Pascal, and Kierkegaard, Tillich finds that the way to God, truth, and Ultimate Reality leads through the desert. It is experience of the ultimate in the moment of despair — experience, that is, of the power of being and the moment when life faces the threat of meaninglessness in nonbeing. Being dawns as a dynamic concept, the power of being as such. It is perceived as the ultimate breaks into man's existence.

Tillich may be said to offer, perhaps quite unintentionally, the outline of a distinctive methodology for comparative religion. Other than what has been said, his outline includes rejection of traditional supernaturalism. The reason for such rejection is that supernaturalism tends to draw the ultimate as a being into a circle with other beings. In Tillich's view, faith in the ultimate can either be an expression of ultimate concern or it is no more faith in God as the power of all being.

Further groundwork for a robust methodology is discovered in this existentialism. It emanates from the very fact that Tillich is simply unclassifiable either as an idealist or a materialist. His is not Schleiermacher's often misunderstood appeal to feeling. His is not Marx's attempt to transvaluate Christian eschatology by introducing the dynamic power of the inner historical process as a drive to fulfillment within history. His instead is Plato's *Eros,* appearing in ecstatic reason. Being is here joined to its depth. Reason is grasped by the ultimate and participates in it.

Marxist revolt against Hegel took the form of a general verdict: Thought is basically the product of a culture. If so, theological thought must be a defensive rationalization of ruling class interests. Indeed, Marxists went so far as to describe thought itself as a mode of economic production.

In such a Marxist analysis Tillich did find some fundamental truth. However, that did not lure him to the conclusion that philosophy is headed toward replacement by either sociology or psychology. The realism that he championed fortifies a specific methodology, for the study of comparative religion.

This is a realism that sees thought as coming out of existence. If thought is the true expression of existential reality, then existence may be viewed as being shaped by thought. Hence the core of Tillich's celebrated principle of correlation.

In Tillich's view, thought which is not correlated with reality lacks reality. Such thought is scarcely meaningful. But truth that really expresses a situation is more than mere speculation. It creates freedom for action. Plato thus comes alive; his insistence that the ground of being is also the ground of thought is rejuvenated in Tillich's new and profound formulations. A formidable methodology is thus distilled for the study of religion and the religions.

Tillich speaks of the *kairos* of religious socialism. It is the moment when time is invaded by eternity. History's *kairoi* are invariably derived from the first *kairos,* the coming of the New Being in Jesus Christ. *Kairos* is the restoring power, the *Gestalt* of grace, the moment of the Eternal breaking into time. Tillich's foremost challenge to modern thought is his call to theonomy, government by God.

A vision of culture is thus flashed on the screen for all serious students of religion. In it an ultimate concern informs the whole web of life and thought. This ultimate concern is also an ever-present horizon. With the idea of theonomy, an easy deification of culture by liberal theology is ruled out. Religion is understood as the root of culture. Culture is reckoned as the effervescence of religion. Tillich succeeds where few others have in singling out an essential relatedness between each cultural expression and its religious groundwork.

Such an emphasis together with the methodology that it inspires prove congenial to a genuinely ecumenical realism. Incidentally, his concept of theonomy provides a concrete base for fruitful Protestant-Roman Catholic dialogue. It may well open the door to wider interfaith wrestling and prepare the ground for the long-longed-for meeting of minds. If Reinhold Niebuhr is rightly credited with having stabbed American theology awake to the fact that despite all optimism, man is a sinner, Tillich may indeed be the one who brought it the other major lesson, namely, that God is absolute concern. Confusing him with other concerns, even the loftiest, will spell disorder for theology, culture, and politics. Hence the ever-broadening base of a methodology called forth by Tillich's masterful strokes.

III

But precisely what role does the idea of God really fulfill in the course of civilization? What determining factors owe to it their origin? How may a scientific estimate be struck of its scope and disposition? Granting the unpredictability of all human eventualities, the unfathomable quality of history as such, how does the idea of God really yield any cogent features?

Certain psychological and cultural phenomena obviously arise beyond the scope of statistics. There are patterns of reality and behavior that obstinately defy ordinary categories of philosophical analysis and intellectual treatment. They refuse to yield to established norms of logical formulation.

Other spiritual vitalities, however, happen to be demonstrable. They tend to comply with common-sense requirements and to them the standards of objective research apply. Convictions that remain a matter of faith are counterbalanced by others that seem both reasonable and rational. These latter lend themselves to inquiry. They may be easily observed, tracked down, and reported. Involved here are such phases of civilization as adorn the historical, sociological, political, and ecclesiastical spheres of culture.

Not one of these spheres stands in full isolation. None is in solitary detachment from the rest. Much less are these spheres torn apart from the total phenomenon of existence. These are spheres that stand, severally and collectively, in mutual interdependence. Together they belong to that total entanglement which constitutes the common reciprocity of everyday living and the unity which glorifies existence.

[A] Historically, the idea of God may be said to summon a dynamic continuity. It is a thread of meaning upon which much else is strung. How little did societies really change? How slight is the radical transformation in human nature itself? A particularly alluring conception of ultimacy takes a firm hold on the popular will and imagination. Hence the immutability of means and ends within which all dynamism of men and institutions must center.

Agra lies one hundred and twenty-seven miles southeast of New Delhi. Historically, it is one of India's most glamorous cities. Its Taj Mahal is a veritable miracle of art, a dream in marble. Shah Jahan, we are told, took twenty-two years (ca. 1631–1653) to fashion these storied halls and inimitable chambers.

Conceived by the mighty Mogul emperor as a magnificent tribute in memory of a beloved queen, Mumtaz Mahal, the Taj (crown) rose as one of the seven wonders of the Old World. It is a portentous monument to man-woman fidelity, an imperishable testimony to conjugal love.

Surely there are buildings that excel the Taj in splendor of design and grandeur of construction. Others may be of more elaborate execution. Yet about the Taj hangs an air of mystery and romance, a glory beyond the fascination of exquisite architecture. It is the kind of otherworldly fascination, a lyrical secret, one may say, which crowns the precincts and interior with a delicacy and charm unrivaled elsewhere. How apt the phrase that describes the Taj as a poem in stone.

One's thought returns to the idea of God and its incarnation in time and space. This idea, we argued, does reflect itself within a historic setting. To it belongs a continuity beyond the ravages of time, the decay of empire. Agra became the residential citadel of the Moguls from the days of Babar, founder of the dynasty, to Akbar, its proudest monarch. Upon the capital, Akbar bestowed a touch of his great majesty. He adorned it with a group of stately buildings including the famous Fort.

Yet something of inestimable significance transcends such forms and symbols of Mogul power as the Fort, Taj, and other relics represent. The last word is by no means uttered by sophistication, political pomp, or dazzling artistry. Agra, New Delhi, and the fabulous range of India's archaeology and architecture are more than what meets the eye. The marvel of it all is a secret to be read in those ever-recurring Koranic verses. On every structure of the glorious Islamic heritage such verses figure as a historic witness to Allah. He is most great: greater than Akbar, Babar, and Shah Jahan. This is an Allah to whom an inscription on one of those sumptuous tombs refers as *ghafurun rahim,* that is, forgiving, merciful.

"Hindu thought," Radhakrishnan[20] reminds the reader, "whether or not we agree with its transcendental claims, has survived the storms of the world for over three thousand years. It has seen empires come and go, has watched economic and political systems flourish and fade. It has seen these happen more than once. Recent events have ruffled but not diverted the march of India's history. The culture of India has changed a great deal and yet has remained the same for over three millennia. Fresh springs bubble up, fresh streams cut their own channels through the landscape, but sooner or later each rivulet, each stream merges into one of the great rivers which has been nourishing the Indian soil for centuries."

Hinduism's historical vitality is traceable, among other things, to its grasp of reality as Brahman the Absolute.

"In spiritual experience, Ultimate Reality impinges on the human spirit. Religion is a living creative power because Ultimate Reality manifests itself to the human spirit. Whether we mean by religion adherence to sect or dogma, an attitude of faith or reverence toward what William James calls the *more* that lies beyond subjectivity, that Platonic pure reason of which Coleridge wrote that it is not 'something which is in us, but something in which we are,' it brings us into contact with something out there."[21]

Adds Radhakrishnan: "The seers have an overpowering conviction of the presence of spiritual Reality. The experience is a compelling vision or intuitive realization of the reality of the Supreme. . . . [Yet] the Supreme Reality is not out there but is one with our deepest self. *Brahman* is *Atman,* the Universal Spirit."[22]

[20] *The Brahma Sutra: The Philosophy of the Spiritual Life,* by S. Radhakrishnan (Harper & Brothers, 1960), p. 8. Copyright 1960 by Sarvepalli Radhakrishnan. Reprinted by permission of Harper & Row, Publishers, Inc.

[21] *Ibid.,* p. 118.

[22] *Ibid.,* pp. 118, 122.

Hinduism conceives the Absolute as a living reality with a creative urge. When this aspect is stressed, the Absolute becomes the living God, Ishvara. The Supreme Ishvara is often identified with Shiva, the deity construed as the material and efficient cause of the universe. In the form of another divinity, Vishnu Ishvara is said to be the source and transcendent God of the created universe. Brahma or Hiranya-garbha is the firstborn emanation of the Supreme Ishvara. As Virat-rupa, Ishvara is the concretization of world purpose. However, Brahman, Ishvara, Hiranya-garbha, and Virat-rupa are four poises of the one Reality.[23]

[B] Sociologically, the impress of such an idea of God can be neither dismissed nor lightly brushed aside. The nature of community life, the status and image of personality, the trends and concerns of social growth, as well as the rate and caliber of fluctuation in traditional and organizational life, reflect in one form or another a people's idea of deity.

That idea is reflected in the type of constitution that proves acceptable. It influences the kind of institution that does emerge. Laws, customs, functional aspects of government, armies, schools, literature, as well as the norms of kinship and marriage, are at the deepest level bound up with a constitutive if at times unrumored idea of God.

Radhakrishnan's[24] idea of the Hindu God must be one of a high and mightily progressive deity. On the issue of caste, it moved him to call for radical surgery in a bitterly contested and stagnating sector of India's social economy.

" The vocation of a person is that which manifests his inner nature. In its origin the caste system represented the division of men into classes according to their capacity and function, *guna* and *karma*. Later it became mixed up with heredity. . . . Some of the great leaders of Indian civilization were of mixed origin. . . . The system of caste whatever its historical significance has no contemporary value. Today it injures the spirit of humanity and violates human dignity. To offer a cup of water is a sign of friendship, not of defilement. . . . There is a story that when Shankara . . . asked an outcaste to clear the way for him, the outcaste who was God himself asked: 'Do you wish my body to leave your body or my spirit to leave your spirit?' If democracy is to be seriously implemented, then

[23] *Ibid.*, p. 135. [24] *Ibid.*, pp. 162–163.

caste and untouchability should go."

Radhakrishnan [25] cites highly cathartic sociological thrusts in behalf of the classic Hindu conception of the Supreme:

"Devotion to the Supreme," he specifies, "opens our hearts to the new life. Spiritual life is the end. That is why the Hindu permits each individual to worship the aspect of Godhead which appeals to him most. The radiance of reality is mirrored variously according to the mediums in which it is reflected. The different aspects we adore are pointers, not halting places. . . . Whatever name we give to the Supreme, it is addressed to the Ultimate Reality."

"Religious intolerance," he warns, "does not make for world unity. Religions which aim at the conversion of the whole world to their own doctrines aim at the religion of power which amounts to sacred egoism, to spiritual pride. Reason should teach us to doubt our own infallibility. Unless we do it, there is no chance for toleration in the world."

He then drives home this Hindu message of immense sociological implication. "If we are convinced of the absolute truth of our revelation and the falsity of others, how can we tolerate those who spread error and lead others astray? It is essential for us to note that while we are convinced of the infallibility of the truth we adopt, others may be equally convinced of the infallibility of their own doctrine."

The eminent apologist of modern Hinduism draws the following sharp distinctions.

"From ancient times, Hinduism adopted a view which would not hurt the religious susceptibilities of others. It enabled the Hindus to welcome the Jews, the Christians, the Parsees, and the Muslims. . . . The Hindu believes that varied as all these religions are, behind them all is the same fire. The experience of fire, though it speaks with many tongues, carries the same message. They all speak of the one realm of spiritual being. Of course, there are characteristic differences among the great religions. They do not teach the same doctrines of God or of man or of the world or provide the same kind of ritual, myth, or norm of behavior."

But these differences, in Radhakrishnan's judgment, are not enough to justify discord and strife. There may be mutual education among religions if they peacefully coexist. There is no doubt in his

[25] *Ibid.*, pp. 170–173.

mind that all religions have helped produce saints of an exalted character. We should be lacking in charity, even piety, he admonishes, if we denied the high degree of sanctity in religions other than our own.

Relevant to its domestic social problems, the Hindu idea of an Absolute seeks applicability abroad. It is recognized that many living faiths are passing through self-criticism. World religions are getting infected with secularism and humanism. Loss of the vision of God is a constant threat. Hindu thinkers are equally aware that many modern leaders regard themselves as priests of a new religion.

Yet the Hindu cry is not for a new religion. It is, rather, for a creative vitality in the practice of the old. This is a call for recognition of the Kingdom of Heaven which lies within man in his integrity, in his inmost truth which is God, the potentiality of every man.

[C] Politically, the idea of what is deemed eternally real transcends earthly institutions and mundane structures. Juridical organization and constitutional frames take their cue from such principles of ethics and moral philosophy as are rooted in religion. Such phenomena are ordinarily geared to a specific idea of deity or the disavowal thereof. In a leading culture, an invariable connection tends to arise between political and legal theory, on the one hand, and, on the other, the concept of an ultimate imperishable order. Yet to this problem, a certain complexity attaches that far exceeds the apparent.

A distinct contribution to the field was rendered by Augustine of Hippo. A realist, he set the Western and Christian world aright on this burning issue — that is, where interaction between political responsibility and faith in God tends to elicit confusion.

Augustine's picture of social reality comes to the fore in his *Civitas Dei*. There he offered an adequate account of tensions and social functions, of convulsions and competitions which are universal and accompany every stage and level of community existence. Yet his picture did not quite conform to the classic Greek notion of a polis. The latter was a simple establishment where order and justice prevailed. In a polis, peace and stability could be achieved if only reason were allowed to bring all subrational forces under control.[26]

With strongly Biblical insights, Augustine viewed the self as an

26 Harry R. Davis and Robert C. Good, *Reinhold Niebuhr on Politics* (Charles Scribner's Sons, 1960), pp. 61–69.

integral unity of mind and body. The self, he acknowledged, was something more than mind and therefore able to use the mind to satisfy its own purposes. Indeed, the self had a mysterious identity and integrity. Such of its functions as mind, memory, and will, it tended to transcend.

In keeping with Augustine's thought, the self enjoyed transcendent freedom. It wielded a capacity to defy any rational or natural system into which it might be maneuvered. Hence nothing short of defeat awaits the philosophy or creed which seeks to unravel the mystery of self.

The blunt truth is that such a conception of self did not originate in philosophy. It was the outcome of devout reading of the Scriptures. Whoever tried to comprehend the mystery of self apart from Biblical religion and the dramatic-historical setting in which it is cast was bound to get nowhere.

A corollary of this doctrine of selfhood is Augustine's conception of evil. The human community is threatened on every side. The source of the evil which threatens it is none other than self-love. That source is not some residual natural impulse somehow to be brought under mastery of the mind.

Superbia is that excessive self-love and pride which is explainable as the consequence of the self's abandonment of God. Abandon God as the true end of self and you discover that self is made an end. Precisely this is what sows confusion in every human community: self-love, egocentricity, the tendency of the self to be governed consistently by its own ordinances.

Augustine's *Civitas Terrena* sums up his view of the city of this world. There self-love prevails to the point of the contempt of God. What a contrast to the *Civitas Dei*. There the love of God actuates contempt of self. Nor is the city of this world to be visualized merely as a tiny city-state in line with classical thought. It comprises the whole human community on its three levels of family, commonwealth, and world.

Realism prompted Augustine to go one step farther. He challenged Cicero's conception of the commonwealth as rooted in a " compact of justice." Commonwealths, declared Augustine, are bound together by a common love or collective interest, rather than by a sense of justice. Without imposed powers they totter and fall. The imperial city to which the republic belongs could scarcely rule over provinces without recourse to injustice. Surely it is unjust for some to rule and others to submit without due consent.

Such realism touches power realities behind most large-scale social integrations. It operated in Egypt, Babylon, Rome, and Britain. It persisted wherever a dominant city-state or home country furnished the organizing power for an empire. It also depicts power realities in national states, even democracies, wherein a group, holding dominant social power, achieves oligarchic rule. This is still the rule no matter how much modern democracy may bring such power under social control.[27]

Yet Augustine rejected the idea that realism with regard to the *Civitas Terrena* must lead to cynicism or pessimism. Such a rejection is embodied in his definition of the City of God. The latter is commingled with the city of this world. Tension between the two cities is occasioned by the fact that self-love is natural in the sense that it is universal. It is not natural, however, in the sense that man has the opportunity to transcend self. He transcends himself as he learns that he can only have God as end of all his being.

How does a realism become morally cynical? When it turns nihilistic and acts on the assumption that the universal characteristics of self-love are acceptable and normative for behavior. Augustine based his judgment in the matter on a solid Biblical foundation. It was solid because it escaped both the illusion of a too consistent idealism and the cynicism of a too consistent realism. Such a foundation as he credited recognized that the corruption of human freedom may make a behavior pattern universal. However, it by no means makes it normative.[28]

Sentimentality is a complicating factor in the relation between faith in God and political action. Any Christian political thought, for example, which exploits the law of love without considering self-love is betrayed into sentimentality. Indeed, Augustine's doctrine of love as the final norm must be distinguished from modern sentimental versions of Christianity which regard love as a simple possibility. The sentimental fad is to assert the obvious proposition that all conflicts

[27] Reinhold Niebuhr, *Christian Realism and Political Problems* (Charles Scribner's Sons, 1953), p. 126.

[28] *Ibid.*, pp. 129–130.

in the community would be avoided, if only people and nations would love one another.

An idea of God has a determining influence on political thought and action. This influence is subject to the distinction between self-love and the love of God. Nor is the love of God reducible to mere sentimental profession. Augustine's contribution gives Christian thought on the subject a certain remarkable character. For one thing, his approach differs from modern forms of sentimental perfectionism.

The difference between Augustine's position and modern perfectionism is clear. He takes account of the power and persistence of self-love on the individual and collective levels. He seeks to establish the most tolerable form of peace and justice under conditions set by human sin. In short, the loyalty of a leavening portion of a nation's citizenry to a value transcending national interests proves dynamic and redemptive. It will save a realistic nation from the error of defining interests in a narrow range of shortsighted terms.

[D] Ecclesiastically, we may safely assume that a particular idea of God will have an immediate bearing on the kind of priesthood, ministry, or congregational officialdom that it inspires. Such a priestly hierarchical, or purely didactic clericalism might spring out of a conventional, cultic, or ritualistic professionalism. Its observances might admittedly be bound up with the social pattern or oracular authority. As such they might develop a small or large sensitivity to political manipulation and pressure. However, they will inevitably draw vitality from the idea of God professed.

Bearing a historic association with the priestly office, as it is universally conceived, are three intriguing areas of primary significance. These are envisaged here as the symbolic, legalistic, and sacred areas where ecclesiastical personnel or their counterparts function.

Symbolism is an integral function of all priestly orders. That it is integral to religion as such seems obvious enough. The study of symbolism owes a debt to depth psychology, that modern science which is heavily indebted in turn to the natural and humanistic sciences.

Depth psychology has devised its own vocabulary. This it did in order to evolve what the positivist philosopher and linguist call an intersubjective language. Relevant to our inquiry are three key words of this special vocabulary: allegory, sign, and symbol. So intimately related are these words to the priestly function under investigation that it might serve our purpose to look up the strictly defined meanings that Carl Jung [29] assigns them.

An allegory, according to Jung, is a view that interprets the symbolic expression as an intentional paraphrase of a known thing. A sign, in his judgment, is an expression standing for a known thing; it always serves as mere sign, never as a symbol. A symbol, however, is a view that interprets the symbolic expression as the best possible formulation of a relatively unknown thing; the thing represented cannot, in other words, be more clearly depicted. Such a symbolism enables a diligent priest to keep the idea of God alive. Drawing upon a set of easily apprehended associations, he sheds the luster of his own special art of communication and illumination upon the treasured faith.

That is not the whole fresh light, however, which Jung [30] sheds upon the subject of symbolism. He advances the theory that archetypes are the basis of all true symbols. Jung concedes that out of its own common unconscious every human group derives whatever symbols it desires. Individual and collective symbols thus arise in outwardly manifold ways. These are ultimately based, he conjectures, on an identical structural pattern or archetype.

To such a universal archetype, Jung would attribute the points of contact among diverse religious symbols and discordant ways of faith. A religious common ground, no matter how it is conceived, tends to evoke fear and trembling among the uninformed orthodox. Such shattering of convictions might even tend to shake ecclesiastical foundations and pervert personal religion. Nothing of the sort need happen, says Carl Jung. Himself a Roman Catholic believer, he assures the faithful his depth psychology can only serve in the end to edify and strengthen the soul.

Archetypes, by his definition, are factors and motifs that arrange the psychic elements into certain formations of images to be known as archetypal.[31] Said to exist preconsciously, these archetypes constitute the structural dominants of the psyche. An unrepresentable factor, an archetype is a disposition that begins to operate at a given moment in the development of the human mind. It tends to arrange

[29] See Jolande Jacobi, *Complex/Archetype/Symbol*, pp. 79–80.
[30] *Ibid.*, p. 106.
[31] *Ibid.*, pp. 31, 53.

the material of consciousness into definite figures.

Jung and his school make one more assumption relevant to this inquiry. The vast array of such symbols as a priest might employ are genuine only to the extent they correspond with an archetype. Rather than disparage the dogmas of his own church, Jung declares them repositories of the soul's secrets, a matchless treasure of knowledge set forth in general symbolical images.

When the vast world of symbols, in their relation to the still vaster world of archetypes, is perceived as an area where priests reveal knowledge or ignorance, its essential character is commensurately enhanced.

On the relation between the phenomenon of legalism and the priestly office, the Pharisaism of Hebrew history provides a classic example. The New Testament portrays the Pharisee as a sanctimonious hypocrite. Indicted is the Pharisee, moreover, for an aversion to what Jesus taught about sinners.

If only to set the record straight, things in favor of the Pharisaic order should be noted. Their legalism notwithstanding, the Pharisees did teach what came very close to the core of the gospel. Their teaching indeed supported what the parable of the prodigal son proclaimed on the love of God for man.

Martin Buber [32] would have us go beyond formal balancing of the Pharisaic record. He offers to defend that selfsame legalism by which priests and Pharisees became notorious. Relaxation of the diatribe against Pharisaic decadence and abuse of privilege fails to satisfy Buber. There is Talmudic authority, he insists, behind due appreciation of sound legalism, the kind that emanates from exalted motivation. Did not the rabbis maintain that the acts of the Torah are to be performed *lishmath,* that is, for the sake of the name, the holy name of God, and not for the sake of reward or the fear of punishment?

Finally, priestly potentialities come to the foreground in the orbit of things sacred as distinct from the secular order. A case in point is Roman Catholic opinion on the difference between sacred and lay civilization. In all that pertains to the sacred orbit priests perform a formidable role. What the Roman Catholic tradition contributes in this field is highly significant. It substantiates the impact of a given idea of God upon society.

Here is an example drawn from the secular order of the Western

[32] See Diamond, *op. cit.,* p. 128.

world. Privileges accorded the clergy in this culture area include exemption from military service. Such an exemption, argues Jacques Maritain,[33] is not a social privilege. To be exempted from having to shed blood, he rightly observes, is a high moral privilege for a man. It is at the same time a socially humiliating condition. Imposed on men consecrated to God, it recognizes their essentially peaceful mission to the human community.

Maritain's recognition that the historical climate of modern civilization is lay rather than sacred is joined to these penetrating insights: "On the one hand, the dominant idea is not the idea of struggle or fortitude at the service of justice but rather that of the conquest of freedom and the realization of human dignity. On the other hand, the great requirement for a sound mutual cooperation between the church and the body politic is not the unity of the religiopolitical body . . . but the very unity of the human person, simultaneously a member of the body politic and of the church if he really adheres to her. The unity of religion is not a prerequisite for political unity, and men subscribing to diverse religious or nonreligious creeds have to share in and work for the same political and temporal common good." [34]

From the foregoing analysis, Maritain [35] draws a number of deductions. First, political power is for him not the secular arm of spiritual power. It is further to be noted that the body politic is autonomous, and within its own sphere, independent. Secondly, he recognized as a basic tenet the equality of all members in a body politic. Thirdly, he stressed the importance of the inner forces at work in the human person, in contradistinction to the external forces of coercion. He accepted the freedom of individual conscience with regard to the state; and the axiom that faith cannot be constrained. Maritain, fourthly, declared that nothing more imperils both the common good of the earthly city and the supernatural interests of the truth in human minds than a weakening and breaking down of the internal springs of conscience.

Assuming the validities of what has been intimated regarding sym-

[33] Joseph W. Evans and Leo R. Ward, eds., *The Social and Political Philosophy of Jacques Maritain* (Charles Scribner's Sons, 1955), pp. 285 ff.

[34] *Ibid.*, p. 249.

[35] *Ibid.*, pp. 249, 251.

bolism, legalism, and things sacred, the office of priest takes on fresh meaning. It is an office of extreme significance for social awakening. For the liberation of personality, mass uplift and deliverance of the mind from the shackles of ignorance and convention, it deserves universal support and faithful training.

The unique opportunity to quicken a common conscience and to foster freedom of inquiry — a feeling for the truth of God — is nothing to be taken lightly. Given such an existential concern for the idea of God, the meaning of Divinity in human experience becomes increasingly vivid and prepossessing.

[Part Two]

RELEVANCE TO THE HISTORY OF RELIGIONS

CHAPTER

4

THE PHENOMENON OF HINDUISM

An early kinship drew the Indus Valley and Western Asia together. Proto-Indian culture was of Indo-European origin.[1] Yet the earmarks of Indian civilization were unmistakable. These included subtlety, simplicity, and compassion, a certain hierarchical design in society, a flair for nonviolence, and reverence for cosmos and divinity. India displays similar traits today in both private and public sectors.

Jawaharlal Nehru delivered a resounding speech in the Rajya Sabha on August 18, 1960. It was in response to a question raised in the course of a foreign affairs debate. He touched upon aspects of a changing Indian defense policy. "I object to our policy being called neutral," said Nehru. "It may be called an uncommitted policy. It should be called an unaligned policy in the sense we are not aligned to militarylike groups. That is the straightforward meaning, that we are not aligned to military blocs."

In that discourse the Prime Minister resumed: "Those who object to this policy only want that we should be tied up with military blocs. It is said that even though we may be unaligned, we are inclined this way or that way. Of course we are inclined this way or that way whenever we feel like it, because ours is an independent people. It is not a negative policy. It is a positive policy derived from our views on the world situation and on our own situation."

[1] Bedrich Hrozny, *Ancient History of Western Asia, India and Crete* (Philosophical Library, Inc., 1953), pp. 195–197.

Nehru explained, furthermore, that India's thought on foreign affairs was conditioned by Gandhi's teaching and example. Resolutions passed over thirty years ago, he recalled, are singularly appropriate today. This may serve to illustrate, he maintained, the fact of continuity in India's domestic outlook and foreign policies.

Despite many failures India has enjoyed a basic cultural pattern, a traditional way of looking at things. Hers has been a way of tolerance, a posture diametrically opposed to what may be described as cold war psychology. Indians will argue their opposition to the cold war is derived from an inherent aversion to hatred, envy, and violence. India's rational spirit, they insist, is irreconcilable with military power politics and diplomacy based on massive deterrence or threat of nuclear weapons. In the fall of 1962, however, a more realistic encounter with world history was occasioned by the rude shock of Red China's attack on the disputed Himalayan frontier.

Nonalignment was therefore a straightforward plan of trying to consider the problem confronting India. It is an attempt to figure out an Indian solution for the ills of society. The aim is to achieve a particular goal. Despite their affluent societies, Nehru believes the peoples of Europe, America, and Russia live in fear and trembling. Theirs is the dread of an evil. Just that is the evil India seeks to exorcize.

India is a secular state. Mr. Nehru's own brand of secularism will stand up in the face of careful scrutiny. Yet his entire public career and the obvious tenor of India's culture leave little doubt as regards the centrality of religion in the nation's consciousness. There is no question that in India religion does carry a stamp of authority.

This has been true for long centuries. The medieval Shiite Muslim physicist and mathematician al-Biruni (973–1048), who sojourned in India and was enamored of Hindu philosophy, testified to Hindu belief in God.[2] "The Hindus believe with regard to God that he is one, eternal without beginning and end, acting by free will, almighty, all-wise, living, giving life, ruling, preserving; one who in his sovereignty is unique beyond all likeness, and that he does not resemble anything, nor does anything resemble him."

In a Hindu classic by Patanjali, al-Biruni presumably came across

[2] Edward C. Sachau, ed., *Alberuni's India* (Trübner & Co., London, 1910), pp. 27–32.

a question raised by a pupil: " Who is the principal one by worship of whom blessing is obtained? " To which the schoolteacher replied:

" It is he who, being eternal and unique, does not for his part stand in need of any human action. . . . He is unattainable to thought, being sublime beyond all unlikeness which is abhorrent and all likeness which is sympathetic. He by his essence knows from all eternity. *Knowledge* in the human sense of the term has as its object that which was *unknown* before, whilst *not knowing* does not at any time or in any condition apply to God."

In the Gita,[3] al-Biruni notes an excerpt from a purported conversation between the supreme Vasudeva and Arjuna:

" I am the universe, without a beginning by being born, or without an end by dying. I do not aim by whatever I do at any recompense. I do not specially belong to one class of beings to the exclusion of others, as if I were the friend of one and the enemy of others. I have given to each one in my creation what is sufficient for him in all his functions. Therefore whoever knows me in this capacity and tries to be similar to me by keeping desire apart from his action, his fetters will be loosened and he will easily be saved and freed."

Such is educated belief in God, observed tenth-century al-Biruni. " They call him Ishvara, that is self-sufficing, beneficent, who gives without receiving. They consider the unity of God as absolute, but that everything beside God which may appear as a unity is really a plurality of things. The existence of God they consider as a real existence, because everything that exists exists through him."

" If we now pass from the ideas of the educated people among the Hindus to those of the common people," wrote the Muslim scientist, " we must first state that they represent a great variety. Some of them are simply abominable, but similar errors also occur in other religions. Nay, even in Islam we must decidedly disapprove, e.g., of the anthropomorphic doctrines, the teachings of the Jabriyya[4] sect, the prohibition of the discussion of the religious topics and such like."

The crux of the matter as seen by al-Biruni was that " hideous fictions are sometimes met with among the Hindus, especially among

[3] Cf. *The Bhagavad Gita,* tr. by Mohini M. Chatterji (The Julian Press, Inc., 1960), pp. 130–133; *The Bhagavadgita,* tr. by S. Radhakrishnan (Harper & Brothers, 1948), pp. 220–225.

[4] Islamic determinism, a doctrine opposed to the school of rationalists which posited man's free will.

the castes who are not allowed to occupy themselves with science."

Yet Hinduism regards religion as duty, *dharma,* in life, good only insofar as it leads to righteous conduct and proper behavior. Duties are of three types. Those of castes, *varna-dharma,* of the stages of life, *ashrama-dharma,* and of cardinal virtues, *sadharana-dharma.* Lost in obscurity, the origin of caste is probably embedded in a variety of social and racial beginnings such as discrimination on account of birth and color of skin. The earliest inception of caste cannot be detached from such things as the division of labor; much less from the necessity to ensure both free accessibility to other cultural groupings as in intercommunal business and trade contacts, and, simultaneously, self-preservation and protection of self-identity through outlawry of exogamy, that is, marriage with outsiders.

In a section of the Rig-Veda occurs the earliest reference to the fourfold caste system which emerged as cornerstone of the community structure in Hindu society. Constituting the four castes are priests, *Brahmana,* custodians of the spiritual culture; noblemen, *Kshatriya,* rulers of society, its political chieftains and military protectors; professionals, *Vaisya,* economists, merchants, and distributors of wealth; and workers, *Sudra,* manual laborers and artisans.

Outside the aforenamed fourfold pale of civilization were the untouchables, whom Gandhi sought to rescue from gnawing misery by calling them God's People, *Harijan.* He regarded untouchability as heinous crime against humanity. He called upon Hinduism to purge itself of this sign before it can be recognized as an honorable and elevating faith. Legislation against untouchability has since been enacted. Yet neither the problem of depressed or scheduled castes nor the inequities of the caste system as such have so far been satisfactorily resolved.

In its self-disclosures the phenomenon of Hinduism transcends preoccupation with caste. Five distinct, though not mutually exclusive, elements are explicit and may be simply stated.

First is the concern of modern India with its ancient historical settings.

Second is a closely related pattern of reappraisal where the ancient Indian heritage is concerned.

Third is popular Hinduism which exhibits itself in ritual, cult, and Yoga, providing an excellent opportunity to test the relevance of a phenomenology that allows a given religious system to speak for itself.

Fourth is the impact of Hinduism upon India's political, social, and economic, as well as ethical, structures.

Fifth is a correlation between Hindu universalism and world cultural currents.

Such are the disclosures of the Hindu phenomenon to be briefly considered in what follows.

I

Modern Hinduism throbs with an adventure into a fabulous past, an ancient heritage continuous with the present. Its resurgence may be described as retrieval of a glorious heritage. Unique among the elements of this tradition are such attributes as toleration and suavity, dialectical reflection, as well as the political and nationalist horizons, visions, and broadening frontiers of an awakened civilization.

Particularly since achievement of her independence in 1947, India has been in the throes of a renaissance. All phases of national life reflected the change.[5] During this era the greatest single influence on Indian philosophical thought was personified in Sarvepalli Radhakrishnan, a statesman-scholar who attained a remarkable and profound appreciation of both Eastern and Western cultures.

This Indian awakening entailed study of documentary source material and evaluation of classical settings. Vedic and historical criticism thus gained in scope and momentum. Eastern and Western scholars forged together and hammered out an enviable partnership as virgin soil was broken.

In 1951, K. F. Geldner's *Der Rigveda* saw the light of day, appearing in the Harvard Oriental Series. Providing a German translation with critical notes, this standard work took into account massive data involving all previously executed exegetical treatments of the subject. To it belongs the palm of preeminence as the most authoritative study of Hinduism's primary Sanskrit source.

Three years later, Raghuvira and Lokesh Chandra of the Inter-

[5] Cf. C. T. K. Chari, "Philosophy in India," in *Philosophy in the Mid-Century: A Survey,* ed. by Raymond Klibansky (La Nuova Italia Editrice, Firenze, 1959), pp. 292–301.

national Academy of Culture, at Nagpur, issued the *Jaiminiya Brahmana,* a veritable mine of myth and ritual. In English translation the reference runs up to some 1,252 sections.

K. N. Dandekar, C. Kunhan Raja, and A. C. Bose have rendered brilliant services to Vedic scholarship. The Poona academy known as Vaidika Samsodhana Mandala brought out the fourth and fifth volumes of its critical editions of the *Rig-Veda Samhita* with the commentary of Sayana.

On the continent of Europe, Indic studies have had a steady growth. There was Louis Renou's comprehensive study of Vedic sources and Indic philology.[6] Mention must also be made of the excellent work done by Barend Faddegon on the *Sama-Veda* and of the investigations carried out in the area of early Vaishnavism by J. Gonda.

J. Sinha's *History of Indian Philosophy*[7] followed up his earlier concern with realism and thought. Under the same title, S. Dasgupta[8] wrote a truly monumental work, which, particularly in Volumes IV and V, dealt with the pluralism of Madhva, the controversy between pluralists and monists, the Caitanya movement, and Southern Shaivism. Both Sinha's and Dasgupta's are literary productions of deft workmanship.

The fact stands out that much scholarly interest in present-day India centers in translations and expository writings. To this department belongs Radhakrishnan's, *et al., History of Philosophy: Eastern and Western.*[9] Also, his prolific contributions to the revival of the cultural heritage. These writings include English translations with commentary and critical notes of the first and third of India's threefold canon of religion,[10] the Gita, Upanishads, and the Brahma Sutra. Radhakrishnan's researches extend far beyond as his texts on nondualistic, pantheistic, and theistic sources reveal. Throughout these notable books, the central issues involved are set in bold relief. Radhakrishnan also edited, in collaboration with Charles A. Moore,

[6] See also Louis Renou, ed., *Hinduism* (George Braziller, Inc., 1961), in series, *Great Religions of Modern Man,* Richard A. Gard, General Editor.

[7] Central Book Agency, Calcutta, 1952.

[8] *History of Indian Philosophy* (Cambridge University Press, London, 1949–1955), Vols. I–V.

[9] George Allen & Unwin, Ltd., London, 1952–1953, 2 vols.

[10] S. Radhakrishnan, *The Brahma Sutra: The Philosophy of Spiritual Life,* p. 10.

an admirable reference work on Indian philosophy.[11]

India's historic impact upon a number of her Asian cultural satellites evokes a fresh approach. Chinese Indian and Indo-Iranian studies in particular have been fostered at Visvabharati University in West Bengal, an institution founded by the poet Rabindranath Tagore. Edward Conze, and colleagues, edited the *Buddhist Texts,*[12] authoritatively based on an array of Pali, Sanskrit, Tibetan, Chinese, and Japanese source materials. Together with Radhakrishnan's English translation of the canonical Buddhist text, *The Dhammapada,*[13] as well as continued researches in Buddhist ethics, these beginnings indicate something of the scope and sweep of contemporary Indian philosophy.

Even more revealing of trends and directions is the preoccupation of first-rate Indian intellectuals with an issue of comparative religious significance and far-reaching proportions. This is an issue that hinges on whether Buddhism and orthodox Vedanta philosophy are basically compatible. In 1954 an entire symposium was devoted to that vexing problem during the session of the Indian Philosophical Congress held in Ceylon.

Furthermore, an immense zeal for historical studies cannot be completely divorced from persistent involvement in philosophy as such. Modern scientific inquiry and research have netted a variety of reaffirmations and reorientations. Yet this is no mere resort to quietism. Lively interest in current and public affairs marks the regular proceedings of the Indian Philosophical Congress. In the person of N. A. Nikam, of Mysore University, the Congress draws upon the unremitting vitality of an able secretary. Two recent symposia gave sustained attention to the problems of existentialism and logical positivism.

The center of the stage in India's intellectual transformation, one needs to reiterate, is filled by none other than Radhakrishnan. This holds true despite overt criticism and dissent across the land. His comparative method aims at a mature synthesis of viewpoints old and new. His comprehensive approach seems to be grounded in recognition of the universality of the spirit and reality of integral ex-

[11] *A Source Book in Indian Philosophy* (Princeton University Press, 1957).
[12] Faber & Faber, Ltd., London, 1954.
[13] Oxford University Press, London, 1950.

perience, *anubhava,* explicit in his treatises. His Beatty Memorial Lectures at McGill University, *East and West: Some Reflections,*[14] convey an idea of his versatile methodology. Intuition, he will admit, ranks higher than intellect. However, Radhakrishnan is too meticulous a thinker to forget there is no real contradiction between the two.

An enduring quality attaches to the name and stature of Sri Aurobindo Ghose (1872–1950). His philosophy in effect postulated a cosmic beatitude, *Ananda,* and a cosmic energy, *Shakti,* as ultimate principles. His message was one of human unity, the "outflowering of the Divine in collective humanity."[15] A host of ranking Indian intellectuals today owe allegiance to Aurobindo's school of thought. Divisive in the extreme, however, is the controversy raging around this figure. In essence the issue is whether or not his ideas sprang directly from the matrix of orthodox Hinduism.

Did Aurobindo strictly repudiate the doctrine of illusion, *Mayavada*? That question happened to be the theme of a symposium held at Calcutta in 1950 upon the occasion of the Silver Jubilee of the Indian Philosophical Congress. G. R. Malkani, distinguished editor of the *Indian Philosophical Quarterly,* fervently professes faith in a self-revealing and self-luminous Truth at a nonempirical level of perception. He is nonetheless inclined to view Aurobindo as a major setback to the cause of classical Advaita. Malkani is not the type of scholar who reserves judgment on matters of significance.

By way of contrast, there are scholars such as Indra Sen, J. N. Chubb, and Haridas Chaudhury who conceded as eagerly as did Malkani the reality of mystical intuition, yet readily hailed Aurobindo as a giant among philosophers. To them he indeed is the maker of a new and vibrant synthesis. S. K. Maitra,[16] formerly of Benares University, lauds Aurobindo's spiritual humanism as an ingenious confluence of Eastern and Western ideas.

As might be surmised such an Indian intellectual revival is acutely sensitive to modern thought. For instance, P. T. Raju's "critico-integral humanism" happens to conform for the most part to the

[14] George Allen & Unwin, Ltd., London, 1955.

[15] Haridas Chaudhuri and Frederick Spiegelberg, eds., *The Integral Philosophy of Sri Aurobindo* (George Allen & Unwin, Ltd., London, 1960), p. 11.

[16] *The Meeting of East and West in Sri Aurobindo's Philosophy* (Sri Aurobindo Ashram, Pondicherry, 1955).

Radhakrishnan patterns. It represents a generous and judicious synthesis of various aspects of idealism both Oriental and Occidental. What Raju attempts in *Idealistic Thought of India*[17] is a reconciliation of intellect and intuition, the rational and suprarational, the human and divine.

In *The Chief Currents of Contemporary Philosophy,*[18] D. M. Datta deprecated the rivalry of systems and pleaded for a catholicity of thought adduced from recognition that philosophy is for life and action both outwardly and inwardly. T. M. P. Mahadevan in *A Study of Early Advaita*[19] and *Outlines of Hinduism*[20] sought " rediscovery " of man in the context of a nonanalytic philosophy. His teaching tends to center in the assumption that time is but the threshold of the timeless.

The irrevocable claim of kindred though unorthodox systems drew out T. R. V. Murti's *The Central Philosophy of Buddhism,*[21] an exploration of the Buddhist tradition according to its Madhyamika school of thought, and interpretation. What could be more illuminating for a full-orbed study of Buddhism than that acknowledgment of Madhyamika, a school that rejects nihilistic and pragmatic interpretations of Buddha's great " silence." Murti's contention was, moreover, that any discrepancy between Buddhist and Vedanta transcendence was largely a matter of emphasis.

A more realistic endeavor to crystallize the rudiments of Hindu philosophy came to the forefront in A. C. Chatterjee's *The Fundamentals of Hinduism*[22] as in the work of Ras Vihary Das, who recoiled from the excesses of Absolutism. Yet in following the course of existentialism he avoided an extreme rationalism characteristic of certain die-hard existentialists. His was no easy shrugging away from belief. What captivated his mind was, rather, a philosophy of affirmation. The viewpoint specifically affirmed by Das was that the life of reflection had a right to an autonomous spiritual activity of its own.

Conspicuous in all this intellectual upheaval is the convergence of multiple forces and influences. Shankara and Kant, Hegel and Rama-

17 George Allen & Unwin, Ltd., London, 1953.
18 The University, Calcutta, 1952.
19 The University, Madras, 1952.
20 Chetana, Ltd., Bombay, 1956.
21 George Allen & Unwin, Ltd., London, 1955.
22 Das Gupta, Calcutta, 1950.

nuja, Thomas Hill Green and Tulsi Das, all are there. This can be witnessed in the epistemology of A. C. Mukherjee who regards thought in its universality as a precondition of the philosophical categories. Prof. C. T. K. Chari, of Madras Christian College, has pushed back the frontier of knowledge concerning modern Indian thought. Broad in outlook, scholarly and highly perceptive, his essays deserve more than casual perusal.

Professional philosophers apart, literary critics, such as J. Krishnamurti, take up the challenge to rehabilitate India's spiritual heritage. His volume *The First and the Last Freedom* [23] champions pursuit of a " choiceless awareness " or an " alert passivity."

In book after book, on pages that glow with wisdom and conviction, Radhakrishnan has transmitted this great tradition in form which both East and West appreciate even where dissent rises to more than a whimper. Radhakrishnan achieved far more than the presidency of the Indian Republic. Not since Fichte and Schelling has there been such a precipitate stream of inspiration.[24] Except for an occasional Marcus Aurelius, philosophers never will be kings.

Sometimes, however, a philosopher wields an influence that a king might envy. Such an influence is wielded by Radhakrishnan and those who, like him, creatively contemplate India's historical settings. For to mediate creatively between India's historic tradition and her meaningful present is to bear grave responsibility before East and West.

II

That storied intellectual and religious armory featured by India's classics is thus today under enthusiastic review, inquiry, and scientific reappraisal. New sciences may steal the show. The status of philosophy nevertheless remains relatively secure. Less secure apparently is that tradition-born wedlock between religion and philosophy. Indisputably the center of the stage in national enlightenment has shifted in favor of such attractions as those of technology, industrialization, trade, and economic welfare. Yet in the intellectual sphere,

[23] Victor Gollancz, Ltd., London, 1952.

[24] George P. Conger, " Radhakrishnan's World," in Paul Arthur Schilpp, ed., *The Philosophy of Sarvepalli Radhakrishnan* (Tudor Publishing Company, 1952), p. 86.

the lure of thought and history of religion inevitably enlists the respect and admiration of many.

An impressive facet of contemporary Indian learning hinges in no small degree on the philosophy of religious symbolism. Through its Institute of Culture at Calcutta, the Ramakrishna Mission sponsors a publication, *The Cultural Heritage of India.*[25] Therein appear forceful disclosures of modern Hinduism's many-sided genius for reappraisal.

Concomitantly, a healthy regard for the pursuit of comparative religion is in full view. Scholarly undertakings are alive not just to the significance of Hinduism but as well to the importance of Islam, Buddhism, and Christianity. Chinese and Tibetan faiths have a way of their own in drawing attention. Mir Valiud-Din has explored Islamic Sufi mysticism with a canny grasp of primary sources.

Ever in vogue is discussion over the religion of Mahatma Gandhi. D. M. Datta [26] offered a philosophical interpretation and treatment of the subject. He depicted Gandhi's faith as a pluralism and theism rather than as an unqualified monism, *advaita.*[27] Indian scholars interested in research acknowledge their debt to the West. For example, the writings of the eminent Swiss psychologist, Carl Jung, evoke rapt attention. Likewise acknowledged are contributions of such European students of religious symbols as René Guénon,[28] G. H. Mees,[29] and Jean Herbert.[30]

Actually, Western evaluation of Indian thought during the last century strikes discordant notes. As Chari phrases it, this inclination has ranged all the way "from sheer admiration to absolute contempt." India was an arresting paradox, a challenge and an opportunity to Voltaire, Goethe, Rolland, and Tolstoy. It was a dream, an absorption, a wish fulfillment to Schlegel, Schopenhauer, Emerson, Yeats, and Keyserling. This selfsame India loomed as an obsolescent

[25] Ramakrishna Mission Institute of Culture, Calcutta, 1953–1956. Volumes III–IV contain a significant contribution.

[26] *The Philosophy of Mahatma Gandhi* (The University of Wisconsin Press, 1952).

[27] Cf. L. Fischer, *Life of Mahatma Gandhi* (Bharatiya Vidya Bhavan, Bombay, 1953), Vols. I–II.

[28] *The Reign of Quantity and the Sign of New Times,* Eng. tr. (Luzac & Company, Ltd., London, 1953).

[29] *The Book of Signs* (Kluwer-Deventer, Leiden, 1952).

[30] *La mythologie hindou: son message* (Michel, Paris, 1955).

Asiatic phenomenon, a decomposed society, an object lesson on the vanity of human wishes to Hegel, Gobineau, Spengler, and Macaulay. Even today, as Arthur Koestler's [31] "pilgrimage" reveals, the therapeutic waters of India can prove repugnant.

Heinrich Zimmer's *Philosophies of India,*[32] a voluminous survey, argues that two contesting, cultural strains were fused in the religion and philosophy of India when they were in the mating stage. Vedic thought was essentially joyous, life-affirming. Eventually the pessimism of non-Aryan civilization wormed its way into the religious philosophic texture without altogether quenching the flame thereof.

The idea of incarnation, if Zimmer's research is credited (incidentally his findings reecho earlier studies by Bloomfield, Macdonell, La Vallée Poussin, Deussen, Pischel, and Roth), also had a non-Aryan provenience. By the same token, Jainism was a flashback to non-Aryan piety.

Zimmer and Albert Schweitzer accordingly pursue a parallel course. Both agree that a precarious oscillation marks Indian thought and worship, an oscillation between belief in life affirmation and life denial. Such a dichotomy is attested, moreover, between the idea of a personal God and that of a neutral world ground, between ethics and mysticism.

On the Indian idea of God, perused elsewhere, the foremost exponent of modern Hinduism, Radhakrishnan, comes under heavy attack. Against him writers [33] have advanced a bill of particulars. They include the objection to his "intuition" on the grounds that it is slippery. In question, above all, is his notion of a God both personal and an Absolute, which many find evasive. Doubtful also are his many compromises between tradition and reform. His admirers claim that he has achieved, nonetheless, a remarkable vision of a truly universal faith.

Bernard Phillips [34] contends, not unfairly, that the naturalist critic of Indian spiritualism cannot justly demand verification, on his own terms. In testing spiritual verities, he advises, one must avail himself of the opportunity to divest himself of such trivialities as sense per-

[31] *The Lotus and the Robot* (The Macmillan Company, 1961).

[32] Bollingen Series XXVI, Pantheon Books, Inc., 1951, pp. 219, *passim.*

[33] See Paul Arthur Schilpp, ed., *The Philosophy of Sarvepalli Radhakrishnan* (Tudor Publishing Company, 1952).

[34] "Radhakrishnan's Critique of Naturalism," in Schilpp, *op. cit.,* pp. 125–171.

ception might breed. Charles A. Moore [35] notes that even when Radhakrishnan transcends ethics, it remains indispensable to the ethics-transcending stage.

Western critiques of Indian faith and thought often follow more subtle and sophisticated formats. For instance, F. S. C. Northrop's thesis adorning *The Meeting of East and West: An Inquiry Concerning World Understanding.*[36] His thesis is that the East is concerned with an aesthetic immediacy, whereas the West conforms to a priori postulation as well as a posteriori validation. Compared with such verbalistic refinements, Radhakrishnan's tolerance must shame legions of critics. To all seekers of the truth he does issue a Macedonian call out of any heavy-handed attempt at satire or cynicism. Before the East and West, Radhakrishnan has brought the fruits of a broad and clear-eyed learning. We need not acquiesce in his judgments, but to accord him respect and awe is the least a scholar will do.

The phenomenon of Hinduism disclosing itself in reappraisal of a great tradition is something beyond philosophy and the resurgent spirit. Much of this reappraisal issues forth as a summons to orderly, vigorous self-discipline, and cultivation of mind and spirit. Self-control is a key to Indian culture, declared C. Rajagopalachari, onetime Governor-General of India, in a special Independence Day article.[37] True culture calls on the individual to impose on himself many restraints without waiting for external direction. Said that forthright Indian statesman:

" When we speak of the culture of a people we refer to the pattern of self-imposed restraints to which individuals among the people are also brought up. This special pattern is what those people have after trial and error through generations settled down to accept in the interest of social order and happiness. It is then known as national culture. There is no resentment or pain in obeying this accepted pattern of restraint. On the contrary, there is internal satisfaction and pride."

Rajagopalachari went on to specify further. " It is this which distinguishes culture from the state regulations of the Communist countries and those who follow their example. . . . But neither state

[35] " Radhakrishnan's Metaphysics and Ethics," in Schilpp, *op. cit.,* pp. 290–294.
[36] The Macmillan Company, 1946, pp. 294, 315, *passim.*
[37] *The Mail* (August 14, 1960, Madras).

regulation nor mere freedom can solve humanity's difficulties. What is wanted is self-control. Education at home, and in schools, through religion, literature, and example must be directed to this end."

The former Governor-General was of the opinion, furthermore, that self-control is the message of Indian philosophy. It is the essence of that culture that can be justly claimed by India as her own special culture, he maintained. For material advancement is not civilization. The civilization of Greece was bound up with the sense of beauty. That of Rome was developed around order and law. India's civilization, however, was built around the central idea of self-control.

The way of self-control emerges as the standard Indian pattern for manners, morals, social organization, and interfaith relations. Such is the pattern of behavior esteemed by the people of India as worthy. This is the format regarded as correct throughout the ages by the common folk as well as by the enlightened. It can be read in the Upanishads and in the Bhagavad-Gita and in other authoritative texts.

As Rajagopalachari sees it, these scriptures did not lay down anything particularly new. They recorded what was universally accepted. They communicated what had already been acknowledged by the elite of society and acquiesced in by the masses. At the profoundest level self-control meant recognition of a soul within and pervading the material body.

Man's control over environment formed the pattern of other civilizations. For such civilizations conquest of nature came to be the aim and reward of achievement. Brilliant records were thus established. Yet the Achilles' heel of such records and patterns was not far to seek. It soon came to light. In the absence of stress on control of self, control over nature and environment might be extended beyond all expectations. In that event, it might spread out to a dangerous field. To exercise control and psychological mastery over the minds of men might reduce humanity to the status of material objects.

The rulers of the modern world, Rajagopalachari notes, have improvised techniques for control over men's minds as if these were merely raw materials like coal and iron. Small wonder that civilization, wrongly so-called, has thrown up its most deadly devices so far. How successful it has been in the introduction of weapons more lethal than the world has ever conceived before.

He asks what the enemies of good character, humanity, equanimity, tolerance, kindliness, purity of thought and action, might be. Some of the enemies he cites in reply are greed, lust, and anger. Modern life accentuates rather than curtails desires. Greed and anger are on the rampage at a terrific rate. Such a fantastic increase in self-gratification leads nowhere except to destruction.

As painful evidence of the above, he points to increasing crime statistics. Modern society, he fears, runs a terrible risk in abetting desires without instilling a sense of duty, or awakening an ear for the voice of conscience.

How does one go about nurturing self-control? Rajagopalachari's counsel is that such nurture ought to proceed from faith; that is, faith in divine ordinance as an indispensable state of mind. Otherwise all talk of self-control fails to carry conviction or reality. Apart from religious faith, self-control is neither acquired nor retained. Nothing but faith in divine ordinance enables an individual to experience self-control actualized in self-realization, fruitful in joy and harmony.

He reminds his countrymen that what they have acquired for themselves was procured at the price of unwearied religious observance. It is wrong to assume their heritage will stand of and by itself. It will not stand unsupported by what gave it being.

Then comes this clinching insight. It is an error to suppose that the people of India will in the course of time give up religion. His surmise is that no established community in India will readily relinquish commitment to religion. Religion is here to stay, he assures his audience, whether it be Hinduism or Islam, Judaism or Christianity. The people of India, Rajagopalachari said, will not settle down to the business of life without some form of worship. Apart from what will or will not happen, it would not be wisdom to seek to dispense with religion. If four hundred million people hold together, he concluded, we must realize that it is God's will that holds them together, not public regulations.

III

The phenomenon of Hinduism displays a practical catholicity disposed to explain deviations, even idolatry, within the framework of symbolism, iconography, mythology, and the anomalies of saints and village gods. Beyond the pale of this broad and inclusive catholicity are such major historic deviations as Buddhism and Jainism. As regards the popular religion of the masses, Hindu scholarship [38] tends to draw a distinction, in its evaluation of practices and beliefs, between the two areas of ritual and cult. A third area, that of Yoga, is a corpus of techniques providing effectual means for obtaining liberation.[39]

[A] The Hindu rituals are of two kinds: Vedic and Agamic. The Vedic rituals are of the nature of sacrifices to the gods. The Agamic rites are mainly connected with the worship of idols. Each Veda consists of four parts: Mantra, Brahmana, Aranyaka, and Upanishad. Of these the first two constitute the ritual proper. The mantras are formulas to be used in sacrifices. The Brahmanas explain how such formulas are to be used. Further explanations are to be found in what are known as the Kalpa-sutras. The smritis also detail several of the Vedic rites. To the hermit who retires to the forest, the Aranyaka (forest books) provide a substitute for the rituals, preparing the mind for the philosophical wisdom of the Upanishads.

When in consequence of the Buddhist revolt faith in the sacrifices came to be shaken, the sacrifices, *yagas,* which entail injury to animals fell out of use. With the institution of temples, moreover, the worship of idols took the place of mere sacrifices. However, elements of Vedic rites were incorporated into the elaborate process of worship.

There are different Agamas for the different parts of India. These offer guidance for the building of temples, installation of idols, modes of worship, as well as other instructions.

Integral to popular Hinduism are Agamic rites connected with the worship of idols and observance of feasts and fasts. Idol worship is not a subject of reference in the Vedas. Excavations at Mohenjo-daro reveal, however, that idol worship must have been a characteristic feature of the Indus Valley civilization. In the popular sacred texts known as *Puranas* specified objects are designated for worship. Such specifications take on the form of rule and set up order. Regulations

[38] For example, see T. M. P. Mahadevan, *Outlines of Hinduism,* pp. 40–53, 180–216.

[39] Cf. Mircea Eliade, *Yoga: Immortality and Freedom,* tr. by Willard R. Trask (Routledge & Kegan Paul, Ltd., London, 1958), p. 3.

were thus enacted for idol worship in home and temple.

Coming to the heart of the matter, Hindu scholars contend that idol worship is by no means peculiar to Hinduism. They regard it as an expression of exuberance in religious sentiment at a particular stage of its development the world over. Since child humanity cannot help thinking in terms of images, the function of an idol is basically symbolic.

No Hindu, however unlettered, this apologetics goes on, regards an idol as exhaustive of the being of God. Nor are Hindu scriptures unaware of dangers inherent in all extreme pursuit of idolatry. The worship of idols, they inculcate, is but the beginning of religion, not its end. A Sanskrit verse arranges the different grades of worship: First is the worship of idols; next comes the muttering of mantras and offering of prayers; superior to all these is mental worship; and best of all is contemplation of the Absolute.[40]

Be it in temple or household, images that are worshiped represent either Vishnu and his incarnations or those of Shiva and Shakti. The most popular and democratic of the deities, however, are Krishna in the north and Kartikeya (son of Shiva and Parvati) in the south. Both are portrayed in innumerable images.

Temples dedicated to these deities are indiscriminately frequented by Hindu masses. The people are inclined to see the same God in all idols and to adore him. In the home, we are assured, the Hindu treats a given deity as he would an honored guest. To the temple he bears flowers and fruits as homage to the King of kings.

In its popular expression Hindu ritual may be said to center in worship, festival, and birthday observances in memory of teacher and saint.

1. In broad outline a worship, *puja,* service follows what might be construed as formal devotion tendered a royal figure or distinguished visitor. "The presence of the deity is invoked, *avahana;* a seat is offered, *asana;* the feet are washed, *padya;* an offering of sandalwood paste and rice as a token of respect is made, *arghya;* the sacred thread is put on the idol, *upavita;* sandalwood paste is smeared, *candona;* flowers, *puspa,* are presented; incense, *dhupa,* is burned; the lamps, *dipa,* are waved; food, *naivedya,* is sacrificed and then betel, *tambula,* followed by camphor, *nirajana,* are burned, and gold is given, as a

[40] Mahadevan, *op. cit.,* p. 48.

gift, *suvarna-puspa.* Finally, the deity is bidden farewell, *visarjana.*" [41]

As already intimated, the priest attends on the deity of the temple as he might a king. The King of kings is awakened from sleep early in the morning to the sound of music. Soon after the ceremonial bath, royal robes are put on him and he is decked out with flowers and ornaments. Before him, artistic lights are waved and at regular intervals food is offered.

The King presides over a daily court. He grants audience to devotees, hears complaints, and bestows grace upon the people. On festive occasions he rides forth in state with pomp and regalia befitting royalty. Throughout the changing scenes of such a mystery play, the Hindu interpreter maintains that the action of God is plain. So in a sense India's temples fulfill a high and noble purpose, we are told. At least they shed a little light where darkness prevails. Backward and underprivileged multitudes are thus drawn out of drab and shabby existence into a brighter vision and more spiritual outlook.

2. Integral to such popular Hindu worship are festivals and ritual symbolism. Observances of fasts and feasts intermittently mark the entire calendar year. Such high days are intended to brighten an otherwise worldly and routine life. The fasts are said to give man an opportunity to look within and to examine the depth of his being.

Many a festival commemorates some major event which the Puranas record. Celebrated thus are the advents of incarnate beings, *avataras,* such as Narasimha, Rama, and Krishna, as well as momentous occurrences such as conquest of the demon Naraka by Vishnu and the burning of the god of lust by Shiva. On such festive days, Indian village and town overflow with joy and thanksgiving. A setting for colorful pageantry is thus provided.

In the view of many an intelligent modern Hindu each of the festivals honors and glorifies God. They are considered a tribute to the mighty hand of God, a hand that casts down evil and suffers good to prevail. Therefore, these feasts are reckoned as symbolic of victory over all that is base in man by a higher, real self.

Another order of festivals consists in the so-called purificatory fasts. In the course of the year, followers of each cult observe a set of special days exclusively devoted to prayer and worship. For many those

[41] *Ibid.,* p. 49.

are occasions of nocturnal fast and vigil. Readings from the sacred texts keep the mind engaged in meditation upon God.

Sacred to Vishnu, for example, is a day known as Vaikuntha ekadashi. Not only Vaishnavas but other Hindus as well join on that day in observance of fast and prayer. Auspicious for the worship of Shiva is a holy night known as Shiva-ratri. Still other days are kept by the women. They fast and offer prayer to Devi in her manifestations as Gauri and Lakshmi.

3. Birthdays of remembered religious giants are also celebrated. To the teacher, *acharya,* as such, Hinduism also accords special honor. Recipients of veneration at temples include other than idols of deities. Luminaries and saintly devotees come up for hearty acclaim and veneration. Hinduism has traditionally maintained that the veritable elite of mankind are those who lift the veil of ignorance and let the lamp of God knowledge shine upon society.

Such are the truly valiant heroes, *dhiras,* of the race. Through spiritual audacity and divine valor, they overcome the powers of evil. They assist others to cross safely to the sea of transmigration, *samsara.* What could be more appropriate than to recall once every year the advent of these redoubtable men?

Hindu scriptures stress the symbolic character of ritual.[42] The opening section of the Birhada-ranyaka Upanishad, for example, interprets the horse sacrifice allegorically. Overlordship of the earth may be achieved by sacrifice of a horse in the duly prescribed manner.

However, spiritual autonomy is contingent upon renunciation. To be renounced is the entire universe conceived by the Upanishad as a horse. The Upanishads also teach that meditation is of the essence. That is, to meditate upon the significance of such sacrifice is spiritually as beneficial as actual performance of the sacrifice itself. Worship of God in the shape of idols largely replaced Vedic sacrifice in later Hinduism. Even so, it was conceded that mental obeisance, *manasa-puja,* surpassed ceremonial worship in efficacy. Clearly then, ritual consisting of ceremonial acts was to be regarded as just an aid in the preliminary stages of inward life.

What the modern Hindu interpreter is trying to say seems obvious:

[42] See T. M. P. Mahadevan, "Myth and Ritual in Hinduism," *The Journal of Madras University* (July, 1950), p. 7.

As one progresses in spirituality, he seems to think, the need for reliance upon external props diminishes. In the case of saint and sage particularly, injunctions and prohibitions lose their priority. Where an absolute spirit has been realized, both deeds and ideas are transcended.

[B] The other great branch of popular Hinduism is discoverable under the rubric of cults. Even Advaita philosophy acknowledges the value of cults in the upward groping of the soul. Basic to a given cult is the mode of worship it engenders. In the Hindu view, the purpose of worship is to lift man up from the level of sensibility to that of divinity by utilizing his very senses.

India has come to know the techniques for such uplift as Tantra. The word may also serve to designate certain initiation books standard for the cult. Cults dependent on these techniques and standards are therefore referred to as Tantrika, be they orgiastic or not.

Literally, the word "*tantra*" refers to that wherewith knowledge is purveyed. The *Kamiḳa Agama* says that the Tantra is so called because it elucidates the meaning of principle, *tattva,* and hymn, *mantra,* and thus liberates man from bondage. If so, Tantra and Veda have the same end in view.

The orthodox Hindu tradition goes farther. Since Tantras or Agamas are based on the Vedas, between the two there can be no point of divergence. In *Kularnava-tantra,* Shiva tells Parvati there is no difference between Tantra and Veda truth.[43]

In fact, popular Hinduism bears the marks of heavy Tantric influence. Tantra procedures govern household and temple ritual as well as observance of fasts and feasts. Whereas Vedic rites are subject to caste reservations, there are no restrictions on observance of Tantras. These are open to all seekers irrespective of cult or caste.

Tantras lay claim to a long record abroad. The word "Bharatavarsa" denotes the vast domains of Hindu culture and faith. These extend far beyond the geographic and historic frontiers of India. Lands as far as Java have felt the impact of Tantra worship. Buddhism which came to be the religion of countless non-Indian generations of Asians created, of course, its own peculiar Tantras.

All in all, there are five distinct Tantras in Hinduism. These are known as Ganapatya, Saura, Vaishnava, Shaiva, and Shakta. Only

[43] Mahadevan, *Outlines of Hinduism,* p. 181.

Vaishnava and Shaiva may be regarded as major cults today. The first two seem to have faded out and are lost, Shaktism fell under the inroads of immoral practices, under the " left-hand " if not the " right-hand " type.

Whereas right-hand Shaktism relied upon the feminine energy or power to elicit grace and provide a channel of salvation, the left-hand variety exhibited wantonness, intrigue, and vengefulness in the goddess' name. Bengali saint Ramakrishna and his faithful disciple Rabindranath Tagore might find the Shakti worship of Kali rewarding. Yet left-hand Shaktism might prove quite another thing. Under whatever name, Kali, Durga, or other, it included indecent, orgiastic rites magical in essence and intent, accompanied by the use of wine, animal flesh, fish, grain, and women. Lower Shaktism has recently experienced a certain transformation thanks to education, radio broadcasting, and social as well as press guidance.[44]

The Ganapatya cult idolizes the elephant-faced Ganapti and the Saura cult makes the sun the object of its worship. The Vaishnava, Shaiva, and Shakta cults, however, are centered in more alluring philosophical and popular teachings. Hence their continuing favor with the multitudes.

1. Common to the many schools of Vaishnava philosophy is identification of highest reality with Vishnu. In every section of India, there are large segments of society committed to Vishnu. In myriad forms, he is adored in temples consecrated to his name. He appears as Nara-Narayana at Badrinath, as Krishna at Mathura, as Jagannatha at Puri, as Vithoba at Pandharpur, and as other manifestations elsewhere.

In the mythology of the Puranas, reports of sages such as Narada, Shandilya, and Shuka occur. There, together with certain celebrated mystics of historic times, they disseminated the Vaishnava faith among the masses. The Alvars of Tamil-land, the saints of Maharashtra, Kabir, and Tulsi Das in the Indo-Gangetic valley, and Caitanya in Bengal are all makers of the Bhakti movement. In their wake the Vaishnava religious revival gained strength and momentum.

Within this tradition arose a special type of teacher known as

[44] John Clark Archer, " Hinduism," in Edward J. Jurji, ed., *The Great Religions of the Modern World* (Princeton University Press, 1947), pp. 83–84.

acharya. Among these endowed men, Ramanuja, Madhva, Nimbarka, and Vallabha were of the highest caliber. Such were the architects of philosophical systems based upon the foundations of Vaishnavism.

Like other religiophilosophical traditions of India the Vishnu cult was transferred to the foreign colonies where Indian emigrants had settled. Even among foreign residents of India were some who embraced the Vaishnava cult. Of these a Greek ambassador, Heliodorus by name, adopted the epithet "Bhagavata" in an inscription at Besnagar. He referred to the erection of a Garuda-dhvaja in honor of Vasudeva, the supreme God.

Vaishnavism has other names: Bhagavata, Pancaratra, Sattvata, and Ekantika. Bhagavata simply means the cult of Bhagavat, the Lord. Those who espouse the Bhagavata tradition draw inspiration for their beliefs from the Bhagavad-Gita, the Bhagavata-purana, and the Narayania section of the Mahabharata.

Topics treated in these and related texts include: (1) knowledge, *jnana;* (2) method of mental concentration, *yoga;* (3) construction of temples and installation of images therein; (4) observance of daily rites and celebration of festivals.

Hindu scholarship corroborates the view that diverse streams of early Indian thought fed the ocean of Vaishnavism. Primary among these was the concept of Vishnu, the god with three strides as depicted in the Vedas; the concept of Narayana, a cosmic and philosophic deity; the concept of Vasudeva, a historical god; as well as that of Krishna, the pastoral deity.

In keeping with the Vaishnava tradition, the ultimate goal of the cult is enjoyment of the presence of Narayana, the Lord. Vaishnavas differ, however, on the question whether effort toward attainment of this goal is required of the devotee or not. Agreement there is, nevertheless, that apart from God's grace, *anugraha,* no one attains the goal.

Such divine grace is held to be natural *svabhavika,* and unconditional, *nirhetuka.* God ever awaits an opportunity to save the soul. Even an unwitting utterance of God's name is deemed enough to set the redemptive power of grace in operation.

Meaningful and distinctive in this respect is the office discharged by Sri, chief consort of Narayana. Toward all souls, who are her children, she exercises warmth and tenderness. In their behalf, she offers to intercede with her Lord. Being mother of all souls, as well as spouse of the Lord, Sri admirably qualifies, as devotees believe, for the role of mediatrix between men and Narayana.

The highest stage in God-love is consummate self-surrender, *prapatti*. This is open to all men regardless of social status, intellectual accomplishment, or sex. How to effect such a surrender is the burden of a passage in the Gita (18:66), where Krishna exhorts Arjuna:

"Renouncing all duties,
Take refuge in me alone.
Grieve not, for I shall
Relieve thee from all evil." [45]

Explicitly enjoined is such self-surrender as the only means for the soul's release. Every other spiritual discipline, *sadhana,* be it external worship, formal piety, or study of scriptures and Yoga meditation, is but an avenue to the final act of surrender.

2. Shaivism is no less a Tantra than Vaishnavism. Devotion here is addressed to Shiva, whose votaries inhabit representative parts of India. Temples dedicated to Shiva dot the countryside. From Amarnath and Kedarnath on the western Himalayas and Pasupatinath in Nepal, through Kashi (Benares), Avantika, Ujjayini, and Somanath to Cidambaram and Rameshvaram, situated at the gateway to Lanka (Ceylon), the name of Shiva is adored.

Viewed from inside Hinduism, these magnificent temples bear witness to Shaivism's pervasive and bountiful power. Surely it ranks as a towering spiritual edifice in India's daily life. Like other Hindu cults Shaivism has been historically a pilgrim faith of migrants. Indians have carried it along to new frontiers in the Far East, as far as Java and Bali, Campa and Cambodia.

Shaivism is rich in philosophical content and variety. As in Vedanta, variations of philosophical doctrine range from pluralistic realism to absolute monism. Extremist Shaiva subsects observe the great *Mahavrata* vow. This consists in use of a human skull as an

[45] Cf. Mohini M. Chatterji, *The Bhagavad Gita,* p. 266; Radhakrishnan, *The Bhagavadgita,* p. 378.

eating vessel. Its practice involves besmearing the body with the ashes of corpses.

The schools of Shaivism agree that Shiva is supreme reality. Identified with Rudra, Shiva for the Shaivas is god of every Hindu Tantra and not simply a member of the Hindu trinity: Brahma, Vishnu, and Rudra. To his devotees Shiva is supreme Lord, *parameshvara,* self of all beings, immutable, ever perfect.

Procedures for ritual and contemplation are set forth in the *Shaiva-Agamas.* These serve to release the soul from bondage. In *Atharvashira Upanishad,* the following description of the Pasupata rite is prescribed: " This is the Pasupata rite. ' Agni is ashes, Vayu is ashes.' Having taken the ashes while uttering these words, and rubbing himself with them, let a man touch his limbs. This is the Pasupata rite for removal of animal bonds."

Ceremonial initiation, *dikṣa,* imparts the necessary competence to perform this and other rites. The ceremony varies according to the degree and depth of spirituality. However, an identical procedure and the same undergirding principles inform all such performances.

The office for initiation ceremonies involves use of receptacles, *kundas,* where sacred fires and mystic diagrams, *mandalas,* are received. Pots, *kumbhas,* filled with water, are used to invoke the presence of Shiva and fire offerings; *homas* are made to the accompaniment of appropriate devotional formulas, *mantras.* The belief is that Shiva himself is present at the festival to initiate the devotee in the god's own path. The conviction is also deep that initiation is a prerequisite for purification of the soul and its preparation for release.

3. Of all the Tantrika cults, the Shakta have suffered most. Misconceptions and distortions are evidently the cause of Shaktism's decadence. To many the Shakti cult is " replete with silly and vulgar superstition," and is regarded as a tissue of " lust, mummery, and black magic." Shakta-darsana is, nonetheless, a type of philosophical nonduality.

Basic Shakta faith conceives of reality as nondual, *advaita.* Reality is depicted in terms of existence, consciousness, and bliss. Reality takes the form of *nirguna* in the sense that there are no distinctions therein. Nothing apart from this view is real. Everything that is real must be identical with it. Nondual reality manifests itself as the world of plurality through the power of *maya.* The *advaita* of Shaktism and that of Shankara agree in this respect.

Yet Shankara's and Shaktism's nonduality do not uniformly coincide. Shankara's *Maya* is the principle of illusion. It veils the real Brahman and projects the nonreal world. For Shaktism *maya* is real power manifest in the form of a variegated universe. In this respect, Shaktism comes closer to Kashmir Shaivism. Both regard Ultimate Reality as Shiva-Shakti, consciousness-power. Shiva is the stasis of consciousness whereas Shakti is its kinesis.

Such an image is concretized by the Shakta Tantras in the form of five corpselike Shivas. These support the throne of the world mother. She is set in the wish-granting groves of the Isle of Gems, *Manidvipa,* whose golden sands are washed by the still waters of the Ocean of Immortality. Both stasis and kinesis are required for the evolution, preservation, and involution of the world. Whereas Shiva is the basic foundation of creation, Shakti is the moving principle.

Extremely important in Shakta Tantra, as indeed in all Tantra, is the instruction conveyed on the ways of worship. A specific way of worship is needed if one is to attain a human goal: realization of the nonduality of the Supreme Spirit. The cardinal difference between Shaktism and Advaita needs to be stressed. In Shaktism, the power of the process whereby the One becomes many is real, for Advaita no such thing can be real.

An art by itself is the technique of Tantrika worship. It involves moral phases, ranging from gross physical forms to subtle mental modes. Deeply significant is every item of such technique. The spiritual aspirant, *sadhaka,* is asked to start with outward worship. However, he is not to stop at this point. Stage by stage he progresses, from chants and hymns to muttering of mantras and meditation. Finally he arrives at unity with nondual reality, *advaita bhava.*

In the *Tantrika-sadhana* images are employed as objects of worship. Sometimes these images bear no definite shape. Step by step, the worshiper trains himself to contemplate the deity in the form of a diagram, *yantra,* or disc, *cakra,* a kind of mystical wheel centered in the spinal cord. Contemplation of the deity also proceeds from linear designs and takes the form of recited formulas, *mantras.*

The process of ritual worship is rigorous and intricate. The worshiper must first purify his body composed as it is of five elements. He then performs *nyasa,* touching the different parts of the body with fingertips and the right-hand palm. This must be done to the accompaniment of an appropriate mantra. The worshiper next invokes the presence of deity in the image and thus beholds it enlivened. Gestures are then made with the hands to indicate different intuitions and wishes.

These are the characteristically Indian *mudra* gestures. Following such preliminaries, the worship of deity begins. In order at this point is bathing the image and adorning it. A crucial objective of all such ritual acts is to make the mind pure so that attention may be constantly directed toward God.

[C] No treatment of the Tantras would be adequate that did not take notice of Kundalini yoga. Kundalini is the psychic power that lies dormant in the soul, coiled up as it were. The purpose of the yoga is to arouse this power. More, it is to make such power ascend and achieve union with Shiva, the supreme Reality.

The concept of power, *shakti,* noted already, is central to Tantra cults. Identified with ultimate reality, this is power that creates, preserves, and annihilates the universe. Such power, together with its possessor, are one and the same thing. In a living organism, the characteristic breathing process depicts mystical power. Breathing, however, is but a tangible expression of psychic power.

Between psychic power and the physical organism, a degree of correlation is envisaged. In fact, Kundalini, the psychic power, is, as stated above, construed as coiled at the base of the vertebral column. Centers of consciousness are imagined to exist in that column from the lower parts up. The first five centers are said to correspond with the five elements: air, earth, fire, water, and ether. A sixth constitutes the region of the mind.

Centers of mystical power in the vertebral column are recognized as *cakras,* discs each depicted by a diagram. Pressed into service in this connection are the fifty letters of the Sanskrit alphabet. These letters serve to designate an equivalent number of lotus petals, symbols of psychic power in the anatomy. Sahasrara is the abode of Peramshiva, seat of supreme consciousness and bliss, Sahasrara has for its symbol a lotus of a thousand petals. Carriers of hidden meaning, the fifty letters of the alphabet obviously run through twenty cycles as they pass on through a thousand petals.

Lotus petals serve hence as symbolic channels, *nadis,* for mystical nerve power, points of convergence where psychic force and dynamism emanate. Along with the nerves they symbolize, the *nadis* constitute an armory of vital spiritual energy. Of these nerve centers, three are noteworthy: Ida, Pingala, and Susumna. The last is by far the most important.

Whereas pale Ida is technically called the Moon, the red Pingala the Sun, they actually connote female and male attributes, respectively. Located between these two, in the interior of the cerebrospinal axis is Susumna, fiery red in color, abode of supreme Shiva.[46]

The principle behind this subtle imagery seems to be an attempt to dissolve the grosser in the nobler manifestations of the Real. In short, this yoga Tantra methodology consists in guiding psychic power along with the living being, or soul, *jiva,* from one stage to another.

IV

This inquiry into the phenomenon of Hinduism has now reached a point where serious investigation of vital interaction between religion and life, faith and social ethics, becomes necessary. The psychological moment has perhaps been reached for certain pertinent questions to be raised even though definitive answers are not to be pretended. What is the nature of the cultural change wrought within India during recent decades? What bearing does such change exert on the religious situation in the country? What of poverty, mendicancy, and disease in relation to the political and spiritual transformation? How does Hindu public opinion react to such formidable problems as that of population explosion? What is a proper and valid evaluation of Indian nationalism and the issue of a national language? Whereas a direct answer to any of the foregoing questions is not contemplated, their background in the Indian ethos might here be explored.

[A] India's attainment of independence was a major event in world history. That fact stands out in the thinking of India's leaders and statesmen.[47] The method of attaining the freedom of some four

[46] On the signification of this erotic symbolism, see Eliade, *op. cit.,* pp. 246–249, *passim.*

[47] See Foreword by Rajendra Prasad, the first President of India, to R. P. Masani, *The Five Gifts: The Story of Bhoodan and Vinoba Bhave* (William Collins Sons & Co., Ltd., London, 1957), pp. 9–15.

hundred million persons had an impact on them, on Great Britain, and on what was known as colonialism. Of the essence were means and methods utilized in that movement for liberation.

When Mahatma Gandhi[48] in 1915 returned to India from his historical residence in South Africa, his homeland was seething with dissatisfaction and unrest. That had been the prevailing mood ever since the establishment of British rule. India had tried the method of open revolt and failed. She had also adopted and tried constitutional methods, inspired by faith in British history and in the British constitution. She had relied on the good faith of the British based on declarations by Imperial authorities.

What Gandhi advised for attainment of independence was a course that steered clear of both the terrorist and the constitutional strategy. The Rowlatt Act, however, passed in March, 1919, impelled Gandhi to proclaim March 30 of that year a day of mourning and general strike. The Act was seen as a slur on Indian responsibility and as a reflection on the sincerity of declared British intentions. It proposed to combat subversive activity by giving judges power to try political cases without juries and by giving provincial governments power to intern suspects without trial.[49]

That date marked the inception of noncooperation. It was not until 1920–1921, however, that he abandoned solidarity with the then ruling regime and took the ending of British rule in India as an aim. Gandhi arrived at such a decision only after constitutional alternatives open to him had proved futile. His efforts along those lines had failed to secure redress for what came to be known as the Punjab[50] and Khilafat wrongs.[51] Thereupon Gandhi began to advo-

[48] Gandhi was a voluminous writer. For years he wrote letters, editorials, and articles regularly for his famous newspapers *Young India, Navajivan,* and *Harijan.* He published books and in 1927 crowned his literary labors with a two-volume *Autobiography: The Story of My Experiments with Truth,* one-volume American edition (Public Affairs Press, 1948). See Homer A. Jack, ed., *The Wit and Wisdom of Gandhi* (Beacon Press, Inc., 1951), pp. 205–216.

[49] Percival Spear, *India: A Modern History* (The University of Michigan Press, 1961), p. 345.

[50] The "Punjab wrong" referred to British decision in Amritsar and elsewhere in the Punjab (1919) to treat Indians as an inferior race. See Raleigh Parkin, *India Today* (Longmans, Green & Co., Canada, 1946), pp. 191–192.

[51] The "Khilafat wrong" or "Caliphate wrong" denoted fear by Indian Muslims, supported by Gandhi in 1920, that unless Ottoman Turkey were restored, Islam would be in danger. That fear deepened anti-British hostility. See R. Coupland, *The Indian Problem* (Oxford University Press, London, 1944), Part I, p. 73.

cate a method of noncooperation and the country chose to follow him.

Gandhi's approach was novel. On the one hand, he repudiated violence. On the other, he refused to cast himself upon the mercy of the British.[52] He was sustained throughout by an independent source of strength. Home rule and independence, *swaraj,* were to be wrung from unwilling British hands by a consistent policy of withholding support. In all this the masses of India gladly accepted his leadership and challenge. Even terrorists suspended operations till his novel approach had been tested.

Nor was it surprising that the world community by and large took pause as it watched the Indian experiment unfold. Gandhi was to emerge as a unique personality hailed and revered around the globe. Yet attainment of *swaraj,* indisputably a matter of priority, did not constitute the maximum objective of Gandhi. It was but a singular victory on the road to more resplendent objectives.

Gandhi's ultimate goal was nothing short of radical transvaluation of values in human society. Realization of that goal was to come in a new social order founded on truth and nonviolence. Such an order was to be rid of exploitation in any form or substance. Inequality was to be replaced by equality, competition by cooperation, hatred by goodwill, and hostility by love. He lived to see the fulfillment of *swaraj.* He was bitterly disappointed and utterly distressed, however, to witness the tragic events attendant upon the achievement of political independence.

[B] What Gandhi did not live to see in the field of social liberation became the task of his heirs and successors. Poverty, disease, and illiteracy remain largely unrelieved. Yet under two five-year plans, and now a third, economic, health, and educational gaps were partially filled. If we are looking for solutions inspired by the Hindu religious ideal, there is no finer example to cite than that of the movement called land-gift, *Bhoodan,* personified by its contemporary prime mover Vinoba Bhave.[53]

The endeavors of Bhave have been regarded as an extension of those which Gandhi formulated but scarcely found the opportunity to inaugurate. For a hard core these efforts had the theme that man's

[52] Prasad, *op. cit.,* p. 10.

[53] See Jayaprakash Narayan's "Introduction," in Vinoba Bhave, *Talks on the Gita* (The Macmillan Company, 1960), pp. 7–10.

strong attachments to property should be tempered. To do this, a new spirit of trusteeship permeated by the motive of nonpossession is required. The profoundly Hindu concept and practice of nonviolence had figured as a determining factor in the attainment of independence. To it, another novel factor, the equally Hindu principle of nonpossession was now added and became an effective measure for social change.

Hindu thinkers are by no means unaware that other world movements strive for the establishment of an egalitarian society. Better distribution of wealth and equality of opportunity for all is a message and concern of such movements. None of these movements, however, is based on anything like the Hindu idea of nonpossession. Each of them is therefore likely, in the Indian view, to carry seeds of its own decay. Since a stated objective of all such systems is possession, higher and still higher standards of material comfort are ever in order. To be sure, some of these systems fix limits on the accumulation of wealth. Yet save under Communist dictatorship, which is another story, a basic curb on ownership and possession is nowhere conceded.

The Hindu scholar reminds us that in his scheme of things a contribution to the finest thought on the subject has been made. This grows out of the insight that there are men who derive profound joy in willingly relinquishing possessions. The Hindu poet Tulsi Das once said that greed increases as more and more is gained. Therefore, to resolve the problem one must begin at the source. An Indian way out is to extol the superior efficacy of nonpossession over possession.

Ownership of property and possession are neither inhibited nor frowned upon. There is no intention to dampen initiative or repress the profit-making motive. Proposed instead is the placement of a just and faithful value upon the ownership of material goods. The ancient Hindu virtue of nonpossession is thus dressed up in modern garb to fit the concept of trusteeship or stewardship.

The Bhoodan movement calls upon Indians to join in the giving of land, the most highly prized of all properties. Rich and poor alike thus come to know the true meaning of possession as trusteeship. Involved is something more meaningful than the mere giving of land. What is envisaged is a new social order patterned after Gandhi's philosophy. It is a vision bound to enkindle hope of social uplift and community welfare. The serious problems which the land redistribution movement has encountered in recent years leave little doubt that other methods need to be adopted if social change is to come. Operative already, but due for marked acceleration, are programs for education, progressive farming, industrialization, and birth control.[54]

Modern Indians will point out [55] that if their country is sunk in awful poverty today, its wealth and splendor once dazzled the world. Greek and Latin writers like Herodotus, Strabo, and Pliny were not unmindful of India's affluence. Such an impression of wealth was documented by early travelers and ambassadors from Greece and Rome. Available to us is the data and detailed information they recorded. "The wealth of Ormuz and Ind" stirred the imagination of Jacobean and Elizabethan poets. It whetted the appetites of European adventurers.

Spokesmen for Indian culture go even farther. They argue there was no problem in those bygone eras as to land ownership or unequal distribution of wealth. Long before Christianity had taught Europe that "the earth is the Lord's," the Indian had learned to say "the earth is my mother." By this dictum was affirmed his right to be fed. Man did not then hunger for land. The land was there pleading for him to till it. This seems to have been common belief across an Asia of divergent religious horizons. "Whoso sows corn, sows righteousness," said Zoroaster, philosopher of ancient Iran, a prophet whose voice is still heard among the Parsis of modern India.

It was not only the wealth of ancient India that drew the attention of the nations. Within its clan and family appeared man's first attempt at civilized living. Even when families came together to form protective communities, individual ownership of land was not recognized. Members of groups lived together as a single family and shared the fruit of joint labor. Only when economic advance led to interdependence did the division of labor sharpen the gulf between one group and another. Communities that were once united

[54] For a statistical report, somewhat dated yet thoroughly useful, see Kingsley Davis, *The Population of India and Pakistan* (Princeton University Press, 1951), pp. 221–231.

[55] Masani, *op. cit.*, p. 25.

began now to break up into individuals of self-employed, employer, and employee standing. Even then the basis of continuity remained, rooted as it was in memory of common ancestry, as well as in consciousness of a blood kinship.

Hence the foundation and development of corporate life as the Indian historian sees it. In the early Vedic, Epic, and Pali literature of India, fully developed and influential local bodies had already emerged. Long before Europe developed self-governing institutions, India's towns and villages had an elaborate system of administrative and judicial councils. Of these, the best known is the *Panchayat,* a council of five village elders, which continues to the present day.

The land-gift movement, *Bhoodan,* the ideal social order, *samyayogi,* the total good of all, *Sarvodaya,* such are the focal points and catchwords of the new society foreshadowed by Gandhi and today spearheaded by Acharya Vinoba Bhave. Perhaps more than any other Asian country, India's national architects have been men of profound religious faith and experience. Beginning with Ram Mohan Roy, on through Mahatma Gandhi, and finally in the figure of Bhave, this has been the norm in the modern era. Exponents of Sarvodaya currently claim that from earliest times Hindu society had sought to develop social ethics. On the basis of monism they see the early maintenance of such social principles as those of equality and simplicity.

[C] The objective of this ancient yet new sociology, according to qualified Hindu critics and planners, is to establish a classless, casteless, and conflictless society. Every individual and group will then get opportunity and means for all-round development. Such revolutionary and radical change can be brought about, they hope, by means of nonviolence and truth.[56]

Essential to all the above is a time-honored Indian belief that the world is kept going by holy men. Through their lives of piety and authority, humanity lives on. Holy men, recognized as Rishis, identified the individual self with the universal self. They thus instructed men in the knowledge of their kinship to God and in a universal outlook on life and things. Such a universality and comprehension

[56] Paul David Devanandan, "Renascent Religions and Religion," in *The Ecumenical Era in Church and Society,* ed., Edward J. Jurji (The Macmillan Company, 1959), pp. 151–163.

of goodness provides the groundwork of Vinoba Bhave's mission. It is a doctrine voiced some twenty-five hundred years ago by Gautama the Buddha who thus communicated it to his disciples: "I do not want to go to heaven until everyone has entered."

That blessed doctrine of universal goodness (*Sarvodaya* was Gandhi's word for it) has often been called the Gandhian way of life. It is equally the Vinobian way of life. Indeed the Bhoodan movement itself is Bhave's stupendous effort to penetrate more deeply into the Sarvodaya doctrine. Thousands upon thousands are thus inspired to strive and to live for the good of all.

Bhave trudges from village to village. He enters the hearts of people and influences their thoughts, inclinations, and wills. He has succeeded in no small measure in changing the lives of men. Landowners have been converted. Rich and poor have shown a desire to lift the burden of poverty and misery from fellow creatures. There lies a most encouraging feature in Hinduism's social consciousness. In rural India, at least, the spirit of Gandhi remains as a source of strength.

V

An idea of the universal transcends India's relations abroad, particularly its contacts with the Western world. An alternative cultural pattern is thus offered as a distinctively Indian contribution. That the whole is one and that within such a wholeness, the truth is pluralistic, those are the two central assumptions of Hinduism. Whatever the philosophy of history may be, and however the doctrine of man may be phrased, the above assumptions provide the initial clues.

[A] Ethics, sociology, and politics are the general spheres where Hinduism's universalist gospel operates. An overriding ethical concern marks contemporary Indian philosophy. The themes of two recent conventions of the Indian Philosophical Congress are proof positive: "Naturalism and Values" and "Can There Be Ethics Without Metaphysics?"

A preoccupation with ethics rather than hedonics is easy to perceive, for instance, in M. Hiriyana's *Popular Essays in Indian Philosophy* [57]; also in such therapeutic ethics as that of Bhagavan Das and Swami Akhilananda of the Boston Ramakrishna Mission.

[57] Published posthumously (Kavyalaya, Mysore, 1952).

As might be expected, this emphasis on ethics accents a growing literary output surrounding the name of Gandhi. Similarly accented are the multiplying expositions of the Bhagavad-Gita. Pronounced in this connection is the above-mentioned emphasis on Gandhi's doctrine of total good for all, *Sarvodaya,* and its implications in Vinoba Bhave's land-gift, *Bhoodan,* movement. To the same genre of social ethics belong a number of new writings. These include B. Kumarappa's edited work, *Sarvodaya,*[58] and an evaluation of Tagore's social philosophy by J. Sinha.[59]

A. R. Wadia's *Religion as a Quest for Values*[60] finds that a maya-ridden world and nostalgia for pilgrimage offer inadequate incentives for values. Wadia wonders whether those who like Radhakrishnan are wont to redefine caste do not in effect compromise the issue. But D. Mackenzie Brown's survey, *The White Umbrella: Indian Political Thought from Manu to Gandhi*[61] suggests that *dharma* has been pivotal to Hindu ethics and politics. Humayun Kabir, so prominently associated with the Indian Philosophical Congress, discusses Islam, democracy, and education in the overall structure of modern India.

Materials are not lacking for the study of Hindu ethics and moral philosophy along modern critical lines. J. Brough's *The Early Brahmanical System of Gotra and Pravara*[62] probes the early exogamic family, *gotra,* and clan system of the Vedic epoch. Radhakamal Mukerjee examined the " dynamics of morals " from the standpoint of modern social philosophy and sociology.[63] Human relations and international obligations figured in a symposium in which UNESCO and the Indian Philosophical Congress concerted their efforts.

N. A. Nikam, editor of *Human Relations and International Obligations,*[64] believes that " the need of an international community is

58 Navajivan Press, Ahmedabad, 1952.

59 *Tagore's Approach to Social Philosophy* (Modern Books Company, Calcutta, 1952).

60 The University, Calcutta, 1955.

61 University of California Press, 1953.

62 Cambridge University Press, Cambridge, 1953.

63 Formerly Vice-Chancellor, University of Lucknow, Prof. Radhakamal Mukerjee's other works include *The Theory and Art of Mysticism* (The University, Calcutta, 1960), a scholarly contribution concerned with the bearing of religion upon the health of human institutions.

64 Indian Philosophical Congress, 1956.

ethical. A world community is necessary for survival." It is no exaggeration to say that a majority of India's thinkers hold that *homo politicanus* can barely function apart from a broadly conceived spiritual democracy.

[B] Hinduism's own variety of comparative religion is indeed impressive. We are frequently told that the Hindu religion, without an acknowledged founder, enjoys a range, universality, and catholicity which Christianity, more uncompromising and proselytizing, has seldom mustered. Did not the French novelist and Nobel Prize winner Romain Rolland (1866–1944) write to Rabindranath Tagore: "I have often wondered at the spirit of religious toleration in India, unlike anything we have in the West. The cosmic nature of your religion and the composite character of your civilization makes this possible. India has allowed all kinds of religious faith and practice to flourish side by side"?

Many enlightened Hindus are convinced all faiths lead to God; all religions have a hold on the truth. That was the burden of Swami Vivekananda's celebrated address in Chicago before the Parliament of Religions in 1893. In that speech, Swami Vivekananda said to the audience: "Sisters and Brothers of America! The Hindu refuses to call you sinners. 'Sinners'? It is a *sin* to call a man so!"

It is quite conceivable, as C. T. K. Chari [65] intimates, that the case for Hindu tolerance and universality has been somewhat overdrawn. Even if we disregard heterodox Jainism and Buddhism and confine ourselves to the orthodox religiophilosophical systems of India, *astika darshanas,* we encounter a wide range of theological and metaphysical speculation and practice. This might signify little more than that the texts — *Vedas, Upanishads, Gita,* and *Vedanta Sutra* — whereupon orthodox Hinduism rests, are cryptic in the extreme in certain crucial issues and admit of conflicting interpretations. The fact remains, however, that conflicting doctrines lead as a rule to intolerance and discord.

A famous saying, *maha vakya,* of the Upanishads is *tat tvam asi* "That Thou Art." Of that saying there have been three divergent interpretations. According to Shankara's elaborate interpretation, formulated in line with the belief that the world is illusory, *maya*

[65] "The View-Point of a Hindu Theist," in *Religion and Society* (Vol. VI, No. 1, Feb., 1959, Bengalore), ed. by P. D. Devanandan and M. M. Thomas, pp. 20–24.

vada, the saying implies there is no difference between the soul, *Atman,* and the Godhead, *Brahman.* Ramanuja expounded the same saying in keeping with the doctrine that God, soul, and world are intimately related yet distinct the one from the other. Madhva proceeded to explicate the saying in his own way. He did set it forth in the light of a radical pluralism and theism. Now all three are renowned teachers, *acharyas,* venerable and admired. Yet where such diverse ingenuities arise, schism among believing souls is bound to result.

Hence an almost instinctive aversion among qualified Indian scholars, aware of incompatible views in their religious tradition to some such expression of opinion as that of Will Durant in *Our Oriental Heritage.*[66] Durant there said the *Upanishads* propound three cardinal truths: the reality of Brahman, the reality of the Atman, and the complete identity of the two.

What injustice that generalization does, for instance, to the Shaiva-Siddhanta religiophilosophy with its thousands of adherents in South India. One case out of many, this school of religious life has the following for a central postulate: the distinctions of the soul, *pasu,* and the Lord, *Pati* (Deity). Nor is Shankara's doctrine of nonduality, *advaita,* any more than his affirmations on the illusory nature of all things, admissible as normative for Hinduism.

In vain, one seeks to extract a theory of nondifference from that memorable passage in the Gita:[67] "Whoever in love offers to me a leaf or flower or fruit — that, given in love by the purehearted, I accept" (IX:26). Even the "Vasudeva (the Supreme) is all that is"[68] of Gita VII: 19 would seem to suggest a panentheism, the doctrine that all things are within the being of God who is yet not merely the whole of actual things, rather than theophany or pantheism.

[C] Setting aside for the moment such distinguished Indian philosophers as Radhakrishnan, who espouses a sort of perspectivism, let us take a hard look at popular Hinduism. But before doing so, let it be noted that perspectivism admits different levels of reli-

[66] Will Durant, *The Story of Civilization: Our Oriental Heritage* (Simon and Schuster, Inc., 1942), pp. 412–415.

[67] Chatterji, *The Bhagavad Gita,* p. 155.

[68] Radhakrishnan, *The Bhagavadgita,* p. 220.

gious experience. There is indeed a perspectivism that admits personal values and a personal God to be valid. Yet such a perspectivism can see personal faith transcended at the ultimate nondual level.

What popular Hinduism achieves is a peculiar syncretism won at the cost of philosophical consistency and religious certitude. A religion uncertain whether a personal God is ultimate will drift into obscurantism. Incidentally, the religious sages, *acharyas,* were both more candid and uncompromising than their followers.

George Bernard Shaw once came up with an astute comment on popular Hinduism. "The apparent multiplicity of gods is bewildering at first glance," he conceded. "But one soon discovers that they are all the same God in different aspects and functions. There is always one uttermost God who defies personification. This makes Hinduism the most tolerant religion in the world. Christ is there as Krishna who might also be Dionysius." But a Christ who might be Krishna and Dionysius as well makes the serious Christian and the serious Hindu alike uneasy.

Not to be minimized is reexamination of *ḳarma* as a key doctrine. Popular expositions of Hinduism delight in rehabilitating this doctrine along modern scientific lines. The subtle doctrine of Karma enables them to interpret the moral government of the world. Karma is thus made satisfactory to science and recognized as a universal law of cause and effect. What we sow, we reap. If we sow the wind, we reap the whirlwind.

Prof. C. T. K. Chari,[69] Hindu of the Hindus and a scientifically trained philosopher, expresses certain misgivings on the significance of Karma. There are many questions to be met, he confides, before the doctrine of Karma can be regarded as unassailable and universal. He asks probingly, "Does effect follow cause in the moral as in the physical domain?" Scruples have been raised about causality in quantum physics, also in the psychobiological sciences. The status of causality is therefore hardly unambiguous.

Modern thinkers like Bergson regard the extensions of the principles of causality to the moral and spiritual domain as gratuitous. Is Karma cosmic, retributive justice? Many texts seem to imply just that. But does a retributive theory of punishment, albeit cast in a cosmic and impersonal mold, really satisfy the requirements of

[69] *Op. cit.,* p. 22.

modern ethical theory? To be sure, as we noted above, a striking verse in the Gita (XVIII: 66) reads: "Renouncing all duties, take refuge in me alone." Be that as it may, Hindu thinkers have yet to decide what precise construction to place upon the theory of Karma before they commend it to others.

With characteristic perception, Radhakrishnan ably rejects the retributive interpretation of Karma. The relevant texts he explains away as allegorical. According to him, Karma is the principle of moral continuity if not a principle of moral causation. Goodness leads to more opportunities for the good. Badness results in freedom to do evil. Unfortunately even such an ingenious exposition fails to settle all issues.

Does a principle of moral continuity in line with Radhakrishnan's understanding entail the hypothesis of rebirth? On this subject, too, ambiguity in modern Hindu thought is not lacking.

[D] There is furthermore the issue of dialectic in the domain of Hindu mysticism. Here again sympathetic reconsideration of the sources of Hindu religion proves illuminating to a non-Hindu. Indeed, one is inclined to agree with Chari that the dialectic of Hindu mysticism warrants reappraisal in a far wider context than that of Hindu philosophy.

Even if God is supremely personal, the relation of Creator to creature cannot be fathomed by our logical categories alone. Therefore it is important that in comparative studies of mysticism one should go back to medieval Christian mysticism. There one should seek to comprehend what Meister Eckhart,[70] for instance, did with the Athanasian Creed, "Neither confounding the Persons nor dividing the substance."

Each Person in the Trinity gives his whole substance to the others and receives it wholly. God gives his whole substance to the others and receives it wholly. God gives himself to the soul beyond all categories. Meister Eckhart had no hesitation in affirming the transcendence of God. He needed no elaborate demonstration of the spirit which dwells in the inner "little castle," *Burglein,* of the soul. It was the ground, *der Grund,* the spirit of the soul, *der Seelengeist,* the spark of the soul, *das Funkeln der Seele*. These were reminiscent

[70] Franz Pfeiffer, *Meister Eckhart,* tr. by C. De B. Evans (John Maurice Watkins, London, 1924), Vol. I, pp. 35–38, 86–90, 169–171.

of the *scintilla* of Plotinus and the *scintilla animos* of Aquinas, Peter Lombard, and Jerome.

Walter Robert Matthews, in *The Problem of Christ in the Twentieth Century: An Essay on the Incarnation,*[71] remarked that any modern Christology has to reckon with man, " the great amphibian," interlocking two worlds, the changing and the changeless. In this, a contemporary Indian philosopher sees a pointer to the Greek *Nous,* mind, Hindu *Atman,* soul, and German *Grund.* Nor is Christian *Logos* irrelevant.

Vladimir Solovoyev's great dream of the " deification of all mankind " was not the climax of Hegelian dialectics but a return to the mystical vision of Sergius of Radonezh (1314?–?1392). The latter saint gave Russian Christian theology its *sobornost,* " ecumenicity, catholicity," in a most characteristic form: contemplation of the divine Trinity enabling us to overcome all hateful divisions of the world. In a parallel vein, a South Indian saint once testified, " I have seen," *nan ḳandu-ḳ-ḳonden.*[72]

[E] Finally, the phenomenon of Hinduism would be incompletely sketched if one crucial question were not raised within its context. " Is a world faith possible? " Hegel set the fashion of reducing various faiths to " moments " in a preconceived dialectic. One is not too happy over such ventures.

In his Hibbert Lectures, *Living Religions and World Faith,*[73] William Ernest Hocking examined three possible courses to world religion. The first pointed in the direction of radical displacement. Karl Barth and Hendrik Kraemer stood, according to Hocking, as the two high priests of this school. In its considered judgment, this tradition would let each faith harden its particular outlines to exclude what are regarded as faiths alien to it.

Hocking isolated, secondly, a course that commends itself as a way of synthesis. The primary motif here was to allow a given faith freedom to assimilate such contents as it may choose to draw from outside, albeit with some modification of original elements. This is a school that wins the approval of such enthusiasts as might

[71] Oxford University Press, London, 1950, p. 74.

[72] Cf. Gordon Matthews, *Siva-Nana-Bodham: A Manual of Saiva Religious Doctrine* (Oxford University Press, London, 1948), pp. 22–24, 26–27.

[73] George Allen & Unwin, Ltd., London, 1940, pp. 143–208. Cf. his *The Coming World Civilization* (Harper & Brothers, 1956).

be expected to let zeal run away with discretion.

Hocking himself espoused a third approach to the subject. His was a course alternative to the foregoing two. This was to be a pattern of " inclusion by reconception," a solid groundwork of earnest idealism attuned to advanced thinking, realism, and conscientious objectivity.

This last course evokes hearty response in more circles than the conservatives are ready to concede. It furthers and fosters valuable insights and provides a keen approach to the prospects for a world faith. The proposal crystallizes along this line: each faith without distortion of its own genius widens its base to embrace what it finds valid elsewhere. Also it thereby recovers what it will find infinitely more valid in its own heritage as it deepens its self-understanding. Generally that is an approach that conforms reasonably well with a Hindu outlook on comparative religion and the relations between living religions. However, few modern Hindu scholars will take kindly to an avowedly eclectic program for their own religion.

Will Durant[74] projected a pattern that might closely resemble the requirements of a phenomenon of religion nourished from within Hinduism. Perhaps in return for conquest, arrogance, and spoliation, he aspired, India might teach us the tolerance and gentleness of a mature mind.

We might indeed take seriously what India has to teach: the quiet content of an unacquisitive soul, the calm of an understanding spirit, and of integrating, pacifying love. From such a profile of their own faith, few modern Hindus will intentionally dissent.

[74] *Op. cit.*, p. 633.

CHAPTER

5

THE PHENOMENON OF BUDDHISM

When Burma in 1961 established Buddhism as a state religion, she reverted to the ways of her ancient kings. An oral Buddhist tradition in that country goes back to the third pre-Christian century or earlier. However, a historical record is not available for any Buddhist ruler prior to King Anawrahta of Pagon (A.D. 1044–1077). At any rate, Buddhism's new status in Burma sheds light on the contemporary resurgence of that religion.

A religion claiming universality, Buddhism ranks as a missionary faith. It also ranks as third among world religions, next, that is, to Christianity and Islam. A total of about three hundred and twenty million people make up its international constituency in the Far East.[1] Widespread across East Asia, Buddhism is a faith of Indian origin and beginnings, historically an offshoot of Hinduism. It overran China and Japan as well as Ceylon, Burma, and Thailand. It penetrated several other important countries such as Tibet, Korea, and Indo-China.

Burma's recent welding of temple and state was voted as a constitutional amendment by a joint session of parliament. It fulfilled a campaign pledge which Prime Minister U Nu made in 1960, having previously taken the vows of a Buddhist monk. He had thus committed himself to Burma's twenty-two million inhabitants whereof 85 percent are Buddhists. Yet the state-religion act was bitterly opposed by Burma's religious minorities: Muslims, Animist Kachins, Christian Chins, and even Buddhists of separatist Karen and Shan states.

[1] W. Schneefuss, "Religionsstatistik," in *Religionswissenschaftliches Wörterbuch*, ed. by Franz König (Verlag Herder, Freiburg, 1956), pp. 752–756. Cf. Benson Y. Landis, *World Religions* (E. P. Dutton & Company, Inc., 1957), p. 126.

Such heightened religious emphasis, symbolized in the official establishment of Burma's ancestral faith, coincided with the country's political orientation. Ever since independence from Great Britain in 1948, neutralist Burma took a firm stand against communism. However, as a deterrent to bigotry, religious liberty was written into law. Religious and political protection were guaranteed non-Buddhists. Yet in public school and college only Buddhist doctrine is taught.

Introduction of Buddhist "sabbath" days in Burma was a significant aspect of the state-religion regulation. Such official holidays generally corresponded with the four phases of the moon. On those sabbaths offices, schools, and bars are closed. Said Brigadier General Aung Gyi, dynamic figure in Burma's military hierarchy: "The state-religion bill has aroused the suspicion of the minorities. Only time can show it is not as dangerous as we think." He further volunteered the view that the country's real problem was something else: "The biggest danger for a country is that if it has a poor economy it will prove attractive for communism. If we cannot survive economically in the next decade, the Communists will come into power." [2]

Whether in Burma or other kindred nations, Buddhism clearly arises as a people's arsenal of strength. It provides spiritual power. It translates itself into a multiplicity of social capabilities. What radiance does Buddhism beam upon Asia that draws such confidence and esteem? Whence that quickening élan, evoking a national ardor as in Burma and eliciting a wonderful massive dedication as in many other lands? In a wider Oriental, if not global, context what does the Buddhist doctrine really amount to? An objective scrutiny of the phenomenon of Buddhism might ready the mind to draw more worthy responses to the foregoing questions. It is with the phenomenon itself that we are concerned: its religious essence, its community discipline, and its monastic orders; its transnational sweep and its contemporary renaissance.

I

As an international religion and world faith, Buddhism fosters a remarkable ethos. Distinctive of it is a fundamental strategy prom-

[2] *Time* (Sept. 15, 1961), p. 36.

ising to abrogate suffering. Buddhism historically crystallized in two classic formations:[3] A primitive formation was initiated by the Buddha himself. Another formation in the course of time flowered in North India about A.D. 200.

This second formation considered itself the "Great Vehicle," *Mahayana.* For its more archaic sister tradition, it reserved the title "Little Vehicle," *Hinayana.* The Mahayana doctrine was duly proclaimed across East Asia. There it acquired the attributes of an essentially Buddhist, universal, religion.

In the face of pre-Buddhist Brahmanism, the Little Vehicle could scarcely remain unchanged. Confrontation between the two was bound to elicit transformation in both. Conspicuous enough is the debt of the Buddha himself for a Brahmanical world outlook. Equally indebted was he for the concept of *samsara,* that indefinite transmigration of living beings leading from birth to endless rebirths. As for the idea of *karma,* where else could the Master have come across it if not in Brahmanism?

A further view the Buddha owed to the same source was this: that the value and nature of former existences will be perpetuated in subsequent births. Common to the two systems is the ideal of salvation. In both religions, the believer strove for an impersonal state of being, for freedom from eternal return. Yet a remarkable holy path determined the course of Buddhist faith and ethics; and radically altered a world outlook it had inherited from Brahmanism.

As indicated above, Buddhism may be described as a religion that aims at the abrogation of suffering.[4] Its idea of suffering is not soundly understood merely on the ground of physical pain and creature misery. Buddhism suggests instead a novel religious category, a consciousness of futility investing the whole fabric of existence. Such an assessment of being presupposes the transitory character of individual existence. A pessimism regarding both suffering and pleasure is inherent here. Both figure as a backdrop to inevitable distress and doom. Not to recognize suffering: that is the height of

[3] At this point we defer consideration of a third formation, the so-called "Diamond Vehicle," *Vajrayana,* a Tantric variety of Buddhism with erotic and obscene indulgences. Cf. Helmuth von Glasenapp, *Buddhistische Mysterien: Die Geheimlehren und Riten des Diamant-Fahrzeugs* (W. Spemann, Stuttgart, 1940). See Gustav Mensching, *Buddhistische Geisteswelt* (Holle Verlag, Darmstadt, 1955), p. 17.

[4] Cf. Gustav Mensching, *Die Religion* (Curt E. Schwab, Stuttgart, 1959), p. 52.

human ignorance, so runs the core of Buddhist wisdom. But reduction of suffering to the dimension of physical pain would be a banality. For the tragic sense of living is really hidden from no one.

Who in the natural order is so bereft of feeling he does not see the transitory character of his total existence? According to the Buddhist view of life, all individual existence is ephemeral and unreal. As regards individual reality, Buddhism advanced its own mode of thinking.

This was a theory that averred, as does modern physics, that an enduring quality is lacking in all appearances of the experienced world, even in the depths of personality. Fleeting are all those forms and appearances. Save under the aegis of eternal truth, *dharma,* they bear no semblance to perfection or ultimacy. Their essential motivating power is the will to live, a corrupt desire, *tanha.*[5] Independent of all determinations is only one factor of existence, *nirvana.* The peaceful surge of Nirvana is like that of the sea. No tidal wave disturbs that perfect peace. In such depths of bliss neither differentiation nor movement are discernible. Attained there is the goal of deliverance: a great calm descends and the billows cease.

The way thither, as the Fourth Noble Truth prescribes, is the Noble Eightfold Path.[6] It opens with instructions for cultivation of ethical and ascetic behavior. It carries the seeker along till he reaches an abode of the four gradations of mystical equanimity. Thereafter the Path guides the wayfarer on the assumption that the mysterious awakening of an inner enlightenment will dawn.

In this experience of deliverance, the desire for personal existence is extinguished. A foretaste of such bliss arrives when even in its earthly garb the self tends to become impersonal. Broken are its fetters, chains that bind it to the world. Upon death it passes on to Nirvana. It will not return to any such thing as individual existence.

In contrast to this primitive Buddhism later Mahayana recognized another evaluation of the Buddha's teaching. Under various sectarian patterns, Mahayana, willy-nilly, developed belief in a paradise of personal bliss. This is what a revised judgment on the Buddha and his doctrine involved. Recumbent in the assembly of the believers he

[5] Robert Lawson Slater, *Paradox and Nirvana* (The University of Chicago Press, 1951), p. 57.

[6] Dwight Goddard, ed., *A Buddhist Bible* (Dwight Goddard, 1938), pp. 33–60.

was no mere symbol of blessedness as Hinayana tended to portray him. He was no mere benign teacher of an impersonal doctrine of goodwill.

The Buddha of Mahayana faith emerged as a savior-god.[7] Belief arose in a whole galaxy of Buddhas and Bodhisattvas, the latter being candidates for Buddhahood. Toward this order of personal deity, the believer's adoration seemed drowned in emotional dedication. Inevitably, however, the devotees committed themselves in worship of a Buddha whom the historical founder of the faith could scarcely recognize.

Another deviation from Hinayana consisted in the concern of the pious not just for their own salvation but for that of others as well. In the Great Vehicle, the believers longed for deliverance of as many others as could be reached. Saintliness thus added to itself altruism. This chapter is far too limited in scope to permit inclusion of Mahayana's diverse sects. Suffice it to note in passing, however, that the axis upon which the Great Vehicle revolves does not essentially differ from that of the Little Vehicle.

Such an axis consists in salvation from an oppressive cycle of rebirths. It is an escape from the ocean of existence. It is an oversimplification to equate such a salvation, however, with a psychological escape. Nourished was the hope that in a personal Nirvana many a former bliss might be continued. Identification of Buddhism as a religion of pessimism is something of a platitude. Yet, what other image does a negative and skeptical outlook on the world's meaning and reality suggest?

As regards the value of faith, however, Buddhism not unlike other religions stakes a claim to optimism. An utterance of the Buddha cites this order of values: "Some people are born again; evildoers go to hell; righteous people go to heaven; those who are free from all worldly desires attain Nirvana."[8]

Sociologically, a world-denying Buddhism attached but little weight to a community structure such as that of Indian caste. The walls of partition whereby caste split up society and alienated man

[7] Erich Frauwallner, *Die Philosophie des Buddhismus* (Akademie-Verlag, Berlin, 1956), pp. 256, 302.

[8] *The Dhammapada,* tr. from Pali by F. Max Müller (Charles Scribner's Sons, 1901), p. 35.

from his brother could hold no special fascination for the Buddha, his order of monks and lay adherents. Charitably, Buddhism might regard caste as just a step toward admittance to the monastic order. If so, then caste might be in order to salvation. But there was no closed-deal assurance of salvation even for those who became monks. The hope of Nirvana was held out, nonetheless, to all who yearned for cessation of that dreary passage across many births. Yet freedom on the oposite shore was ever beyond comprehension.

In Buddhism as in India generally individual salvation is not reckoned in terms of a life-span but rather of countless eons. It is self-explanatory why on this doctrine Buddhism lacks a firm prophetic sense of urgency. In its missionary appeal, there can be no real emphasis on redeeming the time. Lacking is an imperative note for conversion now. In vain does one look for a call before it is too late to a holy and ethical disposition and conduct.

The Buddhist view is that man mellows over a long period of time. The pace is slow at which the human capacity for spiritual growth and enlightened intuition moves. But the Buddhist medallion has another side. Monk and nun orders are open for those conscious of imperfection. Another way of life was envisaged for the laity. Indeed, a code of morals was prescribed for laymen as well as for the family, community, and state. In line with the law of the deed, *karma,* all were required to examine their lives. Communities were urged to order their affairs in keeping with the Buddha's spirit. In the case of saints, a more rigorous discipline was ordained.

However, the order of monks founded by the Buddha does not bear too close a resemblance to the society of the redeemed, the beloved community, instituted by Jesus and furthered by his disciples. Initially, the order of Buddhist monks sought to undergird its own community. This took the form of kindly love, *metta,* and common possession of goods. That is, the Master's injunctions were grasped in terms of self-support. To this theme of the Buddha's intention we now turn.

II

Buddhism is the long shadow of the Buddha. Of vital relevance are the life and legend, the thought and doctrine, of the founder. Myth and tradition obscure the life of one who among the Buddhas must be singled out as Sakyamuni, Buddha of the Sakyas.[9] Controversy forbids exact determination of his dates. Western research, itself divided on this issue, fixed the Buddha's dates at about 563–483 B.C.

Scholarly research in the primary sources agrees on a set of biographical data of which a gist follows. The Buddha was not born a Brahman. He belonged to a princely family established at Kapilavastu, equidistant from the middle course of the Ganges and the Himalayas. Actually, his home state was in Nepal, marginal to the strongholds of Brahmanism. The region had not as yet been fully permeated by Aryan civilization with its hierarchical society, horse sacrifice, and philosophy of an absolute.[10]

At the age of twenty-nine, Gautama abandoned family life. He sought to learn at the feet of the masters. By their conventional erudition, those masters failed, however, to capture the young seeker's imagination. Neither did ascetic mortification bring him any greater degree of satisfaction. At thirty-nine he arrived at an awakening, *bodhi*. This latter experience of the Buddha rates as a turning point in the history of religions.

Gautama now became an awakened, enlightened person, *buddha*. That is, he was awakened from the slumber of ignorance and took to the truth as guide. Such a truth he presumed inherent in the reality of the world. It consisted in the fact of suffering. Opened to his mind was a discovery. It involved the abrogation of suffering. Opened to him, moreover, was the making of a faith that led to that abrogation.

Hence the Four Noble Truths: [11] suffering, its causes centered in desire, curtailment of desire, and the path that leads to salvation. Upon these four parts, the Buddha based a celebrated sermon, his first, preached at Benares. It was not without much hesitation that he determined thus to break his silence on those profound issues. Once the first step was taken, however, he never turned back. To the end of a long life, he continued " to paddle the wheel of the law."

That first sermon netted the Buddha five disciples. They became

[9] Paul Demiéville, "Le bouddhisme," in *Encyclopédie française,* ed. by Gaston Berger (Librairie Larousse, Paris, 1957), Tome XIX, p. 5213.

[10] See E. J. Thomas, *The Life of Buddha as Legend and History* (Alfred A. Knopf, Inc., 1927); Edward Conze, *Buddhism: Its Essence and Development* (Philosophical Library, Inc., 1951), pp. 34–38.

[11] T. W. Rhys Davids and Hermann Oldenberg, *Vinaya Texts* (Charles Scribner's Sons, 1899), Pt. 1, pp. 95–96.

the nucleus of the community or order of monks, *sangha.*[12] There followed forty-five years of wandering across Central India. In his teaching, the Buddha followed a threefold methodology. He taught personally, by word of mouth; he taught by sheer force of personal example; and he taught by silence. Upon his death at eighty, he qualified for extinction, *nirvana.* To his community, by then considerably grown in number, he bequeathed nothing but a law. Yet this law came increasingly to be recognized by all as master and refuge.

The foregoing is simply a vignette. In miniature form, it reproduces the image of a Buddha alive in the sacred tradition. No believer ever wished to see in that image anything save an exemplary and benign character. To the Buddha of the Sakyas, the sources ascribe a variety of documents. What went under the heading of tradition, *agama,* surely was open to divergent interpretations.

Whatever those doctrines meant, they were in part insights drawn by the Buddha from his literary and human heritage. There were certain standards of religion and ethics which he was too reluctant to disturb. As noted already, this heritage included the retributive law, *karma.* It was the emblem of an inevitable mechanistic principle, a law of the deed, behind good and evil. Included among beliefs which he allowed to remain was also the concept of transmigration, *samsara,* an endless cycle of successive deaths and rebirths.

There were Buddhist doctrines consistently at variance with the philosophical implications of the then contemporary Brahmanism. It so happened that the philosophy from which Buddhist doctrine deviated was none other than that enshrined in the Upanishad.[13] The latter rested the hope of salvation on identification of the human self, *atman,* with the universal principle, *Brahman.* It was an identification of the empirical self with the absolute. For Buddhism, however, there could be no being in self whether on the moral or ontological plane. Personality was deemed illusory. It was viewed as no more than an unstable aggregate of aggregates.

Buddhism insisted all is composed and hence " decomposable." All that is, save extinction which spells the abrogation of suffering. As a flame is extinguished so is suffering abolished. Yet the Buddha

[12] Regulations for the order are the subject matter of the *Vinaya Pitaka* in the *Pali Texts.* See Davids and Oldenberg, *op. cit.,* p. ix, *passim.*

[13] Commentaries on the *Vedas* are known as *Brahmanas.* Each *Brahmana* has a special section or chapter on theology for forest meditation, *aranya.* The Upanishads form part of this section. The oldest Upanishads date from the seventh century B.C.

withheld comment on the exact nature of such extinction. He did not define it as annihilation in the sense of "nothingness." There are, therefore, differing conceptions of *nirvana*.[14] It is the final state of one who has attained deliverance.

The Four Noble Truths might be construed as an essentially therapeutic formula. Recognition of suffering is diagnosis. Designation of desire as cause of suffering is etiology, causative origin. Abolition of suffering through curtailment of desire is healing. In a word, the whole path leading to abolition of rebirth is the therapeutic goal of Buddhist law. Under the Second Noble Truth, which designated desire as cause of suffering, an analytical formula reduced the origin of suffering to a series of twelve items, *nidana*.

The twelve items led step by step from ignorance to knowledge. Featured was everything from birth to old age and death. It was a simple chain of cause and effect, both relevant and "logical" in being geared to a series of experiences and events. There was no first principle singled out for mention here. There was no eternal substance or essence, no god either personal or impersonal.

Buddhism did not, however, eliminate the divinities of Brahmanism. Nonetheless, it did relegate them to a secondary position. In an empyrean of sense perception. Brahma occupied in Buddhist cosmology the lowest rank where desire held sway. The superior celestial stations were reserved for those beyond the range of sense. All thought about matter was discarded there. Beheld there were deities immersed in mystical states. Men were admitted thereto on disavowal of any desire to resume birth.

If men are to attain perfect peace, they must venture out beyond sense. For even in the highest stations of mystical experience one does not really escape the chains of anxiety and pain. The law of retribution continues to dog man's existence, preventing attainment of extinction. This reservation fully applied to the trance which played a major role in Buddhism as indeed in all Indian religions. A basic technique of the trance was a concentration, *samadhi,* a Sanskrit word corresponding with Greek *synthesis*. Yet neither this specific concentration nor any other mystical state held any guarantee of salvation.[15]

[14] Pali, *Nibbana*. See Henri de Lubac, *Aspects of Buddhism,* tr. by George Lamb (Sheed & Ward, Inc., 1954), p. 190.

[15] Conze, *op. cit.,* pp. 100–101.

Of necessity the devotee needed to be equipped with a morality in action, *sila,* and with intellectual wisdom, *prajna.* Only the essence of three disciplines — contemplation, morality, and wisdom — set the wayfarer on the proper road to abrogation of suffering and ultimate extinction. It was certainly in order to require beneficial relaxation through a procedure of psychophysical culture. Such a procedure might involve reduction and regulation of breathing; also, alternate inhaling and exhaling, *anapana.* In no such procedure, however, was there anything particularly Buddhist.

Only when as a matter of conscience, *smriti,* one concludes that breathing in itself is transitory will such an exercise have any truly Buddhist validity. It ought in that event to prove conducive to meditation on the impermanence of all things. In other words, it ought to lead to a deeper appreciation of the Four Noble Truths. The trend was to see all India's ancient discipline of yoga in a new rational light. It is purified, evolved, intellectualized, in keeping with the mind of a Buddha whose reform tended to downgrade whatever was mythological in nature.

III

It is clear then that Buddhism is community forming. The Upanishad seers disclosed sacred knowledge only to their own sons and adepts. In contrast, the Buddha drew no sharp demarcation between the inner and outer circle of devotees. He proclaimed his doctrine to the whole world. Buddhism had no tie with the sociopolitical order in India. In the region where it flourished, Magadha and neighboring North Indian territories, the might of Brahmanism was relatively weak.

Among the Buddha's first proselytes, tradition depicts rich city patricians and quite a few affluent Brahmans.[16] Those were the members of the earliest community whom he taught to beg from door to door. Those were the ones he sent out as wandering monks. The Master proved as eminent an organizer as he was a teacher. His community centered in an elite of monks.

A ready-made model for his community was available in Jain Nirgrantha, founded by Mahavira perhaps about the sixth cen-

[16] Max Weber, *The Religion of India: The Sociology of Hinduism and Buddhism* (The Free Press of Glencoe, 1958), p. 226.

tury B.C.[17] Jainism, a mighty Hindu unorthodox sect, still claims several million adherents in India. However, the Buddha's own organization reveals a higher degree of originality and refinement. This was fully in keeping with the distinctive character of his doctrine. Whereas the Buddha could not have been the author of every regulation set forth in the *Vinaya Pitaka* for monastic discipline, the organization does reflect his guiding hand and personal touch.

Monastic life begins when the monk, seeking self-perfectibility, sets out as wandering mendicant. Initially, this is a departure out of home surroundings to the homeless estate. Admission to the novitiate is permissible at the age of fifteen. Most inestimable to the disciples are the Three Jewels, *Ti-Ratana:* the Buddha, Dharma (doctrine), and Sangha (order). Repeated upon joining the order are the standard Three Refuges, *Ti Sarana:*

> "I take refuge in the Buddha!
> I take refuge in the Dharma!
> I take refuge in the Sangha!"[18]

Formal admission to the order of monks comes after the age of twenty. It is signalized by ordination. There is no initiation into divine mystery or sacred office. There is no investiture into a school of gnosis. Much less is Buddhist ordination a sacramental act. As performed by the Master, ordination began with the words of exhortation: "Come, monks, well taught in the doctrine. Live in the holy life for the utter destruction of suffering."[19] Later, the Buddha set up regulations governing ordination, probation, and the training of novices. He placed the task of monastic administration in the hands of the monks themselves.

The act of ordination strikes an outsider as a nakedly legal transaction. The novice presents a petition, so to speak, which comes up for a hearing before the chapter of monks gathered in solemn assembly. A juridical pronouncement establishes the status of a candidate in the face of any irregularities. In granting formal approval and recognition, the assembled monks confirm the applicant in his

[17] On the history and doctrine of Jainism, see Heinrich Zimmer, *Philosophies of India,* pp. 181–279.

[18] Nyanatiloka, *Buddhist Dictionary* (Frewin, Colombo, 1956), p. 164.

[19] J. Kashyap, "Origin and Expansion of Buddhism," in *The Path of the Buddha,* ed. by Kenneth W. Morgan (The Ronald Press Co., 1956), p. 34.

new office. They so act through the silent consent of a presiding "abbot." The ceremony is conducted in an atmosphere of simplicity and decorum. A formula of rules is addressed to the novice. But the Buddhist monk is under no kind of "eternal vow." When and if he chooses, he is at liberty to resume secular life.

A Buddhist order of monks is a community of mendicant friars, *bhikkhu.* They own no property and perform no manual labor. Other than a saffron robe, an individual monk owns just a begging bowl, a sewing needle, and a sieve, to filter insects from drinking water. Originally, a mendicant monk led the life of a wanderer. Subsequently, the monks occupied an "abode" during the rainy season, a cloister, *vihara.* This served as assembly center, temple, storehouse, refectory, and bathhouse.

The begging rite has been retained. Silently, a monk stands at the door, alms bowl in hand, and receives gifts of food, without a glance at the giver. A common meal, as a rule served once daily at noon, consists of bread, rice, vegetables, and water. Meat and fish, although not forbidden, are rarely eaten. The regular monastic schedule includes meditation, recitation of holy texts, discourse on doctrine, and preaching. Transition from the oral to the written tradition gave rise to the necessity for transcription and translation of sacred texts. This in turn occasioned scholarly and scribal pursuits among the monks.

The first Buddhist community knew next to nothing of corporate prayer. Highly esteemed instead was silent meditation. Either in a cave or in open-air gatherings, the monks met on the new and full moon days. There was a ceremonial confessional litany, *uposatha.* The senior member read the Disciplinary Code, *Patimokkha.* Any monk who had violated a rule was called upon to disavow it publicly.

Following the rainy season, prior to the period of "wandering," the monks of a given chapter held a special session. They sat on the floor, hands folded. Then the rite of "loading," *pavarana,*[20] began: each monk entreated the other to mention any offense the former might have committed. Thus from the oldest to the youngest, they inquired of each other if during the period of their association any ill-feeling or misconduct had occurred.

As regards the orders of nuns, their discipline generally corre-

[20] Davids and Oldenberg, *op. cit.,* pp. 325–355.

sponded with that of monks. Such rules were added as were required for women. To the nun, the same title, mendicant, *Bhikkhuni,* was applied. They receive a similar ordination and lead a religious life almost identical with that of monks. Whereas nuns do gather in assemblies, to them are forbidden both the life of a hermit and that of wanderer. Their order, furthermore, is subordinate to that of monks.

In the countries of Theravada Buddhism, the modern nun no longer regards herself as a ward of the monks. The grounds which formerly prompted withdrawal from ordination vows are gradually passing. The modern nun has finally won emancipation from the supervision of monks. She is presently under the direction of an abbess. She occupies a position halfway between that of traditional Buddhism and the status of a laywoman.

Undergirding the orders of monks and nuns is a world community of admirers, the vast body of laymen, *upasaka,* and laywomen, *upasika.* Buddhist laity assures the orders of monks and nuns a decent livelihood. Lay people afford support to the poor. They flock as pilgrims at holy places. For reward laymen and laywomen entertain the hope of rebirth in a heaven of bliss. They cherish the vision of a hereafter, a really holy path, and the opportunity of ultimate arrival at Nirvana.

Thus life in the Buddha's community demonstrates vitality along two polar lines: householder and houseless believers enter upon an exchange of religious values. Both live in admiration of their exalted Master. Each in his own way participates in the noble doctrine. Each contemplates an incomparable salvation.

IV

Buddhism is a transnational faith. The first historical and authentic document on Buddhism consists of Emperor Asoka's inscriptions. Asoka [21] ruled around the middle of the third pre-Christian century. His inscriptions witness to the existence of a well-established Buddhist community. The Buddhism to which Asoka was converted in-

[21] E. Hultsch, *The Inscriptions of Asoka, Corpus Inscriptionum Indicarum* (Oxford University Press, London, 1925), Vol. I. Consult Etienne Lamotte, *Histoire du bouddhisme indien* (Publications Universitaires, Louvain, 1958), pp. 244–261.

cluded both monks and laity. It extended over a major part of India. The Kingdom of Magadha over which Asoka ruled embraced the regions from Kashmir to the Ganges Valley, and south almost to what later became Madras. From India, Buddhism spread to Ceylon. It also fanned out apparently to Afghanistan and Baluchistan.

Asoka affirms that he furthered the " victory of the Law " as far as the Mediterranean. The Mediterranean world which felt Asoka's thrust included the states which had arisen in the wake of Alexander's conquests: Hellenized Syria and Egypt as well as Macedonia and Greece. To those lands he said missionaries had been dispatched as well as medical doctors for relief of man and beast. Such a contact between Buddhist India and the Occidental world was evidently ended by Parthian Iran (250 B.C.–A.D. 224).

The Asoka inscriptions refer to a number of texts in which sayings of the Buddha were enshrined. Reading of those sayings was recommended for edification of the Buddhist community. The titles of such texts correspond with those of certain canonical Buddhist writings known to modern scholarship. No such identification, however, goes beyond the matter of titles. It is therefore considered inconclusive. Indeed, such canons as are known to us must have been established after the age of Asoka.

Tradition preserves the memory of certain councils which the community held following the Buddha's death. Codification of the Buddha's sayings was said to be the outcome of authorized recitations. The Buddha's discourses as well as the record of his doctrinal encounters with the disciples came to be known as the thread, *sutra*. Under the rubric of Discipline, *Vinaya*, the corpus of monastic regulations was collected.[22]

In the course of scholastic discussions, the Little Vehicle, *Hinayana*, school emerged. Those were discussions documented in such exegetical treatises as the *Abhidhamma*, literally, " on or against the law." A return to study of the law, *dharma*, was indicated. These treatises were eventually incorporated in a canon, the so-called Three Baskets, *Tripiṭaka:* Texts, Discipline, and Exegesis.[23]

[22] André Bareau, *Les premiers conciles bouddhiques* (Presses Universitaires de France, Paris, 1955), pp. 21–24.

[23] Consult Edward Conze, ed., *Buddhist Texts Through the Ages* (Bruno Cassirer, Publishers, Ltd., Oxford, 1954), pp. 9–14, 207–310.

Each principal school tended to develop its own Three Baskets. In India, the canonical language happened to be a relatively pure variety of Sanskrit. As was to be expected, the canon received anything but uniform exegesis. Epigraphical remains dating from about the beginning of the Christian era attest the advent of two schools: conservative and liberal. Conservatism was spearheaded by the Sthavira, a school so named after its presiding elders. The liberals adopted the title "Great Community," *Mahasangika,* as their designation. The issues that divided conservatives and liberals included such matters as monastic discipline and textual interpretation.

Relatively obscure are the beginnings of the Great Vehicle, *Mahayana.* Whatever the exact time and place of its inception, the Great Vehicle shook the schools dating from the first Christian century to their foundations. To earnest believers, it offered a highway recommended as exceptionally superior since it afforded real progress in religious experience. It is an open question whether Northwest or Southern India provided the first setting of this mighty creed. At any rate, the Mahayana school pressed with vigor for the basic character of ontology. It reminded the Buddhists that the Little Vehicle had either but faintly hinted at ontological considerations or actually evaded them altogether.

An ingenious Mahayana analysis confirmed the Absolute under different names. Invariably safeguarded, however, was the integrity of the canonical tradition. An imaginative, though highly dangerous, distinction was drawn between two truths: the truth of Ultimate Reality and that of convention. It was a distinction which tended to permit compromise on practically everything. Mahayana acquired a solid reputation for the doubtful gift to approve whatever seemed expedient.

The following is an illustration of Mahayana flexibility. If the Buddha of the canonical tradition was silent on the question of the Absolute, it was because he addressed an uninitiated audience. To such an audience, only conventional truth was suited. As for learned and wise men, they had little trouble in discovering the intention behind his silence: that the Absolute transcends language and words.

Hence the two profiles of Sakyamuni mirrored in biography. Among the simple folks, and in popular literature, he was depicted as no more than a mortal with a metamorphic body, *nirmana-kaya.*

But in the elevated view of speculation, he was conceived as identical with an absolute metaphysical reality, the Body of the Law, *Dharmakaya.*

Ethically, Mahayana accent falls on action, an action made vivid in compassion. In the Little Vehicle, the saint had extinction for ideal. This amounted to coiling upon oneself and observing indifference to the world as the highest virtue. Such a saint sought to perfect his own salvation: an eternal repose through abrogation of suffering. In contrast, a Great Vehicle saint emerged as an awakened person, a *bodhisattva,* concerned with the relief of others and hence a different type of believer, an aspirant who was potentially an enlightened "buddha."

The notion of grace broke through in Mahayana in a manner too remote for the Little Vehicle. Hinayana made man the sole perfecter of his own salvation. Emanant in the Great Vehicle, moreover, was a type of devotion that throve on an ever-increasing number of savior-buddhas. In contradiction to the Christian counterpart, it projected a vision of multiple heavens.

Crystallized in the findings of two speculative schools, Mahayana greatly enriched the development of Buddhist philosophy. The first of these schools was the Madhyamika. Its theorists were committed to the central position of Buddhism. This was a philosophical view that said: "There is no entity that is not dependent. An absolute nonrational entity does not therefore exist."[24] Silence was the singular method for arrival at the truth. It means a wisdom, *prajna,* involving critical renunciation of the vain sport of reason in favor of intuition. Prajna wisdom is conceived as a suprarational intuition, a mystical experience where all duality is neutralized. Nagarjuna, founder of this school in India about A.D. 150,[25] defined prajna as the negation of all views. This negation is the Doctrine of the Void, *Sunyata,* the pivotal concept of Buddhism.

The other Great Vehicle school came into being in North India during the fourth century A.D. An idealism known by its theory of knowledge, *Vijnavada,* colored its philosophy. It held that nothing existed, whether spiritual or material, outside the range of cognition.

[24] T. R. V. Murti, *The Central Philosophy of Buddhism* (George Allen & Unwin, Ltd., London, 1955), pp. 58, 104–105, 218–220, 228–229.

[25] Robert Linssen, *Living Zen* (The Macmillan Company, 1958), p. 35.

A rope may look like a snake, but it is inherently devoid of the snake reality. It is by no means devoid of its own intrinsic nature as a rope. With this logic, Vijnavada schoolmen contended that the reality of consciousness, *vijnana,* needs to be posited since it cannot be denied at all. Hence the trend toward analytical examination of all being.

Such were the summits of Buddhist speculation in the early centuries of the Christian era. An apogee was reached in the reign of Harsha during the seventh century. The Gupta period extended from the crowning of Chandragupta in A.D. 320 to the end of Harsha's rule in A.D. 647. It brought the Buddhist art of India toward great perfection. This art was an expression of the zeal and inner feelings of devotion shared by the artist. Examples of painting have been preserved at the Ajanta caves; and in the sculpture at Mathura and Sarnath another aspect of this art is revealed.[26]

Throughout that epoch the development of Tantra became rife. That is, a ritualistic and symbolic form of magic came into vogue in the popular practice of the faith. Tantric Buddhism retained an ideological superstructure borrowed from Madhyamika emptiness and the Vijnavada theory of knowledge.

There were those who rated the Tantric elements erupting in Buddhism as reproachful perversions bearing the stigma of Brahmanism. Similarly suspect in the philosophical domain was the Great Vehicle's absolutism. On its part, Brahmanism, as noted above, also registered the impact of Buddhist doctrine.

About A.D. 800, Shankara reformed the Vedanta. His system owed a heavy debt to Buddhism. The Islamic conquests had by this time brought ruination upon institutional Buddhism. The outcome was that by about A.D. 1500 Buddhist institutions had practically disappeared in most of India. Other than an array of monuments and Tantric survivals it left hardly any visible trace in the country. As for the penetrating though invisible impact of Buddhism upon Indian thought, culture, and faith, it most certainly endures, forming an integral part of a great heritage.

The disappearance of Indian Buddhist texts is unparalleled in the history of world literature. Without exception lost to India are manuscripts of an immense Sanskrit Buddhist literature. Such fragments as are extant were preserved only in neighboring countries to

[26] Kashyap, *loc. cit.,* p. 43.

which Buddhism was transplanted: Nepal, Kashmir, Central Asia, Tibet, China, and Japan.[27] In order to acquire a fuller grasp of those vanished treasures, recourse is necessary to Tibetan and Chinese translations of the original texts.

In Southeast Asia, Pali Buddhism holds sway. The story opens with the transmission, to Ceylon, of the Buddhist canon in recension. It had been drawn up in Pali, an Indo-European language which was related to Sanskrit as Italian is to Latin. An Indian idiom, Pali is thus indigenous and original. Where it was spoken, if ever, no one seems to know. Indubitably, however, Pali belongs to Central India. Thence it was introduced into Ceylon, as has been observed above, through Asoka's Buddhist emissaries.

In point of doctrine, this corpus of Pali scriptures belonged to the tradition of Sthavira (Pali, Thera) and is therefore known as Theravada, " Doctrine of the Elders." Ceylon's Theravada Buddhism vied with all major Buddhist traditions, not excluding the Great Vehicle. Toward the end of the fifth century A.D., a general revision of the Buddhist texts was carried out on the island of Ceylon. The present millennium has since witnessed the expansion of Pali Buddhism across several adjacent lands: [28] Burma, Thailand, Indo-China, Cambodia, and Laos, where under other forms Buddhism had had an earlier start. In Indonesia and among the Tibetan Champa tribesmen of Kashmir, where Buddhism had long flourished, non-Muslim faiths frequently suffered.

The Pali school does not slavishly observe the doctrines and institutions of the Little Vehicle. It has evolved a luxuriant exegetical literature, partly through authors of Indian background. Yet it fails to match the speculative depth of the Sanskrit tradition. Essentially it is a monastic tradition, somewhat narrow but very much alive in the lands where it is professed.

Central Asia is a crossroad of migrations and civilizations. During the first millennium of the Christian era, it witnessed the coming of Buddhism. This new community emerged as a bridge between the Buddhist religion and the Chinese world. Little kingdoms of

[27] Jack Finegan, *The Archeology of World Religions* (Princeton University Press, 1952), pp. 242–247.

[28] For a Mahayanist estimate of Hinayana, see Bhikshu Sangharakshita, *A Survey of Buddhism* (Indian Institute of World Culture, Bengalore, 1959), pp. 191–196.

Indo-European dialects formed in the oasis of what today is Turkistan. The emergent culture was a mixture of Indian and Chinese elements. Buddhism was practiced alongside other religions such as Manichaeism and Nestorian Christianity.

Buddhists also penetrated Iran. Among early propagandists who in the second and third centuries A.D. carried Buddhism into China many were of Parthian and Soghdian origin.[29] Converted to Buddhism, too, were certain Turkish elements. In these new realms of conquest, the two Vehicles coexisted. The Great Vehicle, however, tended to outshine her sister.

These religious conquests were swept aside by Islam after A.D. 1000. Only in Tibet did Buddhism hold out. It was introduced into the country by missionaries from both India and China.[30] There Buddhism had been jealously guarded till the present day. It gave birth to a curious order of ecclesiastical government dating from the eighth century.

About the same time, the Mongols, if only in the eastern section of their empire, adopted Tibetan Buddhism, better known as Lamaism. The latter word is derived from a Tibetan title, *bla-ma,* applied to Buddhist teachers. To the present day, there are Mongol tribesmen in the Soviet Union who profess Buddhism. Tibetan Mongol Lamaism is tinctured with Tantra magic. To its credit, however, are exegetical, historical, and literary works by no means devoid of originality. It incorporated the Diamond Vehicle, *Vajravana,* the third magical phase of Buddhism.

Chinese Buddhism dates from the beginning of the Christian era. A poet-official, writing about A.D. 130, evokes the first casual reference to Buddhism in China. But the Buddhist observances of Ying, Prince of Ch'u, in A.D. 65, are established beyond reasonable doubt.[31] In China, Buddhism has had to contend with national philosophies and beliefs deeply entrenched in the national consciousness. It was far from equal to the task of effacing Confucianism. This latter happened to be the doctrine of the learned mandarins, the " cultured

[29] Chou Hsiang-Kuang, *A History of Chinese Buddhism* (Indo-Chinese Publications, Allahabad, 1955), pp. 22 ff.

[30] Helmut Hoffmann, *The Religions of Tibet* (The Macmillan Company, 1961), p. 50.

[31] Arthur F. Wright, *Buddhism in Chinese History* (Stanford University Press, 1959), p. 21.

gentry."[32] Their traditional responsibility had been administration of the empire. Their Confucianist ethics was not easily adjustable to Buddhism.

This was the reason Confucianism did not acquiesce in the Buddhist challenge. Buddhism loomed as a soteriology detaching the individual from allegiance to the state. It conflicted with the dictates of filial piety. It violated the norms of a tightly knit social order, centered in the family, and strove to pose as guardian over it. Taoism seemed closer to Buddhism and initially tended to be confused with it. Between these two, at least on the intellectual side, a degree of concurrence shaped up.[33] Such a meeting produced a measure of doctrinal osmosis. This in turn engendered a new type of Buddhism in China.[34]

The new Chinese Buddhism was as different from India's Buddhism and that of Southeast Asia, as Roman Catholicism and Protestantism differ from Jewish and ancient Christianity.[35] The most significant outcome of the Buddhist transfusion in China was the school of meditation: Sanskrit, *dhyana,* Chinese, *teh'an,* Sino-Japanese, *Zen.* Since the Tang dynasty (seventh to tenth centuries), this school created in China a religious psychology as well as an incomparable art and literature. The key teaching of the Meditation school focused on a Buddha nature common to everybody. Pointing to the human mind, it urges man to become a Buddha by seeing his own Buddha nature.[36]

Confucianism carried the day, but not without being thoroughly modified by the heavy Buddhist dose. The encounter with Confucianism evoked vivid shades of that with Vedanta in India. Vedanta was modified by the same Buddhism toward whose overthrow it rendered a capital contribution. After the Sung dynasty (tenth to thirteenth centuries) Buddhism in China barely survived. However, throughout the so-called Chinese middle ages, it had left an ineradi-

[32] E. Zürcher, *The Buddhist Conquest of China* (E. J. Brill, Leiden, 1959), pp. 4–6.

[33] *Ibid.,* pp. 288–320.

[34] On the nature of Confucianism and Taoism, see Lewis Hodous, in Jurji, *The Great Religions of the Modern World,* pp. 1–43.

[35] Demiéville, *loc. cit.,* p. 5216.

[36] Wing-tsit Chan, *Religious Trends in Modern China* (Columbia University Press, 1953), p. 251.

cable mark on Chinese culture. To it, China owes a whole class of masterpieces in art, literature, and philosophy.

Japanese Buddhism dates from the sixth century A.D. Shotoku Taishi (572–621), second son of Emperor Yomei, is recognized as founder and establisher of Buddhism in Japan.[37] The new religion arrived via China, Korea, and Vietnam. It sank deep roots into the native soil. It had to run the Shinto gauntlet.[38] That is, Buddhism had to contend with a primitive cult, devoid of intellectual refinement, and with which competition was scarcely possible. A *modus vivendi* somehow had to be forged between the two systems. When it finally achieved status in Japan, Buddhism performed a far more impressive role than it ever did in China.

This Buddhism of Japan was nonetheless an import from China. Even if traced back to its origins in India, the road must still pass through China. On reaching Japan, everything Buddhist went through a fine sieve of meticulous selectivity. The price of incorporation in Japan's ongoing life was a rigorous process of adaptation and synthesis.

In the upshot, Japanese Buddhism acquired a novel physiognomy. In the Middle Ages, such an adjustment to the Japanese environment meant nothing short of feudalization and militarization of the monastic order. Emergence of hierarchical sects, subsects, and branches was to follow. Each of these clamored for preeminence. Then came suppression of certain sects, of monastic celibacy; and a closer concern of monks for popular pulse and social interests.

Symptomatic of Japanese Buddhism at times was intensification of piety and devotion to the point of fanaticism. Equally apparent was the relative dearth of philosophical productions. Such were the salient features of the country's Buddhism. Today, however, Japan stands, along with Tibet, Ceylon, Burma, and the Indianized parts of Indo-China, as one of the world centers of Buddhist renaissance.

[37] Beatrice Lane Suzuki, *Mahayana Buddhism* (The Macmillan Company, 1959), p. 126.

[38] The reader is referred to a classic exposition of Shinto by Daniel Clarence Holtom in Jurji, *The Great Religions of the Modern World,* pp. 140–177.

V

Buddhism is, finally, a resurgent religion. The clue to contemporary Asia is an expanding Western civilization. Such an expansion does not preclude religion. Concerned over their own destinies, alternative civilizations are invariably on the defensive. Conquerors, negotiators, and educators, no less than scholars, are accompanied if not preceded by missionaries. Faced by Christianity and other forms of ostensible Western encroachment, Buddhism feels constrained to reexamine its position in the world, its role in history.

The Buddhist apologist will take this, therefore, as a central assumption: there is mighty little the Occident offers that Buddhism does not already own. Speak to the intelligent Buddhist about democracy, and he will hasten to draw your attention to the order of monks: egalitarian from the outset, its decisions are ever subject to majority approval. D. T. Suzuki [39] reminds his audience, "One of the first things Zen accomplished in China . . . was to establish a special form of monasticism quite distinct from the older kind of monkish living. The Zen monastery became a self-governing body divided into so many departments, each of which had its own office to serve the community. A noteworthy feature of this institution was the principle of complete democracy. While the elders were naturally respected, all members were equally to engage in manual labor, such as gathering fuel, cultivating the land, and picking tea leaves."

If a critic should bring up humanism, the Buddhist apologist will argue that according to canonical doctrine, man as such is a primary object of concern. Should the challenger turn out to be a communist, the Buddhist might indeed state that his primitive community was classless, and that ownership of goods stood on a strictly collective basis.

Buddhist apologetics might capitalize, further, on the strictly rational character of its dialectics. Salvation, it will insist, is a matter of reason. Wholly beyond the scope of transcendence where the West talks of the Kantian and Hegelian philosophy, it will dwell on its philosophy of equanimity and void, its Madhyamika and Vijnavada. It may even refer to its existentialism. This will, of course,

[39] *Zen and Japanese Culture* (Pantheon Books, Inc., 1959), pp. 3–4.

be justified on the grounds that the contingent and accidental must yield to the reality of suffering. It may even build up its own Vijnavada school of knowledge as a counterpart to, if not precursor of, Freud and Jung.[40]

Nor does the twentieth-century Buddhist feel unduly embarrassed by the spectacle of decadent practices and superstitious mythology in his community. Buddhism, he will claim, has rid itself of much traditional nonsense. There is nothing wrong with the Buddhist religion that adjustment and reform will not cure. Granted such adjustment and reform, Buddhism might well outstrip its rivals, whether Christian or Marxist. Such arguments are not infrequently heard across the Buddhist world. In India and Ceylon, Burma, China, and Japan, they constitute a recurring theme for magazine article and book. " The thought of Enlightenment is the most important event that can occur in the life of a human being. As by the discovery of a priceless jewel a poor man becomes immensely rich, so with the rising of the thought of Enlightenment the devotee is transformed into a Bodhisattva." [41]

Primarily under American pressure, Japan opened her doors to the modern world about a century ago. Buddhism was then in league with the Tokugawa dictatorship. It was a partnership that assured the Buddhists protection and in return called upon them for cooperation against the forces of Christianity. Held accountable for Japan's inertia, the Tokugawa regime was tossed out. Restoration of Imperial authority in 1868 meant the eclipse of Buddhism in Japan. State support for Buddhism was withdrawn in favor of Shinto. Nor were the Buddhists spared persecution.

They saw an imperative need for reform, if hope was to be entertained at all for recovery of their former power. In effecting such a reform, they were bound to look to the Occident for guidance and inspiration. In a bid for reinstatement in Japan, the Buddhist thesis came down to this: in Japan's indigenous culture, there is no component other than Buddhism qualified to cope with Christianity and Western civilization. To know the adversary at close range, that was the primary requirement.

[40] Cf. S. Kulandran, *Resurgent Religions* (United Society for Christian Literature, London, 1957), pp. 16–25.

[41] Sangharakshita, *op. cit.,* p. 457.

Hence the decision of great Kyoto monasteries for instance to dispatch personnel to Europe for study. Such scholars as were then sent did not go as propagandists. Theirs was a far more subtle task: to pursue knowledge, to acquire advanced techniques, and to achieve a full mastery of Western methodology. Among the first of these scholars was Shimaji Mokurai. He sojourned in Europe in 1873–1874, visiting cathedrals, theological seminaries, and universities. Homebound, he stopped off to see the Holy Land of Christianity. He then continued on a pilgrimage to the sacred sites of Buddhism in India. The express purpose of Mokurai was to acquaint himself with Christianity. This was in order the better to equip himself for defense against its intrusive character.

Some years after, Nanjo Bunyu, a colleague of Mokurai and also a Buddhist monk, matriculated at Oxford for the study of Sanskrit. He proudly made known his scholarly interest in the Buddhist scriptures of his homeland, Japan. Other scholars were to follow. Notably after 1882, Buddhist scholars sought knowledge in France. They were attracted by a European school of Orientalists. Lasting contributions had been made toward the revival of Buddhist learning in Japan and the Far East.

Foremost among fields of study that attracted Buddhist scholars were those of history and philology. The scholars were also intrigued by scientific methods applied to the study of religions. They came to know at first hand discoveries of European scholars such as Eugene Burnouf, Sylvain Levi, and Louis de la Vallée Poussin. Through their researches, these savants had literally resuscitated Sanskrit Buddhism.

European study opened the eyes of Japanese scholars, moreover, to another essential facet of the Buddhist tradition. This pertained to the Pali Canon of which they scarcely recognized even the name. In keeping with the Chinese Buddhist practice, the Japanese had practically ignored the Pali texts, authentic standard of the Little Vehicle. A serious blind spot was gradually remedied.

Nor did such Japanese pioneers escape the penalty incurred by all who dare to challenge an established though decadent tradition. It was a day that saw the excommunication of innovators by their religious superiors. Their offense was that they had had the audacity to question the Sino-Japanese traditions of Buddhism. They had gone as far as to speak of a " historical Buddha," such a Buddha as was portrayed in the Pali tradition and interpreted by ephemeral Occidental scholars.

Japan was soon caught up in the full bloom of a Buddhist renaissance. Intriguing was the prospect of self-extrication from Western motifs and outlooks. In the case of Zen Buddhism, this took the form of vital confrontation with the Western mind.[42] Outcome of intellectual vigor and first-rate scholarship, this renaissance was mediated in services to Buddhist learning. As for methodology, there is little left that Japan has not learned from the West. The temptation seems strong to shake off historicism. This in order to concentrate on one thing: reevaluation of Buddhist philosophy in terms of comparative study of Western philosophies. Such projects are generally steeped in competent research and scientific techniques.

This Japanese research centers in numerous Buddhist colleges and universities with a sectarian connection. Seminaries devoted to Buddhist studies are affiliated with most state universities. In 1955, there were one hundred and seventy-six academic chairs assigned to Buddhism. These constituted about 22 percent of the total number of university chairs in Japan.[43] Equally impressive is a social program inspired by Buddhist thought and ethics.

China's Buddhist revival during the past half century was largely due to Japanese influence.[44] In more precise language, Japan's role was chiefly that of mediator. The fact stands out that in China, as in Japan, Buddhist stirrings in modern times owed a primary debt to Western stimulation. The first harvests of this revival were garnered in secular and intellectual centers to which free inquiry had brought a fresh breath of life.

A break with Neo-Confucianism [45] prepared the way. Neo-Confucianism had stifled Buddhism and there were historians who saw the outcome as a drawback to China's cultural structure. Restored

[42] See Christmas Humphreys, *Zen Buddhism* (William Heinemann, Ltd., London, 1949), pp. 39–40; D. T. Suzuki, *Studies in Zen* (Philosophical Library, Inc., 1955).

[43] Demiéville, *loc. cit.*, p. 541.

[44] Cf. Wing-tsit Chan, *Religious Trends in Modern China,* p. 59.

[45] On the Neo-Confucianism of the Sung school, see W. Theodore De Bary, in *Studies in Chinese Thought,* ed. by Arthur F. Wright (The University of Chicago Press, 1953), pp. 81–111.

to Buddhism, therefore, was its rightful place in the social, economic, and intellectual affairs of China. Philosophers readily conceded the superiority of Buddhism. New directions soon began to appear in the general outlook of China's thought, epistemology, logic, and formal analysis. Since the Revolution in 1912, and in keeping with patterns set by Christian missionaries, reforms initiated by the Chinese literati hued to the line of social welfare.

The Buddhism that reached Ceylon in the age of Asoka emerged as the island's state religion. In modern times, the impact of the West upon Ceylon's native faith was more shattering than anywhere else in the Buddhist world. The Portuguese, Dutch, and British came in 1518, 1658, and 1796, respectively. They favored alternately Roman Catholicism and Protestantism. Under colonialist rule, public instruction was "Christianized" and the Buddhist institutions were ordinarily disparaged. About the middle of the eighteenth century, the Buddhist order of monks had all but deteriorated. Monks had to be recruited from Thailand [46] in order to strengthen ordination procedures. Thai influence in Ceylon is preserved in the so-called Siam-nikaya, "Siamese-sect," and remains the principal Singhalese body. In 1801, in a total population of a million and a half, the census of Ceylon showed some three hundred and forty-two thousand Protestants. No Roman Catholic figures for the same year were cited.

The Buddhists are the mainstay of nationalism in today's Ceylon. The independence Ceylon gained in 1947 led to membership in the Commonwealth. Citadel of the Southern Buddhist community, Ceylon is simultaneously involved in study of the Great Vehicle. Allegedly, the Great Vehicle was foretold in the Little. This latter is not recognized as Hinayana in Ceylon. It is rather referred to as Theravada, "Doctrine of the Elders," as was mentioned above. No less determined in opposition to broadening the scope of their tradition are these Elders of Ceylon than were once the Japanese Buddhists at the turn of the century. Repeated in the opposite direction is the experience of the Japanese, who studied the Little Vehicle tenets in Europe. The Theravadin of Ceylon and Burmese monks are currently pursuing in Europe and America studies in the polyglot texts of the Great Vehicle.

[46] P. V. Bapat, *2500 Years of Buddhism* (Publications Division, Delhi, 1959), p. 422.

Critical revision of the Pali Canon along philological lines was meanwhile executed in Ceylon and Burma. Sessions for collating the readings were scheduled in the style of ancient councils. Those were held in Colombo (1950–1956) and Rangoon (1954–1956). The goal was establishment of an authorized Pali Canon text, to be printed in the Singhalese and Burmese script. Collation of available manuscripts entailed comparative textual research, oral reading of the material, and choice of sound versions, the variants being assigned to a critical apparatus.

Nor did this Buddhist renaissance bypass India. There Buddhism was born. Yet there for a thousand years, it suffered an almost total eclipse. In India, as in Japan and China, revival was touched off in circles receptive to Western learning. For over fifty years now, books and articles in English, Hindi, and other Indian languages, have brought the history of Buddhism to light.

Increasingly fascinated is the Indian mind with the art, logic, and philosophy of Buddhism. High-caste scholars have gone to Ceylon for study. The curriculum of many an Indian university offers courses in Pali. Chinese and Tibetan are offered in certain institutions. The Mahabodhi, "Great Awakening" Society, founded in 1891, by a Ceylonese layman, who in old age became a monk, attracted multitudes in India and established many branches. Of these, the chief center is in Calcutta. Several convents are operated where Singhalese, as well as Burmese, Indian, even European, monks reside.

The Republic of India favors the revival of Buddhism. Above the chair of the President of India in the House of the People is inscribed the Buddhist message, *dharmacakrapravarttanaya,* "to turn the wheel of the Dharma." At the center of India's national flag, the same symbol, that of the wheel of the Doctrine, reminds all citizens not only of the Buddha but also of the *dharmavijaya,* Asoka's concept of conquest by righteousness.[47] The declared foreign policy of the government of India is based on the five rules of conduct, *Pancha-Sila,* the very foundation of Buddhist politics. It is a policy that allows for peaceful coexistence of peoples and faiths. In 1949, the British Museum returned to India the relics of two disciples of the Buddha: Sariputta and Moggallana. In officially receiving the relics, Prime Minister Nehru said, "With these relics the truth

[47] *Ibid.,* p. 459.

returns to India." On May 24, 1956, in inaugurating the Twenty-Five Hundredth Anniversary of the Buddha's death, *Mahaparinirvana,* Mr. Nehru declared that " the whole world is the homeland of the Buddha."

Buddhism knows nothing of a central authority on an institutional basis. An exception may be detected in the internal structures of countries such as Thailand. There the king is constitutionally " Upholder of the Doctrine " and Buddhism enjoys a status derived from the state. Another exception is Tibet. Until his recent exit under Chinese Communist aggression, the Dalai Lama was supreme pontiff. He united in his person both religious and political authority. Whereas Burma established Buddhism as a state religion, Ceylon has stopped just short of taking that step.

Even more ambiguous is the status of Buddhist doctrine. Orthodoxy lacks specification and definition. The tradition as such is enshrined in the texts. These are chronically the storm centers of controversy, contradiction, and paradox. Till more recent times, as was already emphasized, the two Vehicles knew next to nothing about each other.

In certain Buddhist quarters, trends toward a rapprochement are at present apparent. These trends are evidenced in general assemblies. They are an expression of internal as well as external solidarity. Doctrinally, adherents of the two Vehicles are disposed to search for conciliatory views. Buddhist associations attract international attention as they acquire universal overtones. In certain instances there seems to be a desire to combine in the face of a dynamic West.

If the People's Republic of China sent delegates to India, Ceylon, and Burma to attend ceremonies commemorating the death of the Buddha, the reason was decidedly political. A vast discrepancy divides the Chinese Buddhist tradition from the Pali records. Nowhere more pronounced is this discrepancy than on the date of the Buddha's death. In 1950, a World Fellowship of Buddhists was organized in Ceylon. Its first session was attended by members from thirty countries. Other general assemblies followed in 1952, 1954, and 1956, in Japan, Burma, and Nepal, respectively.

Burma boasts a Buddhist International Society. There are in the country many other Buddhist organizations of national and international stature. In the rise and growth of these societies, nationalism has played a formidable role. A Chinese Buddhist Federation came into being with the first Revolution of 1912. Reorganized after the Red regime took over, it was accorded official recognition in 1953.

In Japan, Buddhism was split into dissident sects requiring strict state control. After World War II, however, a more lenient policy has been introduced for regulation of relations between civil authorities and religious bodies. In prewar Japan, thirteen Buddhist sects and twenty-eight branches were reported. In 1955, however, there were some hundred and sixty-nine such sects. This proliferation was in part at least a revulsion against former authoritarianism and traditionalism. It is moderated by portents of cooperation and understanding. Toward such intrafaith solidarity, the Japanese Buddhist Federation, established in 1953, renders a substantial contribution.

As a phase of the contemporary Buddhist phenomenon resurgence is inseparable from a particular environment and historic setting where the Buddhist finds himself. Whether in India, China, Japan, or elsewhere, such resurgence needs to be seen as an expression of the Buddhist spirit in its constant battles with civilization and religion. Scholars may dwell on such Buddhist adjustment as the challenge of Christianity and modern science evoke.[48] There is another adjustment that encounters with materialist and communist forces require. Involved in this latter is Buddhism's own conception of change.[49] A new chapter is being written by Buddhism. Its theme is the adaptation of both the monastic order and the laity to novel social patterns.

[48] For instance, August Karl Reischauer, "Buddhism," in Jurji, *The Great Religions of the Modern World,* pp. 139–140; see also Karl Ludvig Reichelt, *Religion in Chinese Garment* (Philosophical Library, Inc., 1951), pp. 174–175.

[49] Richard A. Gard, ed., *Buddhism* (George Braziller, Inc., 1961), pp. 13–57, 203–243.

CHAPTER

6

RELIGIONS BORN IN THE NEAR EAST

THREE MIGHTY RELIGIONS — Judaism, Christianity, and Islam — rose to magnitude within the geographic boundaries of the Near East. The imperfections of human architects and the frailties of interpreters did not long deter these historic faiths from the establishment of widely recognized records of piety and organization. Nor did retreat from pristine quality, indulgence in reaction, perversion, and the setbacks of political misfortune permanently cripple their growth or stifle reform and renewal.

In our time, far more Jews, however, dwell outside than inside their ancient homeland. As for Christians, their numerical ascendancy certainly lies in the Occident. A network of Christian minorities persists in the cradle of the faith where its role is not quite so perfunctory as certain writers tend to report. Islam itself is in this age represented by many millions in Asia and Africa far beyond the confines of the Near East. A population graph of the parent region will undoubtedly show, almost wherever one looks, overwhelming Muslim majorities.

Remarkably, it is not just a common Semitic religious heritage that Judaism, Christianity, and Islam share. In varying degrees, they reproduce a classical Greco-Roman philosophy. Explicit is their rootedness, moreover, in a Biblical psychology and viewpoint transcending the mere vocabulary of revelation.

It is a matter of signal importance that our study refers to those and other religions as phenomena. Deliberately to think of any great religion under that rubric is something of a calculated risk. The nature of the risk becomes obvious the moment one begins to imagine a religion as only an aspect of this or that, even of eternal ultimate reality. On the most profound level, no religion is adequately grasped if it is projected as just an appearance or phantom. Where it is not an experience of an abiding presence, the essence of the holy, as well as the idea, are written off.

Yet use of the term " phenomenon " in relation to our subject carries a distinct advantage. Such an advantage may be said to outweigh any liability incurred. Clarity is its primary reward. A calmer perspective, a more incisive selectivity, those are highly to be prized virtues in any solid critique of religious subject matter. Committed to a scientific methodology, such an objective reading of religious history bids fair to open doors now closed. It implies readiness to listen, hence patience to sift materials. The approach more than justifies itself. It empowers an eager mind to see things just as they are, perchance to arrive at new conclusions.

Saturated with Greek and Kantian particularism, philosophy consistently charges the word " phenomenon " with partial and finite if not narrowly parochial meaning. Not the essentials of things, nor any core of reality, but rather the transitory and nominal facets come to light identified as a phenomenology of a sort.

In the context of the present inquiry, however, the word " phenomenon " conveys what is relevant, universally valid; what is crucial about religious experience; and whatever forms the immediate concern of those who study religion scientifically.

Relevance itself makes such a phenomenology eminently significant. The picture projected is true and faithful. To letter and spirit, and to all that is logical and positive, it stands firmly loyal. Yet such a picture is nowhere oblivious to whatever theologically is normative. To study these great religions as phenomena is to capture what really matters. First, no phenomenon can be religious if not theological; and, secondly, such a phenomenon emerges garbed in an inevitable realism.

Under the eyes of a candid camera, as it were, outlooks and efficacies of Judaism, Christianity, and Islam come alive. Hopefully, an evaluation of them carries considerable weight, at least more conviction. Easier to ascertain from that naked angle must be the implications and manifestations of these faiths on world crossroads.

Better understood, too, in that spirit, is the relative vigor of each religion's response to challenges of humanism, secularism, and nationalism. Visibly at hand are the rapport of each religion to, or its possible wedlock with, culture and society, ethics and politics, no less than with literature and economics.

Hence the ever-receding frontier of an imaginative, serenely envisioned phenomenology on this order. Discoverable therewith are, on the one hand, the acts of a given faith's followers, their discharge of covenanted obligations, and the way they function on the post. On the other, religion comes to the surface as something intimate yet tangible, if and when associated with that loyalty and devotion to essence by which committed persons and groups live. Religion begins to disclose its secret message in the way ordinary men and women, even little children, set out to perform regular tasks and routine chores as sacred duty.

Such a phenomenology inquires into the nature and scope of mutual relations within each of those believing societies. Both in the environment where their doctrinal heritage originated and abroad, this is the kind of question followers of each faith might ask of themselves. What *modus vivendi* governs our reciprocal contacts and what motivation inspires our interfaith exchange? In other words, across far-flung frontiers, how do Jews, Christians, and Muslims respond to the vexing problems of this new age?

Faith needs to be accurately documented and credited regardless of the form it takes. There is a crying need for original source material now available to those who are competent to read the texts at first hand.[1] New writings which treat crucial issues that agitate these religious communities deserve careful scrutiny. If there is to be any future form of integration, any significant meeting of minds, the phenomenology of religion must soon acquire a dimension of serious relevance.

One of the elementary revelations of phenomenology regarding the three religions originating in the ancient Orient is this. At the very heart of their doctrinal groundwork, they are religions of universalism and cosmic vision. Their constituencies embrace representatives of every nationality and tongue, race and color. Their communities and organizations seem to reflect extraordinary intersocietal flexibility and acumen.

[1] A useful volume along this line is Berthold, Carlsten, Penzel, and Ross, eds., *Basic Sources of the Judaeo-Christian Tradition* (Prentice-Hall, Inc., 1962).

Whereas Judaism is a folk religion, both Christianity and Islam figure as world faiths. Withal, each is a highly articulate religion, dramatically conscious of its potentialities. In mundane affairs as well as churchly life and work, they wield massive influence upon men and nations. Apart from due regard for the ingenious resilience of the living religions and their capacity to unite as well as divide humanity, the dream and prospects of a " one world " community must remain an expression of hazy optimism.

A second disclosure of phenomenology about the three faiths springs from the fact of their common ethos, an ethos, as stated above, related to the ancient Orient. Coupled with all that is a European legacy of vanished paganism and extinct mythologies. These, together with more intricate though obscure forces and factors, condition the three religions in contemporary intercourse with and attitudes toward others. Many and diverse are the factors that shape their destiny and set the stage for individuality patterns and social configuration within their respective orbits.

Owing to such impulses and radiations from the past, a certain continuity is noticeable within and between these culture areas. An integrating and consolidating continuity it is. Novel turning points and points of departure are by no means lacking.

A third element that might be cited is not a disclosure at all but rather a corroboration. Phenomenology corroborates that superb service which these religions render the cause of world education. In range and substance, a steady global advance makes the worldwide contribution of these religions cumulatively colossal. In civilizing capacity they excel as carriers of Western ideas, cultural progress, and technology to a developing world. They alternately serve as liaison between one civilization and another.

A fourth revelation of phenomenology attests that without Judaism, Christianity, and Islam, the world's total loss would indeed be staggering. In that unlikely event what would really suffer is faith itself, faith, that is, in the truth that makes free, the truth adored as one, eternal God. In any event, without these three religions the theistic climate might be radically different, possibly far more somber than it has been.

In what sense is this phenomenon of faith a mutation? Could it be due to the eruption of novelty in ideas, the breaking of virgin soil in religious experience? Or is it revelation according to classical theology? Precisely what the incandescent lamp within these faiths happens to be, phenomenology without solid support from theology cannot say. However, that mystery is undoubtedly related to an inner center of being called "self."

This inner center of our manhood expresses itself in the drive for integration and individuation. For we know that where self is not recognized, or if it is repressed, personality will either become rigid and narrow or be broken up. But when self is realized and supported, personality can develop and grow to its full stature as man created in the image of God.[2]

It should be nothing short of fatal to the central task were the reader offered even in capsule form a condensed history of the three religions under study. Nor would it be likely that adequate consideration within space limitations could be achieved of such major areas as the encounter of Judaism with Hellenism or the impact of early Christianity upon Judaism.

As regards Christianity itself, it is doubtful whether church history up to the twentieth century actually constitutes a background or rather a sequel to the luminous personal meaning of the Christian faith to a true believer. Any attempt, moreover, in our confrontation with the phenomenon of Islam to detail Arab and Islamic history is tantamount to setting the cart before the horse.

It is to the essence of a given religious phenomenon, as it exhibits itself, and not to the way it might be strangled by unessential historical data that top priority needs to be given.

Reliable introduction of these three religious phenomena awaits a more systematic examination of their depth and dynamism. Such an examination will not suffice, however, apart from a discerning sensitivity, an awareness of the subtleties of symbol and meaning. Of these religious phenomena, the Hebraic merits a prior claim upon our attention, if only because of its historical antecedence, and to it therefore, we must now turn.

The Phenomenon of Judaism

An array of incisive characteristics illustrates the Jewish religious phenomenon. Those characteristics form an integral part of that

[2] Gerhard Adler, *The Living Symbol: A Case Study in the Process of Individuation* (Bollingen Series LXIII, Pantheon Books, Inc., 1961), p. 410.

Hebraic saga contained in the Old Testament. At the core is the drama of a people's faith and defection. Woven into the Mosaic tradition, glorified by prophetic interpretation of pure religion, and revived through Rabbinic, Talmudic, and medieval epochs, this is a faith that attaches special significance to history.

The hallmark of Judaism is an intense consciousness of vocation. Belief and sentiment are thus evoked, persisting in the grim face of adversity. Hence the singular dynamism and lure of a chosen people's assumptions and outlooks.

Judaism lays just claim to a fabulous backlog of learning. Its heritage includes achievements in scholarship as well as a tradition of ancient wisdom. Such resources of mind and spirit became articulate in academies and centers of culture. An amazing thirst for science, an aptitude for experimental research, are attributes of the Jewish intellect. Those whose Lord was God, and to whom the Torah was law, simultaneously were possessed of an unusual hunger for knowledge and free inquiry.

A community that survived captivity and enslavement, exile and dispersion, ghetto and planned liquidation, demonstrated thereby an inner prowess and an extraordinary will to live. Indeed, many Jews could not have held together but for their faith in God. Eventually a Messianic vision quickened such faith, a faith that was hardly distinguishable from a perennial heartbeat for the Land of Promise.

Psychological and anthropological motivation centered in the age-old conception of Law and People. Such a motivation has come to a focus in Zionism, a phenomenal response to settings and circumstances. In opposition to a heavy concentration of juridical arguments, undergirded by political and military action, modern Zionism apparently has won support of qualified liberal segments of Western society.

Other than their substantial contributions to philosophy, Jews more recently have scored high records in scientific enterprise. Esteemed Jewish scientists carved roles of honor in the field of psychology. Even in psychical research, as in psychoanalysis and psychiatry (presumably antithetical to the ancient faith), Jewish pioneers won high trophies.

There is an affinity, furthermore, for economics and big business, for international commerce and finance. Yet save in the State of Israel, Jews betray little taste for agriculture or factory jobs. More alluring are the stock exchange, proceeds of world markets, and an official bureaucracy. Karl Marx (1818–1883), who sought to reverse this capitalist trend in history, himself came from a well-to-do German family of Jewish origin. His ponderous magnum opus, *Das Kapital,* the bible of socialist utopia, exerted a remarkable influence on Vladimir Ilyich Lenin (1870–1924), founder of Bolshevism and of Soviet Russia.

Instead of total eclipse, Judaism chose to live and outlive. Whatever permanent results a guilty conscience will inflict upon twentieth-century dispossessors of Palestine's rightful citizens, only time will reveal. The transitory stage has been passed. Yet a final settlement seems nowhere in sight.

In what follows, three selected aspects of Judaism as a phenomenon are set forth.

I

Judaism is rooted in an environment. It is creative of a community where religion is clearly a matter of law-abiding observance. Judaism fulfills a distinctive role among mankind's folk religions. It is grounded in the soil of the ancient Orient. Thence it passed into the bloodstream of a world faith, Christianity.

In the seventh century, Islam arose. It drew upon both Jewish and Christian sources; its debt to the former as well as to the latter seems incontrovertible. Although Jesus of Nazareth is related to the Jewish sect of Qumrân Essenes, to whom both Philo and Josephus refer, he stands apart. The church that Jesus founded is not fully patterned upon the Dead Sea community. Jesus was related by common background to the Essenes, whose piety and discipline the Dead Sea scrolls depict. Yet his person and teaching lead us far beyond Qumrân.[3]

Our approach to the religious phenomenon of ancient Israel requires review of traditional outlooks. A number of new departures in an old setting are detectable. A long and checkered apprenticeship apparently heralded the emergence of Israel's faith. Granted the truth of the Eternal is ever the same, man's grasp thereof is bound to falter, and at best can only be gradual. The infancy of Hebrew faith

[3] For critical analysis and source material, see Kurt Schubert, *The Dead Sea Community* (Harper & Brothers, 1959), pp. 147, *passim.*

goes back to Abraham. It also elicits memories of primitive cults.

Those primitive cults are better understood in a new relationship, that is, within the context of Old Testament history. Central to them all is the fact of idolatrous practices and heathen worship: on high places, through orgiastic cults, in sacrifices of blood and burnt offerings, and a host of other pre-Mosaic forms. Such preoccupations were involved as the adoration of trees and fountains, of stars and stones. All those and still more loom across the horizon of time. If that primitive religion stemmed from a simple and single pattern, the pattern in all probability would have had to be primitive totemism. The scenes were frequent where demons paraded in animal form; where references were made to serpents in beguiling shapes; where spirits satyrically roamed fields and hills; and where cults of the dead and especially of ancestors at many a stage appeared.[4]

Moses then comes into the spotlight. He emerges as a champion of a new, highly significant, break with the past. Of the older tradition, the new religion preserves what was deemed compatible with the infant community's spirit, what was considered of permanent value. Moses calls a Semitic folk from the worship of a tribal deity to faith in an eternal God. He rallied the tribes together and whipped discordant Hebraic elements into a united front.

Thus the religion of ancient Israel came into being. To say it was a folk religion implies there was a new religious community brought into being. Whether or not its theism was from the outset complete is a problem, tailored to order, for scholarly research and academic controversy. Suffice it to state here that monotheism in the earlier period was not an issue; and that, anyhow, a consistently monotheistic community never has existed.

Where high religion may be classified under two orders — folk religion and world faith — the religion of ancient Israel ranks as a foremost example of the former. From its earliest beginnings this prototype of Judaism bore the structural signs and attributes of a specific type of faith to which we refer as a folk religion.[5]

Precisely what was the nature of that radical change introduced

[4] Cf. George E. Mendenhall, "Biblical History in Transition," in *The Bible and the Ancient Near East: Essays in Honor of William Foxwell Albright*, ed. by G. Ernest Wright (Doubleday & Co., Inc., 1961), p. 40.

[5] See Gustav Mensching, *Die Religion* (Curt E. Schwab, Stuttgart, 1959), pp. 48–51.

into the history of religion? Briefly, the radical change consisted in the way ancient Israel reckoned the relation between Yahweh and his people in terms of a covenant.[6] It is particularly this covenant idea that was distinctive of Mosaic religion.[7] Distinctive, too, was the fact that in subsequent history, this covenant idea lent itself to interpretation and reinterpretation.

If Yahweh was to be Israel's God, other peoples might also have gods of their own. Yet Israel's covenant relation with Yahweh differed: it was based upon a historical experience and certitude. The certitude grew out of a recognized deliverance. Yahweh actually took initiative and delivered a number of Hebrew tribes out of Egyptian bondage.

Surely, then, that was a unique type of folk religion. It was fit to be set apart from all other religions. It called forth a peculiar spirit of the time, to it belonged the unique quality of a people's faith in God. He was, and ever shall be, the God of history. In the covenant, he established his people, a nation unlike other nations since the Eternal had chosen her for himself.

The authority behind that covenant relation between Israel and her God was the law. There Yahweh manifested his will. Beyond and transcending God's self-revelation in nature and history stood the law. In it, above all else, the will of the Almighty took concrete form. Across the vicissitudes of ancient Israel's history, and throughout all phases of its religious unfolding, it was the Torah that unilaterally and inexorably determined Hebrew thought, faith, and action.

Whatever else Israel's relation to Yahweh meant, it was primarily fulfillment of the law. That was to be the glory of Israel's ancient faith. Therein lurked also the greatest danger Israel ever faced. In substance the danger was this: that the law tended to achieve an independence all its own. When that unhappy outcome was reached even the Eternal himself might come to be patronized by an excessive legalism.

Inherent in the law, moreover, were certain tendencies that betrayed its weakness to pry itself loose from human desires and hopes.

[6] See Keith R. Crim, *The Royal Psalms* (John Knox Press, 1962), p. 53.

[7] See Henri Frankfort, *Kingship and the Gods: A Study of Ancient Near Eastern Religion and the Integration of Society and Nature* (The University of Chicago Press, 1948), p. 339.

Such a legal system might end up as a legislative complex. It might give rise to a proliferation of injunctions, a mass of rules and regulations literally unrelated to the dictates of conscience and only remotely consonant with the truth of revelation.

Hence the constitutional crisis in Israelite history. It was not only legal and legislative, but juridical as well. It was a time of stress and strain which saw the rise of the great prophets. Called directly and spontaneously by Yahweh, they inveighed against the people's brazen defection.

Further grounds for prophetic censure were such things as human sacrifice and sacred prostitution. Equally reprehensible were popular weakness for externals of the cult and fear over the cause of national security. Yet even where Israel was seduced by alien practices, she still imagined the covenant with Yahweh held firm and provided protection.

"And they have not cried unto me with their heart, when they howled upon their beds: they assemble themselves for corn and wine, *and* they rebel against me," said Yahweh by the mouth of the prophet Hosea. (Hos. 7:14.)

Again a new interpretation of the covenant relation was advanced: Yahweh judges the inward disposition and conscience. He is not satisfied with the outward and formal keeping of the law. Yahweh indeed may cause his people to be tempted. He will discipline them if they go astray. That is, if they refuse to turn to him in their deepest and most inward being.

The crux of these prophetic insights eventually was incorporated in the law. But not till after Jerusalem lay in ruins. In 621 B.C., King Josiah attempted a cultic reform. His act has been construed as a momentous event, a constitutional renaissance, an outcome of the prophetic message and impact. It may be truer to say, perhaps, that the reform proved abortive, that the bid for religious consolidation failed. Presumably the reform was initiated through a creedal and juridical manifesto, the so-called Fifth Book of Moses, Deuteronomy the "Second Law." [8] Actually, discovery of an old lawbook in the Temple did not of itself change many hearts. It did no more than furnish a program for return to old traditions. Other than the small

[8] Cf. Ivan Engnell, "Methodological Aspects of Old Testament Study," in *Supplements to Vetus Testamentum* (E. J. Brill, Leiden, 1960), Vol. VII, pp. 29–30.

band of prophets and their adherents few souls were permanently stirred. The syncretist and secularist trends persisted.[9]

Subsequent to the Babylonian exile Israel's religion was specifically to become a book-and-law religion. In confrontation with strange peoples and cultures, possession of this code of laws was to insulate the uniqueness of Israel's faith. It heightened the consciousness of the Jew and enhanced an awareness of his rich inheritance.

It thus had come to pass that perpetuation of Israelite religion was to be contingent upon the immutability of the law — the same law slavish applicability whereof had raised eyebrows among the prophets. Yet the canonization of the Pentateuch is nothing short of an innovation in the phenomenology of religion. For all future time, it did furnish a foundation for the development of Judaism, Christianity, and Islam. That this canonization took place when a new Jewish community had come into being in Jerusalem under the Persian Empire suggests a possible Iranian influence.[10]

The spirit of the prophets was thus set aside, if not disavowed permanently. Only certain aspects of their teaching had been accorded approval under the law. Provisions of the law came to be decisive and mandatory, a matter of life and death. Obedience to immutable laws came to be the measure of righteousness. Such laws it was firmly believed reproduced the divine will and hence were of religion's very essence. For all time, the religion of Israel had thus set up a life situation without which the faith could not be fulfilled.

What Israel exhibits is a sociological phenomenon, a model example of a genuine theocracy in operation. Yahweh is King. A basic conviction was early to take hold with the power of a mighty idea: blasphemy against God is treason. The law itself is nothing but a gift from Yahweh. Israel's wars are Yahweh's. Earthly thrones and monarchs are essentially an expression of waywardness from God to whom all sovereignty, authority, and power belong.

With the onset of the monarchy its need for such religious guarantees as might provide for national stability became real. From Saul to Zedekiah, however, the kings repeatedly came under a barrage of heavy prophetic condemnation. Yet the significance of the

9 Mendenhall, *loc. cit.*, p. 47.

10 Cf. George G. Cameron, "Ancient Persia," in *The Idea of History in the Ancient Near East*, ed. by R. C. Dentan (Yale University Press, 1955), pp. 91 ff.

Hebrew monarchy calls for careful consideration.[11] For the prophets did not represent more than a segment of the Yahwist structure. Only in the North, after the schism, did the monarchy fail to obtain permanent religious endorsement.[12]

Revealed by Yahweh, the law even in the area of state justice retained a sacred character. Yet the royal cultus was not devoid of special significance.[13] The cultus as such was servant of the monarch. Nor should we underestimate the importance of such a royal cultic institution. All religious ideas and practices were construed within a threefold structural design: law, prophet, and cultus.

An earthly setting was everywhere a matter of paramount concern. Beyond the realities of environment lay a relatively undeveloped image of the hereafter. Always the Israelite community retained its collective personality through a cultic way of life. So long as the earth shall endure, Israel's distinctive forms and religious phenomena are to center in such a holy community as the law creates and sanctions.

A remarkable shift was to overtake that neat balance. By the first Christian century, Judaism had come to live in a time between the times. On the one hand, the past with all its moving drama held sway. On the other, a Messianic hope was eloquently expressive of the era's deepest religious longings. The past and the future, time and history, jointly determined the experience and aspirations of the Jewish people. Such was the world in which Jesus appeared. It was a world caught between the past and the future, and for which the present held no special meaning.[14]

II

Another characteristic response that Judaism makes, particularly early in the face of strange surroundings, is Zionism. In its modern expression, Zionism is apparently a reaction against familiar types of emancipation techniques improvised in the Western world. The fact

[11] See Aubrey R. Johnson, *Sacral Kingship in Ancient Israel* (University of Wales Press, Cardiff, 1955), pp. 127–134.

[12] A. Alt, "Das Königtum in den Reichen Israel und Juda," *Vetus Testamentum* (1951), Vol. I, pp. 1–22.

[13] See Ivan Engnell, *Studies in Divine Kingship in the Ancient Near East* (Almqvist & Wiksells boktryckeri A.B., Uppsala, 1943), pp. 174–177.

[14] Günther Bornkamm, *Jesus of Nazareth* (Harper & Brothers, 1960), p. 55.

is that historical Christian and Islamic persecution of the Jews forced the latter to keep Judaism alive. Yet Christian and Muslim rulers there were who invited Jews to take refuge in their countries. There were popes who supported the Jews and befriended them. Christian authors and clergymen have increasingly recognized the world role of Judaism. Christian expectations of the Second Coming of Christ have kept the Messianic expectations of Judaism alive. Indeed, Zionism is in a historical sense a special form of Messianic expectation.[15]

Zionism is in diametric opposition to all emancipation patterns that offer a solution to the Jewish problem along the line of assimilation. Zionism offers a Jewish solution for anti-Semitism in its social, political, racial, and religious aspects. This solution takes the form of a Jewish state.

Modern Zionism became a movement through the indefatigable effort of Theodor Herzl (1860–1904). Herzl's twin monuments are a book, *The Jewish State* (1896), and the First Zionist Congress, held at Basel in 1897. Zionism has had to wrestle with the objections of an orthodox Judaism that saw its hopes for a personal Messiah dashed by the strategy of an earthly state. It had to reckon, moreover, with the mentality of a liberal wing that all but looked to " America as Jerusalem of the Jews, and to Washington as its Zion."[16]

The British Government's Balfour Declaration of 1917 brought the Zionists a step closer to the realization of their dream. Finally, in the wake of many ups and downs, an independent Jewish state, *Eretz Israel,* was proclaimed in 1948. From its very inception, however, it bore an earthly character. But a minority of its citizenry were devout believers, and of those just a fraction professed Jewish orthodoxy.

The Hebrew University of Jerusalem[17] emerged as hub of cultural Zionism. A somewhat religiously oriented institution, it set a high standard for scientific and scholarly research. It is made famous by eminent scholars of whom Martin Buber (1878–   ) is

[15] Cf. William F. Albright, "Israel — Prophetic Vision and Historical Fulfillment," in *Israel: Its Role in Civilization,* ed. by Moshe Davis (Harper & Brothers, 1956), p. 37.

[16] Friedrich Heiler, *Die Religionen der Menschheit* (Reclam-Verlag, Stuttgart, 1959), p. 614.

[17] See Norman Bentwich, *For Zion's Sake: A Biography of Judah L. Magnes* (The Jewish Publication Society of America, 1954), p. 220.

a well-known representative. Classical Jewish mysticism, a brilliant literary outpouring of the nineteenth century, found in Buber a masterly expositor.

Yet Martin Buber's stature is not merely a reflection of his role as expounder of Jewish mysticism. To a sizable world audience, he stands as a remarkable philosopher and theologian who renders a profound contribution. In the realm of religious philosophy and morals, Buber's voice reaches many ears far and near. The new Jewish mysticism borders on the frontiers of Christian theology and piety. It is not confined to cabala research.

Yet restoration of their ancient homeland did not bring the children of Israel a longed-for and highly deserved peace. In defiance of all sober expectations, their new predicament was to be a life of constant peril, an existence fraught with fear, encompassed with hatred and intermittent anxiety. For the present at least, Buber's message is to be heard and esteemed elsewhere.

" Of all the manifestations of the history of religion," wrote Buber, " Hasidism is that one in which two lines meet in full clarity, lines which it is usually assumed cannot meet by their very nature: the line of inner illumination and the line of revelation, that of the moment beyond time and that of historical time. Hasidism explodes the familiar view of mysticism. Faith and mysticism are not two worlds, although the tendency to become two independent worlds ever again wins the upper hand in them. Mysticism is the sphere on the borderland of faith, the sphere in which the soul draws breath between word and word." [18]

With Hitler's seizure of power in Germany, the anti-Semitic movement, which had originated in the middle of the nineteenth century, reached its zenith. The fiercest persecution of Jews in all history began. The newly unleashed destructiveness proved radically different from previous European waves of vengeance against Jews: it did not spring from the silly notion that Jews were corporately and personally guilty for the death of Christ. It owed its venom instead to the nationalist socialist doctrine of racial superiority. Upon the Jewish minority it inflicted a penalty due an inferior stock who held back the progress of a master race.

[18] Martin Buber, *The Origin and Meaning of Hasidism* (Horizon Press, Inc., 1960), p. 239.

In the "crystal night" of November 9/10, 1938, almost all synagogues in Germany were set on fire. In 1941, Jews were assigned to ghettoes and forced to carry the yellow star of David as a badge of shame. In that same year, systematic extermination of the Jews began in Germany and occupied countries.

The total of victims has been variously estimated. The figure has been set at four, five, or six millions. Such unprecedented failure of human feeling was shockingly distressing to all who had somehow identified ethics and modern progress. Fully justified seemed the dictum of the church historian Ignaz von Döllinger:[19] The destiny of the Jewish folk is possibly the most shattering drama of world history.

But fifty-one years after Zionism's first congress, an independent Jewish state was established. A New Palestine came into being as a focal point of world Jewry. Next to the restoration of the homeland in significance was institution of modern Hebrew as a national language. A touch of homogeneity was thus introduced to knit together immigrants of every conceivable background and national origin.

The religious foundation of the new state, if any, was not, however, related to a uniform Hebraic confession of faith. Israelis were generally under the influence of political, national, and social ideals, rather than theological. In the State of Israel, the dominant groups are generally secular. They represent the labor movement and the pioneering elements. The Zionism of the pioneers was a revolutionary movement and the culture they espoused was secular. All reference to Deity was omitted in the Declaration of the Establishment of the State of Israel.[20] Left-wing Mapan is in opposition to religion, whereas the ultra-orthodox Agudat Israel Party favors a more theocratic state.[21] A pertinent question does arise as to which impulse, the secular or religious, ought to prevail in personal and communal relations.

In the homeland a multiplicity of mores and outlooks is in vogue. A number of values and yardsticks are involved, running the full gamut of possibilities. In principle, at least, whatever Judaism has

[19] Heiler, *op. cit.*, pp. 614–615.

[20] *Iton Rishmi* (May 14, 1948, Tel Aviv, Israel), p. 2.

[21] Joseph Badi, *Religion in Israel Today* (Bookman Associates, Inc., 1959), p. 50.

bequeathed is equally tolerable. This means that ideological and religious affiliation varies widely — all the way from the Torah, heritage of pious orthodoxy, to the variegated hues of liberalism and irreligion.

Liberal interpretations of ancient outlooks and rites will turn up in embarrassing patterns of stark worldliness. Withal, such elements as do exist are thrown together under a single unified and for the most part combative enterprise. It is a solidarity that Judaism has demonstrated the will to preserve, lo these three millennia.[22] Israel cannot become, however, a clerical state. Mosaism creates no centralized structure of religious administrative power and control. Yet separation of religion and state does not exist. The government does give religion a traditional place of honor.[23]

A Zionism spurred on by anti-Semitism, indirectly abetted by a nationalist socialism and by a variety of both innocent and not so innocent friends, a Zionism resentful of an environment that invariably seems strange — those are the outward and visible factors that created the modern homeland.

The story has two other facets: what happened was a repercussion of theological Messianism. It also signalized defeat of trends toward symbiosis between Jew and Gentile. In the lands of the Orient such an attempted symbiosis had exploded earlier. Long masked in the West, a symbiosis between Jew and Gentile seemed a clear-cut possibility in the age of freedom.

Many ardent spirits had come to recognize the urgency of a political solution that would amicably effect the divorce between Hebrew and Gentile. It was to be a queer kind of divorce, an annulment of a marriage that had never been really consummated.

Two other determining factors distinguish this Zionism which gave rise to the Israel of today as a state. First, when all has been said and done, the homeland seems to be the sum of religious nostalgia and Messianic calculations, even when Messianism itself has been virtually discarded if not altogether discredited. Second, there is a will to wring out self-emancipation of Jewry in absolute or near-absolute detachment from theological assumptions.

[22] Helmuth von Glasenapp, *Die nichtchristlichen Religionen* (Fischer Bücherei, Frankfurt am Main, 1957), p. 209.

[23] Badi, *op. cit.*, p. 57.

III

Judaism is, above all else, a modern society. A glance at the ideological situation within Judaism inevitably will shed light on the nature of the vast transformation going on; also on the type of society emerging. A spectacular shift in the population centers of Jewish concentration calls for fresh reappraisal of what lies beneath the surface and comes to light only in spasmodic disguises.

Whether in Israeli Palestine or elsewhere in the worldwide Diaspora, modern Jewish society manifests certain trends. Some of these are easy to detect. As already stated, there is, first, an extreme traditionalism that defies all comparison. Declining any semblance of compromise, this is a traditionalism that prefers an isolation of its own. Nothing is ever allowed to disturb an age-old manner of life. Traditional Judaism pursues today a style of existence somewhat reminiscent of its social pattern in Eastern Europe before the hour of revolution had struck.

Another feature of modern Jewish society, to which attention was drawn above, stems from a rabid irreligious nationalism, if not from an integral Marxism. What one comes across in this domain is a deliberately scientific paganism. For it, spiritual values of the past have lost their savor. If these values continue at all, it is because they once formed part of the Jewish patrimony. They must receive reverence even when nothing but a historical or sentimental aspect remains.

This modern society bears, furthermore, the imprint of issues evoked by Zionism. Also, of issues raised by the disasters that befell Judaism since World War I. Currents and crosscurrents previously blurred and obscured have come to the foreground. Contrasts and tensions hitherto concealed begin to shape up.

Within modern Judaism and the society it sustains, Reform means liberal religion. Reform once looked askance at Zionism. But that attitude has since changed. The same change is discernible in the policies of official Jewish organizations in France and the United Kingdom.[24] Volatile and turbulent winds gather ordinarily in youth movements where, at any rate, much of Judaism vitally ebbs and flows.

[24] George Vajda, *Encyclopédie française,* Tome XIX, pp. 4812–4813.

In the absence of a central see or generally recognized seat of authority, no one particularly knows what the voice of catholic Israel will say to this renascent society. As regards the Conservative synagogue, there can be no question of a radical or overly critical departure from classical doctrines. These are basically the time-honored beliefs that every faithful Jew accepts.

These beliefs include faith in God, Creator and Providence; the election of Israel; the revealed Law; tradition, which sets the regulations for life and fixes the hope of an eschatological redemption. No major trend has been registered affecting the principal tenets that involve juridical and ritual structures. These along with the festivals and the Sabbath remain unshaken in the observance of pious Jews.

Actually, however, the generality of modern Jewish society has apparently abandoned standard observances. This blanket statement is perhaps relatively more applicable to European than New World Jewry. Whatever else this abandonment of ancient moorings may mean, it is for the most part an expression of indifference, or it may just be a refusal to commit oneself religiously. The pressures of modern life ought not to be forgotten as a cause of poor attendance at the synagogue.

In the United States, Judaism exhibits deliberate adjustment to the American environment. How many of America's five and a half million Jews are personally caught up in the work and worship of the synagogues? The evidence is inconducive, but probably about one half of that population regularly attends to the cry, "Hear, O Israel, the Lord thy God is one God."[25]

The problem of withdrawal from vital religious participation is most acute in Israeli society. Imperative demands of modern life and the almost total lack of non-Jewish manual labor jeopardize the enforcement and observance of Talmudic regulations.

Other religious issues tax the patience of intelligent Jews and threaten the architects of a strong community spirit. Extremists among the orthodox Jews, for instance, tend to regard the Jewish state restored by secular and selfish means as a Satanic anomaly,

[25] See Will Herberg, *Protestant — Catholic — Jew* (Doubleday & Company, Inc., 1960), p. 195. Also, Edwin Scott Gaustad, *Historical Atlas of Religion in America* (Harper & Row, Publishers, Inc., 1962), pp. 144–148.

its apparent blessings a travesty on redemption. Whereas they themselves enjoy high prestige and privilege, members of the rabbinate volunteer very little toward solution of issues at stake.

Those are but a sample of the type of religious problem which agitates Jewish society today. Symptomatic of unsettling aftereffects of Zionism upon American Jewry was a controversy over dual allegiance (to Israel and to the United States of America) which in 1961 Prime Minister David Ben Gurion [26] evoked. As a sequel to fierce struggle for emancipation, Jews have had a full quota of agony. Judaism has survived at a heavy price.

Whatever its conception of Israel's faith may be, a modern Jewish society must make up its mind with regard to two things: the meaning of its history and the meaning of religion in modern society. Abraham J. Heschel [27] drew attention to the divine dream that the prophets and rabbis have cherished. " It is the dream of a world, rid of evil by the grace of God as well as by the efforts of man, by his dedication to the task of establishing the kingship of God in the world. God is waiting for us to redeem the world. We should not spend our life hunting for trivial satisfactions while God is waiting constantly and keenly for our effort and devotion."

Heschel discloses the phenomenon of Judaism a little further when he warns: " Israel did not accept the Torah of their own free will. When Israel approached Sinai, God lifted up the mountain and held it over their heads, saying: ' Either you accept the Torah or be crushed beneath the mountain.' "

Seeing the mountain of history over its head, modern Judaism inquires, Shall we renew the covenant with God?

The Phenomenon of Christianity

The history of Christianity takes its point of central reference from the career of Jesus Christ (ca. 5 B.C.–A.D. 30).[1] The birth and growth of the early church is reflected in the New Testament.

[26] See his *Rebirth and Destiny of Israel* (Philosophical Library, Inc., 1954), pp. 523–539.

[27] *Between God and Man: An Interpretation of Judaism* (Harper & Brothers, 1959), p. 258.

[1] For literary and historical criticism in the life of Jesus up to and including Origen, see Robert M. Grant, *The Earliest Lives of Jesus* (Harper & Brothers, 1961).

Church history was initiated in The Acts of the Apostles, an account of the spread of Christianity during the first thirty years or so after the earthly life of Jesus.[2] Earliest among the church fathers were those known as apostolic. They were the personal disciples of the apostles or at least sufficiently close to them to be thus identified in the tradition.[3]

In and through Jesus the Old Testament religion was brought to fulfillment. The faith he proclaimed was embedded in the Hebraic heritage. To those who accepted him, Jesus was Christ the Lord, Light of the World, and Redeemer. This situation involving adherence through faith and possible persecution was changed, however, from the moment Constantine in A.D. 313 altered the course of the ship of state and not only recognized the church but in A.D. 324 gave it public favor. The change was deepened when Theodosius I in A.D. 380 made Christianity the sole religion of the state. Up till then, it had required courage to join the church. Thereafter in the empire this quality was generally needed in refusing to join.[4]

By way of inclusive retrospect,[5] Christianity may be seen as preserving, nevertheless, a measure of continuity. This it demonstrated in unfoldings that extend from the primitive church and patristic times to achievements in Byzantine and Western cultures; and from the Middle Ages through Reformation and Counter-Reformation to modern self-revelations on the world stage. In its most recent self-expressions, the church has been articulate in theological and doctrinal restatements as well as in ecclesiastical, apostolic, and ecumenical disclosures.

By virtue of a fourfold tradition, Christianity exerts a worldwide influence. This includes the ancient communions of the Near East and India; the Eastern Orthodox Churches; Roman Catholicism; and Protestantism. A fifth category comprises the Younger Churches, outcome of Western missionary enterprise chiefly in

[2] Bruce M. Metzger, *The Oxford Annotated Bible,* RSV (Oxford University Press, London, 1962), p. 1167.

[3] John Lawson, *A Theological and Historical Introduction to the Apostolic Fathers* (The Macmillan Company, 1961), p. 1.

[4] Hans Lietzmann, *The Era of the Church Fathers* (Lutterworth Press, London, 1951), p. 97. J. R. Palanque, *et al., The Church in the Christian Roman Empire* (The Macmillan Company, 1953), Vol. I, pp. 24, 59, 367.

[5] Kenneth Scott Latourette, *A History of Christianity* (Harper & Brothers, 1953), pp. 1463–1477.

non-Occidental parts of the world.

Along with its entanglement in politics, the church could scarcely escape identification with Western civilization. A cultural upsurge which the European Renaissance entailed was crucially immune to theology. Goethe characterized his hero Faust as an elderly scholar weary of learning and given to romance. His child by Helen of Troy was Euphorion, an embodiment of both classical and medieval traditions. It is well to keep this figure in mind if we are to recall the twin nature of the Renaissance, pagan and Christian.[6]

As the Greco-Roman classics were revived, heavier accent on secularism developed. In the Renaissance and the Age of Enlightenment, vitalities that had once flourished side by side with Christianity were accorded priority. Discoveries, conquests, and inventions, which the world owes the West, were to follow. At a time when there was such passionate interest in classical civilization, the West found in the Byzantine sources a means of satisfying its longing to explore the treasures of antiquity.[7] The Byzantine Empire (324–1453) was indeed an instrument whereby Greco-Roman antiquity survived. Byzantium fell into Turkish hands in 1453, but her spirit remained.

Ivan III (1462–1505), consolidator of Russia, married Sophia Palaeologue, the niece and heiress of the last Byzantine emperor.[8] He assumed the imperial Byzantine double-headed eagle in his coat of arms, introduced Byzantine ceremonial into Moscow, and soon made Russia the leader of the Christian East as Byzantium once had been. If Constantinople was the New Rome, Moscow was to become the Third. The great traditions of Byzantium, its law, political ideas, and administration as well as its Christianity lived on through the centuries in the Russian Empire.

By the end of the twelfth century, the transition from medieval to modern times had already seemed imminent.[9] After 1300, the church

[6] Harry Levin in Tinsley Helton, ed., *The Renaissance* (The University of Wisconsin Press, 1961), p. 128.

[7] George Ostrogorsky, *History of the Byzantine State* (Rutgers University Press, 1957), pp. 508–509.

[8] Ivar Spector, *An Introduction to Russian History and Culture* (D. Van Nostrand Company, Inc., 1962), p. 31.

[9] Frederick B. Artz, *The Mind of the Middle Ages,* A.D. 200–1500 (Alfred A. Knopf, Inc., 1953), pp. 450–455.

steadily declined as an organization and as an intellectual and spiritual force. In the early Middle Ages, it had taken the place of the Roman Empire in holding many national and cultural groups together under the bishop of Rome. European civilization was finally to be carried around the globe. Before the voyages of Columbus and Vasco da Gama, this civilization was shut in the south and southeast by the Islamic peoples spread from Morocco to the Balkans and beyond to India and Malaysia. What the Roman Catholic Church lost, as a result of the Reformation, it gained later in new communicants in the Americas, Asia, and Africa.

The flowering of the arts and sciences saw the rise of great universities to hegemony in the realm of independent research, intellectual adventure, and creativity. In the meantime, political theory began to attract Christian thinkers concerned with contemplation of man and his destiny. The influence of Machiavelli (1469–1527),[10] the Florentine statesman and political thinker, upon the history of political theories can hardly be exaggerated. He was possibly the first of modern political philosophers. It is quite as accurate to say that he ends the medieval era as that he begins the modern.

Western Europe could not be so easily rationalized and paganized. Before the death of Machiavelli, Martin Luther (1483–1546) gave the signal for a movement that was to keep the intellectual energy of Europe fully occupied for a hundred and fifty years in the field of religion and ethics. He was not only the greatest of the Reformers but also one of the most important figures in the history of religions.[11] The Luther research of the past ninety years leaves no doubt that his positive achievement has to be expressed theologically. With all his grievous mistakes, his stand at Worms against the majesty and power of half the world and his insistence on justification by faith alone are historic landmarks of Evangelical Christianity and of the struggle for religious freedom.

Christian theology had not isolated the Kingdom of God from that of this world. It cautioned, however, that a discrepancy divided the two. Whereas fidelity toward temporal authority was enjoined, a

[10] William Archibald Dunning, *A History of Political Theories* (The Macmillan Company, 1923), pp. 322–325.

[11] J. S. Whale, *The Protestant Tradition* (Cambridge University Press, London, 1955), p. 8.

warning was issued against rulers who abused political privilege. Emphasis was laid upon the evil nature of the state. Christianity took a dim view of perfectionism in state and society and scored any thought of man's natural readiness for perfectibility.

The Crusades had had their sequel in international discord and wars of religion, in exploitation of subject peoples, and in imperialism. Yet many such an unhappy episode deepened the imperative demand for reform and fairer understanding of international questions. Christians did not invariably know the answers to social and economic ills; they did not systematically endorse liberty, democracy, and constitutional government everywhere. But among them a sense of compassion and a concern for justice were never completely lost.

To the emissaries of John the Baptist, this is what Jesus said in detailing his role in history.

"The blind receive their sight, and the lame walk, the lepers are cleansed, and the deaf hear, the dead are raised up, and the poor have the gospel preached to them." (Matt. 11:5.)

Whether Protestant Christianity, especially the Reformed tradition initiated by John Calvin (1509–1564), actually produced capitalism [12] in its Western dimension and thrust is an open problem. The truth is that ages before Karl Marx, Christ took the side of the broken of earth and set a standard for relief of pain and misery. The faith of Peter whereupon the church was founded became a reality of confession and proclamation.

The nature and vitality of such a Christianity are examined below in three sections. First, an attempt is made to discover how the Christian phenomenon displays itself as a religion, that is, as a meaningful personal faith and commitment. Second, the faith is seen as an apostolate, a world-mission involving confrontation with such major issues as those of the indigenous churches in Asia, Africa, and elsewhere; involving furthermore, a confrontation with Communism and consideration of the kind of competitive alternative Christianity offers. Third, Christianity is seen in the perspective of ecumenical motivation and longing for unity. At the risk of generalizing from particular trends, those churches are borne in mind which have been drawn together in the World Council of Chuches.

[12] Cf. Max Weber, *The Protestant Ethic and the Spirit of Capitalism* (Charles Scribner's Sons, 1958), p. 2.

There are, of course, important conservative and evangelical bodies and sects which stand apart from this movement in a growing fellowship of their own.

I

Christianity is a religion. It conceives of God as love and of man as his child. Christ, the Risen Lord, is the central reference of the faith. From such a standpoint it must be quite inadequate to distill the peculiarities of Christianity along the classic lines of its various doctrines of God; its views of the world; or its undoubtedly distinctive ethics.

Such distillations of the Christian religion are, of course, valid and justifiable. They can be most significant. They are by no means devoid of value in stressing the unique character of Christianity. However, the fact is they are relatively secondary even if essential. In comparison with the above-mentioned centrality of the risen Lord, those are surely pivotal points, major but not primary.[13]

At the beginning of our era, Jesus of Nazareth founded Christianity. The problem of the historical Jesus has long engaged the attention of scholars. Such research was generally conducted on this assumption: that more exciting historical investigation might succeed in establishing the identity of Jesus with the Christ of community faith and worship.

This problem in all probability will continue in the future to be as close to the devout Christian as it is to the assiduous scholar. The believer ever desires to know how the divine figure of Christian faith and history is to be received. In a world of change and decay, what do the factors of time and place mean for comprehension of the Redeemer's role?

What enkindles the imagination of modern youth, and quickens the faith of the church is not, however, a matter of time and place. Nor is it to be discovered in an essentially historical setting. There is something here far beyond the findings of rational science and its methodology. Something invariably eludes us as we try to read aright what the living Christ meant in the historical situation.

That something has to do with a singular relation, fully mysterious yet true, which consistently arises between Jesus and his disciples.

[13] Mensching, *Die Religion,* pp. 54–59.

If we are to grasp the essence of Christianity, such a relation cannot be esteemed too highly.

The New Testament leaves little doubt that children and ordinary people discovered an immediate rapport with Jesus. He himself was a " child of God." Generally speaking, this connection was not unlike that between " master " and " pupil." Its chief concern was neither understanding nor determination of the will.

Nor was it primarily a relation of doctrine and order. The chief merit of this relation lay in the domain of confrontation between essence and essence. By word and deed, the Master again and again introduced this genuinely mysterious contact which the disciples spontaneously recognized. "And we believe and are sure that thou art that Christ, the Son of the living God." (John 6: 69.)

But what of the pure and true content of such a relation? The question before us probes whether or not in the disciples' relation with Christ a special experience of God became real. Was this an experience of God clearer than anything known before? Clearer than an Old Testament experience which in comparison left God relatively shrouded in obscurity, relatively veiled, so to say, by intrusive and demonic forces? If the answer is in the affirmative, then this new relation indeed revealed a true God formerly known but imperfectly. Such a true God was formerly set apart from the creature by moral grandeur; he was removed evidently by void and the infinite majesty of his divine being.

About the idea of God as Father the history of religion has had much to say. Required in the scrutiny of all such ideas of God is a sense of proportion. That is, enough balance and imagination to state precisely what the essence of this peculiarly Christian experience of God might be. For it is a primarily Christian belief that Jesus led his disciples out of restless questing at the threshold of an inaccessible Being to a new relation with God as " Father."

Such a principle requiring ascertainment of what a religious experience happens to be, and what it claims, ought to apply in the phenomenology of all religions. What is here at stake is no mere idea. It is, rather, the content of such an idea as might be incorporated in a real experience. Nor does a religious experience of this type readily lend itself to description. For in Christ, and through him with God, a contact comes to men. This is above all a contact that evokes shock. In the case of Peter, for instance, the shock was punctuated with these words: "Depart from me; for I am a sinful man, O Lord" (Luke 5:8).

Neither was the foregoing utterance of Peter a response to Jesus' rebuke. It was no retort to a reprimand that apprised Peter of sin's enormity. It was instead an indication of a normative Christian grasp of the meaning of sin. In a word, this utterance is a spontaneous expression of a dynamic idea of God, a God met on the stage of reality and experience. In its Christian connotation sin can never be reduced to merely moralistic terms. It is an attitude of essential being, diametric opposition to God.

Sin spells isolation and self-sufficiency. Involved is an exclusive outlook and posture. To be exclusive toward God might ostensibly mean being true to oneself. It is to trust in the strength of one's arm as indeed we all should. There is a difference, however, between a vigorously wise self-reliance and a naïve immaturity forgetful that man is frail and imperfect. For if all that placates the ego is automatically approved, man comes to be his own worst foe, a victim of self-deception.

Distance from God then comes to be an offense against the Eternal, an absolute apathy of solitude. Exhaustively memorable is the treatment of this alienation offered in the parable of the prodigal son (Luke 15:11-32). In miniature that has been the test of waywardness from God, a test set at the heart of Christian experience. For every case of existential prodigality finds an echo and response, a symptomatic expression, in a sinful deed. Nor is sinfulness in the first degree a breakdown in performance. Primarily it is not failure in normal behavior. Essentially it is a documentary on man's distance from God.

It must follow that for the Christian, a religious experience basically is decisive nearness and proximity to God. The God known in Christ is a searcher of the heart and Redeemer. He is also gracious. He is One who through the Savior calls men to draw nigh to him. No matter how heinous their deeds, men are thus delivered from every prodigality of distance and isolation.

To be thus bound up with Christ is to be lifted to a personal reality of living communion with God. To know the reality of such communion is to be born again and to live a new life. Those to whom such an experience is real are saved from separation and solitude. This is the atonement.

At this point, kindred Christian doctrines arise — relative to faith, adherence, and community. The union longed for is attained through commitment to Christ. No word in the New Testament is more misunderstood than "faith." It seemed reasonable to compare faith with truth. The analogy suggested that before faith could be crystallized in dogma, a rational verification was necessary.

On the contrary, what distinguishes Christian faith is simply this: readiness in confidence and hope deliberately to lay hold upon Jesus' personality at the very core. There is a capacity here which all men share. It is man's capability to transcend his personal essence. It is a capability at the deepest level whereby man joins the essence of his being to that of another.

So thoroughgoing can this coming together be that the one person no longer thinks even in terms of imitating the other. The two are inextricably linked. Individuality and selfhood are, of course, retained. Yet the two acquire a "conciliar" association, a bond that sheds luster on religious experience in everyday life. It is as though thereafter living confronted the two with an identical situation.

What this union represents between Christ and the eternal Father on an infinite level, Jesus renders finitely real between man and God. Thus man begins to live consciously by God's power and strength. That is, he deliberately seeks to live in joy and fellowship with the Eternal, confident that the divine resources are sufficient.

This spells the end, or at least curtailment, of self-righteousness. The posture of solitary reliance upon self gives way to true humility and therefore grounding in the grace of being. Recovery of the basic understanding comes: that all one's being derives from the Eternal.

Essential adherence to Christianity thus involves this: laying hold on the essence of Jesus at the core of being. Man then daily renews his strength and mounts up with wings as the eagle. In such a genuine commitment is the making of Christian character. As a ground of faith and conviction that is the basis of adherence.

Such a change of mind, *metanoia,* engenders new courage. It signalizes attainment of new life, *nova vita.* Although it could, such a new life does not ordinarily find fulfillment in a solitary encounter with God. Rather, does it come to fruition in a living community along with the brethren. Jesus declared the Kingdom of God to be near. Such an eventful imminence filled the mind of Jesus as well as that of the early church. Imminent was a complete break which will introduce the mystery of an otherworldly Kingdom.

That such an expectation ran high was altogether within the limits and scope of a contemporary eschatology. It had to do with an experience beyond time. The claims of an unconditional God were indicated. In relation to that transcending event considerations of earthly values and finite gifts were unessential. A consummation of all worldly structures and realities of time and space was envisioned.

A kingdom of divine sovereignty shall therefore triumph in spirit and in truth. The end of the age shall usher in the Day of the Lord prayerfully awaited by the believers.

Christianity spoke of overcoming the world as Jesus himself said he did (John 16:33). There was not the slightest implication, however, that his disciples should either despise the world or leave it alone. In the Christian conception of ultimate things, the world around us does not constitute an absolute frame of reference. The world of men for the most part constitutes those who have gone astray. As general background the world of men consists in disillusioned and sorrowfully frustrated souls. Insofar as Christians were concerned, no greater hindrance to the progress of the truth or detriment to saintliness could be conceived. The world agonizes under principalities still at large. Of hostile powers far from overcome there seems to be no end.

An alternative attachment tempts man on this planet. It is an alternative road which most religions caution against. Christianity regards this alternative as the world's option to God. Hence the choice everyone must make: either God or mammon. No one can worship the two simultaneously. Mammon is the symbol for blinding world power and arrogance. Literally, " mammon " is " riches." " No one can serve two masters: for either he will hate the one, and love the other; or else he will hold to the one, and despise the other. Ye cannot serve God and mammon." (Matt. 6:24.)

Christianity advocates a bond with God inevitably involving a transfer: the transfer, that is, of life's center of gravity to location in divinity. However, the end of all care for things of the world is not envisaged. Such an end to worldly concerns might seem to be a logical sequence to fellowship with God. This is not the case, however, if only because of the Christian's status and responsibility as his brother's keeper.

As regards " good works " it is patent that Christianity preaches no " world flight." Attachment to God and a bond of union with him are a summons to service. Love must be revealed in service. Love toward all kinds of beings in a God-created cosmos of values and orders stems from love of God and parallels love of self.

What are the sociological consequences of the Christian religion? The course of church history displays a variety of social forms. The need to look at them separately is vital. Christianity's centuries-long development is scarcely intelligible apart from its social phenomena.

The first disciples formed a sacred community easily recognizable as a reconstituted Jewish sect. A desegregation program for which Paul bore chief credit was soon set in motion. National walls of partition were ordered removed. Believers in Christ were to become a free society. Thereafter the road was to be open.

About the opening of the second Christian century, the " church " took visible form. A solid organization was thus instituted, as Christ had ordained, with exclusive claims to the truth and an impelling urge to proclaim the gospel.

An abundant and unlimited range of values was introduced by Christianity. It is therefore exceedingly difficult to define this faith in a generally acceptable formula. This is specially true since these values were experienced and crystallized in concrete forms, as indicated above. Van der Leeuw [14] saw Christianity in essence as a religion that conceives of God as love.

On the one hand, however, human notions of love seem inimical to a concept of God's decisive love for man revealed in Jesus Christ. On the other, it does seem gratuitous to reflect on the Christian understanding of divine love without proper exegesis of the New Testament Greek word for love, *agapē*. Presentation of a theological thesis followed by precise commentary and exposition is involved.

Gustav Mensching [15] seemed inerrantly correct in adopting a critical attitude to such an oversimplification of what Christianity

[14] *Phänomenologie der Religion,* pp. 582–584. [15] *Op. cit.,* p. 59.

is. He decided in favor of a somewhat fuller definition. He designated Christianity as a religion of filiation to God and of love. Whatever the aptness of either definition, it must be emphasized that the Christian religion is most strikingly a gospel.

II

Christianity is also an apostolate. The contemporary era of world mission is of necessity wrapped up with a changing global situation. In a world geographically drawn together and culturally interlinked, mission fields, once remote and isolated, tend to constitute a single neighborhood. Astonishingly new modes of transportation, of which the jet airplane is a harbinger, had an inescapable influence on missionary strategy.

A missionary now reaches his post not within a year or a month but the same day he leaves home. Travel facilities are available so that anyone who desires to see for himself what a mission field is like may do so. By way of exchange, hosts of international Christians and non-Christians currently visit, travel, study, teach, and work in the so-called Christian West. Christian civilization, Christendom in all its varieties, is now examined by multitudes of outsiders at first hand.

Roman Catholics, for instance, have achieved fellowship with each other across national frontiers. This has been described as inter-Catholic understanding, along a horizontal plane. Added to a long-established connection with the Vatican, vertically, it assures greater solidarity and a common purpose.[16]

Christian missions in today's world, as emergence of the Peace Corps reminds us, are no longer to be dissociated from the technical revolution sweeping non-Occidental lands. Everywhere men and women are involved in a social and economic drama. Upon men and nations, an age of intercommunication forces itself. The challenge is this: cooperate or move out of the way.

On the erstwhile mission fields, conditions are abysmally and chronically depressed. In most of Asia and Africa, three fourths of the population are undernourished. Public welfare and health

[16] Alphonsus Mulders, *Missionsgeschichte* (F. Pustet, Regensburg, 1960), pp. 501–504.

agencies are at about one tenth of the level required under Western Europe's standards. Most such welfare departments are understaffed, too ill-equipped to meet basic needs and to cope with overriding problems.

A million and a half in those countries annually die of malaria. One fourth of the children born will not live beyond their first year. Wherever industrialization takes hold it inflicts penalties of slums and unemployment similar to those the West has long endured.

In his encyclical letter *Evangelii preaecones,* of June 2, 1951, Pius XII stressed the responsibilities of missionaries. The pontiff took note of new developments in Roman Catholic missions during the preceding quarter century. He stressed the need for a trained native clergy. The pope recognized growth in Roman Catholic missionary effort during the period 1926–1951: "The Catholic missionary movement both in Christian and pagan lands has gained such force and momentum and is of such proportions as perhaps was never witnessed before in the annals of Catholic missions." It is likely that Roman Catholic missionaries in 1956 outnumbered Protestant missionaries at an approximate ratio of 5 : 3, a significant reversal of an aproximate 3:4 ratio in 1925.[17]

Pope Leo XIII in a celebrated encyclical, *Rerum novarum,* "Of Things New," had said in 1891 that the social question is above all a moral question. The encyclical *Mater et magistra,* "Mother and Teacher," issued by Pope John XXIII, July 14, 1961, reaffirmed this tenet of Roman Catholic sociology. Pope Leo's message had dealt essentially with the relations between capital and labor, property, professional organizations, and the state's right to intervene in social affairs. He rejected socialism and proposed a Christian solution of the social question that has become part of the program of Christian Democratic parties and movements in many parts of the world.

Rerum novarum is the basic document of the Roman Catholic Church's attitude toward social problems. It has been looked upon as the church's answer to Karl Marx's *Das Kapital,* the bedrock of communism. Pope Leo opened up a middle ground in 1891 between the extremes of the Marxists, who were said to exploit the "poor man's envy of the rich," and irresponsible capitalists who were labeled

[17] Yorke Allen, Jr., *A Seminary Survey* (Harper & Brothers, 1960), p. 295.

"covetous and grasping men." Leo condemned both extremes, defended unions, and asked for governmental protection for the workers. The failure of communism to destroy social mobility and stratification has become abundantly clear.[18]

Pope John's encyclical expanded on the second encyclical in the social series, Pope Pius XI's *Quadragesimo anno,* "Fortieth Anniversary," issued in 1931 to commemorate Leo's action. The second letter cited economic collectivism, on one side, and economic individualism, on the other, as the "twin rocks of shipwreck." It asked for added protection for the laborers.

Mater et magistra's opening lines are: "Mother and Teacher of all nations, the universal church has been instituted by Jesus Christ so that all who in the long course of centuries come to her for loving embrace may find fullness of higher life and a guarantee of salvation." What followed set forth "new aspects of the social question" and recommended means for the "reconstruction of social relations in truth, justice, and love."

Pope John did not designate communism by name but he did point out, "Experience has shown that where the personal initiative of citizens is missing, there is spiritual tyranny." He then skillfully thrust through to communism's most vulnerable spots: its promise of a temporal paradise, its scoffing at man's deeply felt religious needs, its persecution of Christian believers.

The pope noted that individuals were growing increasingly convinced of the need for mutual understanding and cooperation, but their leaders seemed unable to understand one another. The reason, wrote Pope John, is that "men, especially those more responsible, are inspired in the unfolding of their activity by different or radically opposed concepts of life. Unfortunately, in some of these concepts, the existence of the moral order is not recognized: an order which is transcendent, universal, absolute, equal, and binding on all. Thus, they fail to meet and understand each other fully and openly in the light of one and the same law of justice, admitted and adhered to by all. Mutual trust among men and among states cannot begin or increase except by the recognition of and respect for the moral order."

[18] See Pitirim A. Sorokin, *Social and Cultural Mobility* (The Free Press of Glencoe, 1959), pp. 15–16.

Christian missions are furthermore sensitive to the fitful mood of world politics. In the modern era, missions have long been identified with the expansion of Western political power. In carrying out their multiple ministries, they have depended indeed upon the reality of such political ascendancy as the Western nations exercised. Today not unlike the emissaries of colonial states themselves, missionary statesmen and personnel are convinced the episode of colonial authority is virtually gone.

The emergence of indigenous churches is one specific response to a changing world order. Missionary societies of all Christian traditions witness the coming of age of national congregations and hierarchies. The underlying cause behind the emergence of such national bodies is not far to seek: the missionary obligation can no longer be articulated in European or American garments.

Exclusively indigenous churches are the order of the day. They are staffed, managed, and theologically as well as pastorally administered by a national hierarchy, ministry, or episcopate. It is the express desire of such younger churches in Asia and Africa that their own ecclesiastics and religious rulers be citizens of the country where they labor.

A foreign missionary may occupy an office only at the behest of an indigenous bishop or other church official. He renders service as adviser, assistant, teacher, doctor, or fraternal worker. But such restricted opportunities may not be permanent. Even where vacancies remain unfilled, political and cultural adjustments to independence in a host country may not have reached such a stage as would permit entry and residence of foreign churchmen.

Neither the backing of a powerful state nor the prestige of race will determine the success of a missionary in today's world. Far more decisive are the nature of his personal contacts, his contribution to community welfare, and also his practical tolerance and willingness both to share, and to enter into partnership, with those of another background and faith.

National churches will take over full responsibility for the apostolate. Even so there will be much essential work for those sent in from abroad. In the new age, there can be neither national nor alien believer, neither westerner nor easterner, but a single apostolate for a single world.

Ecclesiastics and men under holy orders thus regardless of homeland find themselves beneath the same standard. In like manner, native and foreign laymen in whatever walk of life draw together on an international scale. Spiritually, they seek salvation of souls; humanistically, they intend to resolve social ills. The two categories of body and soul are intimately and indissolubly knit.

It is thus that the church universal ceases to be a hollow phrase. It comes to be a living organ of the Lord. It is of the essence that an organized world communism be confronted with a socially alerted and ordered world church poised to take bold action. Against communism, only the true, the clear, Christian faith can hold its ground. If we fail to participate in it completely afresh, said Karl Barth, then we shall also lack its steadfastness.[19] In the developing countries of Asia, Africa, and Latin America, as well as the Middle East, Christians under massive corporate bodies seek to evolve a better social structure and to promote a more abundant way of life. In a partnership of obedience, Christians discover that the principle of fellowship and goodwill is ideally suited for this age of constructive dynamics.

The world crisis itself is indeed pregnant with meaning if it serves to bring about definitive mobilization of all missionary forces and agencies. In the overall missionary obligation of Christianity, as well as in certain other services, consolidation and cooperation offer a clue to vexed problems. To meet the challenges of a world revolution is to plan together on a global basis and for the good of all mankind. Inevitably the fellowship of all religious people everywhere is involved and the pooling of all resources for the good of human society is a noble purpose.

In the last analysis, one admits that Marx's diagnosis of social pathology was substantially sound. But, as Nicolas Berdyaev held,[20] Marx prescribed the wrong cure. Marxist communism is false because God exists, a higher power and a source not only of economic but of spiritual power. If capitalism has failed at its task, so has Marxism.

A glance at the present missionary situation in the world reveals

[19] Karl Barth, *Against the Stream* (Philosophical Library, Inc., 1954), p. 142.

[20] Matthew Spinka, *Nicolas Berdyaev: Captive of Freedom* (The Westminster Press, 1950), p. 18.

there are countries still closed to the apostolate. Closed doors are the order of the day in countries such as Saudi Arabia, Afghanistan, Tibet, and Bhutan. Elsewhere, an inordinately forbidding ethos is experienced. In still other regions, the mood might vary from insidious to precarious.

The redoubtable state of Red China has not only turned against the missionary; he has been ridiculed, jailed, maligned, expelled, and above all, rejected. In North Korea, all that is left of a once promising and refreshing mission field is a remnant of starving, homeless, and aching humanity. A Vietnam population, for the most part Roman Catholic, has fallen victim to Communist repression.

India and Indonesia admit missionaries under strictly enforced immigration laws. Even what cracks in the walls of exclusion remain open are under constant surveillance. New legislation is an ever-present threat. Always in store, too, are stricter interpretations of immigration rules, regulations, and procedures. Considerable segments of public opinion across the non-Christian world support once and for all exclusion of the foreign missionary.

There are some observers who entertain high expectations that Japan is different. They foresee the rise of a moderate, enlightened policy. A Christianity might then come into being in Japan, nationally tolerated and recognized, relatively secure. Even in that hoped-for event, large-scale conversions are scarcely anticipated at all.

The last quarter century saw an African Islam which added twenty million new adherents. For the full Christian picture at exactly the same time, statistics are not available. The Roman Catholic Church reports just ten million converts for the same period. At present, 40 percent of Africa's Negro population are Muslims, whereas but 7½ percent owe allegiance to Rome.

No wonder devout Christians are prone under the circumstances to question the validity of missionary programs. Such questioning finds its best answer in church history itself. Missionary enterprise, for one thing, happens to be an expression of Christian faith in action. For another, the faithful are persuaded the church received its mission from its divine Founder. The missionary movement is, furthermore, not only a singular attribute of the faith, it is an obligation — that is to say, an obligation corresponding with belief in an invisible fundamental of life and growth through self-realization in service.

As an act of faith, the mission is an apostolate: a ministry of reconciliation rooted in creative, redemptive, and revelatory work of God. It is a form of God's love reaching out to all men.[21] As an act of faith, this apostolate is not sustained by human security. It must inevitably pick its footsteps across stony pathways and rugged conditions.

In the face of aimlessness, fear, feebleness, and cynicism, the apostolate means a ring of triumph is heard around the world. "This is the victory that overcometh the world, even, our faith." (I John 5:4.) The past teaches us with regard to Christian mission that the ring of an apostolate is a determining factor in the faith and destiny of the believer and his church. In the encounter now shaping up between Christianity and the other faiths, the fact of missionary concern is paramount.

The three great world faiths — Buddhism, Christianity, and Islam — are all missionary religions. The Buddha himself was a wandering preacher. The cause of Buddhist mission owes a primary debt to King Asoka who about 250 B.C. designated missionaries to serve in India and abroad. Whatever dynamic spirit Buddhist monks possessed, it was concealed under a thick overlay of mysticism. One looks in vain in the Buddhist gospel and ethics for a prophetic "either-or" challenge. Buddhist mission operated instead under the formula that religious truth was "not only this" but "that as well."

The brunt of prophetic missionary dynamism among world religions devolved upon Christianity and Islam. The early predicament of these two faiths in the environment that gave them birth was one of opposition, persecution, and rejection. Prophetic religions that they were, Christianity and Islam were regarded as alien in every land they entered. They were resolutely and passionately resisted, the attempt to shake them off being rarely relaxed. Such was the sort of reception accorded the early church. Nascent Islam did not fare much better in its native Mecca.

But the pattern of ostracism and attrition did not last forever. The fifteen centuries beginning from Constantine saw the church enjoy featherbedding. After 1800, this situation began to change, owing to new political settings, the advance of science, and the growth of

[21] R. Pierce Beaver, "The Apostolate of the Church," *The Theology of the Christian Mission,* ed. by Gerald H. Anderson (McGraw-Hill Book Company, Inc., 1961), p. 258.

modern rivalries to living faith; although in some respects it remained virtually the same. Islam likewise for over a millennium waxed rich and fattened on the bounties of empire — Arab, Mogul, or Ottoman.

Characteristically Islamic is the notion of a religious humanity encompassed in a political, theocratic world order. It seemed to follow that an Islamic mission prosecuted with fire and sword was not primarily a matter of religious expansion. It was, rather, an attempt to build a political state through exercise of military and strategic domination. "Indeed, we sent forth among every nation a messenger, saying: Serve you God and eschew idols. Then some of them God guided and some were justly disposed to err. So journey in the land and behold how was the end of them that cried lies."[22] The historical fact is clear. When Islam the empire collapsed, the faith saw signs of new birth and the more distinctly religious mission was crowned with signal success.

Christian mission bases itself formally on the Great Commission pronounced by Christ. "Go ye therefore, and teach all nations, baptizing them in the name of the Father, and of the Son, and of the Holy Ghost: Teaching them to observe all things whatsoever I have commanded you: and, lo, I am with you alway, even unto the end of the World. Amen." (Matt. 28:19-20. Cf. Mark 16:15, probably taken from Matthew.) As for the substance of Christian mission, there is a design rooted in the offer of salvation to all mankind. Associated therewith is a prophetic authority. The claim to the truth is absolute, unequivocal. "Neither is there salvation in any other: for there is none other name under heaven given among men, whereby we must be saved." (Acts 4:12.)

Mission is a central living function of genuine Christianity. The first missionary, Paul, considered preaching to the heathen his primary obligation. (Gal. 2:9.) Across the centuries, violent missionary methods and improper tactics were not unknown. However, a persuasive missionary calling and outlook, steeped in prophetic faith, armed with divine mandate, and undergirded by a sense of responsibility and obligation — those are the manifest power of love which incarnate what Christianity really is.

[22] Koran 16:37–38. Cf. *The Koran Interpreted,* Arthur J. Arberry (George Allen & Unwin, Ltd., London, 1955), Vol. I, p. 290.

III

Christianity is furthermore ecumenical. The ecumenical movement took form in the first half of the twentieth century. It had a dual origin. There was, first of all, a trend spearheaded by Charles H. Brent (1862–1929) in his career and contributions as bishop of the Protestant Episcopal Church, missionary, and statesman. Bishop Brent caught the vision of unity among the churches.[23]

In the summer of 1910, the World Missionary Conference was held at Edinburgh. It was an event crucial in ecumenical history. On that conference many nineteenth-century events and trends converged. Edinburgh may be regarded as a watershed between miscellaneous ecumenical strivings and the integral ecumenical movement of more recent times.[24]

Edinburgh was attended by representatives of missionary bodies responsible for action in areas of non-Western cultures. It was the first such major conference of modern history. Present were missionary delegates as well as spokesmen of indigenous churches in Asia and Africa.

Representatives of missionary churches contested at Edinburgh the wisdom of mission boards and societies in perpetuating denominationalism and confessionalism on the field. These divisions, it was argued, obscured the reality of such new communions as had meanwhile come into being: for instance, the Church of India, the Church of Japan, and the Church of China.

Upon his return from the Edinburgh Conference to the U.S.A., Bishop Brent induced the General Convention of the Protestant Episcopal Church to support the cause of church unity.[25] He charged that such estrangement as existed was contrary to the original teaching of Christ with regard to the church. He advocated a rapprochement among the Christian Confessions which implemented the will of Christ as expressed in his great high-priestly prayer: "That they may be made perfect in one; and that the world may know that

[23] Latourette, *op. cit.*, pp. 1344–1345.

[24] Ruth Rouse and Stephen Charles Neill, eds., *A History of the Ecumenical Movement, 1517–1948* (The Westminster Press, 1954), p. 258.

[25] F. L. Cross, ed., *The Oxford Dictionary of the Christian Church* (Oxford University Press, London, 1957), p. 195.

thou hast sent me, and hast loved them, as thou hast loved me" (John 17:23).

Suspended by the war of 1914–1918, the movement was revived upon cessation of hostilities, and pursued with vigor. Patient negotiations and preparatory steps culminated in the First World Conference held in 1927 at Lausanne,[26] whereof Brent was president. This great ecumenical meeting took the faith and constitution of the church as its chief concern. From it came the Faith and Order wing of the ecumenical movement.

When the Lausanne Conference assembled in the handsome buildings of the University, August 3, 1927, there were one hundred and eight churches represented. Most non-Roman Confessions had accepted invitations to attend. Doctrinal divergences were studied in complete freedom and candor and in a moving spirit of charity. The confession of faith, the concept of the church, the sacraments, the ministries, and church unity were examined. A call to unity was addressed to the Christian world: God desires the unity of the church. Our presence here proves our resolve to join our will to his. We will never continue as we were before.

When the Lausanne Conference came to review its work at the close, the full Conference received a report, largely the work of Prof. Adolf Deissmann: "The Church's Message to the World — the Gospel." This was a document accepted by the members of the Orthodox churches as well as by the rest of the Conference. It was destined to play a role decisive in shaping the ecumenical movement. Before the Lausanne Conference dispersed, a Continuation Committee of ninety-two men and three women was appointed. William Temple, the then Anglican Archbishop of York, was called upon to preside after the death of Bishop Brent. With what brilliance did Temple discharge his office till an untimely death overtook him in 1944.

In order to trace the ecumenical movement back to its other origin, we must look in another direction. As the tragic years of World War I dragged on, there was one great churchman whose mind was set on unity. He knew that as soon as an armistice was signed, the churches must concert their efforts toward the making of a more stable peace. That churchman was Nathan Söderblom (1866–1931), Lutheran Archbishop of Uppsala. Söderblom was a statesman of

[26] H. N. Bate, ed., *Faith and Order* (SCM Press Ltd., London, 1927).

note, a prophet of ecumenicity, and a man of thought and prayer. His point of departure was altogether different from that of Bishop Brent.

Archbishop Söderblom did not think in terms of confrontation between church doctrines or along the lines of ecclesiastical structures and governments. His aim was, rather, to organize the practical cooperation of the churches: to attack social questions without undue regard for confessional barriers. He took a stand on the terrain of the church's life and action. Even while the war still raged, he entered upon correspondence with the churches of neutral countries.

As early as 1919, Söderblom called together a preparatory conference in Paris. From all quarters, the churches gave hearty response to the invitations that were issued. However, the Roman Catholic Church declined the bid to the Paris meeting as it also declined to attend the later Lausanne Conference. Out of these multiple soundings and proceedings came the Universal Christian Conference on Life and Work, held at Stockholm,[27] August 19 and 20, 1925, two years prior to Lausanne.

The Stockholm Conference drew together over five hundred representatives of the larger bodies of non-Roman Christendom. For the first time in history, representatives of Eastern Orthodoxy, as well as those of the Old Catholics, sat down with delegates of the churches of the Reformation. As its declared purpose, this Universal Christian Conference on Life and Work resolved: to concentrate the mind of Christendom on the mind of Christ as revealed in the Gospels toward those great social, industrial, and international questions which are so acutely urgent in our civilization.[28]

A moving message was voted. It expressed penitence for failure of the churches to do their duty. It affirmed the obligation to apply the gospel " in all realms of human life "; but it limited " the mission of the church " which " is above all to state principles and to assert the ideal while leaving to individual conscience and to communities the duty of applying them with charity, wisdom, and courage." The Stockholm Conference appointed a Continuation Committee; this

[27] G. K. A. Bell, ed., *The Stockholm Conference, 1925* (Oxford University Press, London, 1926).

[28] Norman Goodall, *The Ecumenical Movement* (Oxford University Press, London, 1961), pp. 60–61.

was reconstituted in 1930 as a permanent body: The Universal Christian Council for Life and Work.

In the view of Bishop Brent and others, the Edinburgh Missionary Council of 1910 did not merely reveal the importance of a great task and enterprise. On the eve of a devastating world holocaust, it set in bold relief an obligation to coordinate all missionary forces. It spotlighted the need to integrate the younger churches within the world communion of churches.

Such was the dual incentive that brought the International Missionary Council into being. It held a great assembly on the Mount of Olives at Easter time, March 24 to April 8, 1928. That was the historic gathering known as the Jerusalem Meeting of the International Missionary Council.[29] Following Stockholm and Lausanne, the Jerusalem meeting was devoted to the evangelistic character of the ecumenical movement.

Thus on the morrow of World War I, a majority of the Christian churches had committed themselves together. By three different highways, which had led to Stockholm, Lausanne, and Jerusalem — eventually to merge in a common procession — they all sought unity and mission. A vivid vision of ecumenical unity was undergirded by more profound comprehension and theological reflection.

As for the Roman Catholic Church, an official declaration stated its inability to do otherwise than remain outside the nascent ecumenical movement. In 1919, a delegation of Protestant Episcopal bishops from the United States was received by Pope Benedict XV. The reception was cordial. But the words of the pope were a prelude to refusal: refusal to join any ecumenical assembly that did not acknowledge the Bishop of Rome as the source and cause of the church's unity.

The Vatican's rejection of an invitation to the ecumenical movement served as a reminder of the papal thesis: The successor of St. Peter, Vicar of Jesus Christ, prays that those who participate in the Lausanne Assembly could, by the grace of God, see the light and reunite with the visible Head of the Church who will receive them with open arms.[30]

[29] *Report of the Jerusalem Meeting of the International Missionary Council* (Oxford University Press, London, 1928), 8 vols.

[30] Cf. Rouse and Neill, *op. cit.*, p. 416.

Under the presidency of Cardinal D. J. Mercier and the initiative of Lord Halifax, conversations between Anglican and Roman Catholic theologians took place at Malines, Belgium, between 1921 and 1925. But these so-called Malines Conversations were disavowed in 1928 by Pope Pius XI in his encyclical *Mortalium animos.* In its initial stages, the ecumenical movement gave rise in Rome to the fear of equivocation and doctrinal confusion. Ecumenicity was thus summarily condemned under the name of pan-Christianity. If the Roman Catholic attitude has remained virtually unchanged, it is only proper to state that at different junctures this attitude has expressed itself in a variety of shades and nuances.[31]

It is difficult to exaggerate the important role of Continuation Committees. Such committees came into being in the wake of the Stockholm, Lausanne, and Jerusalem assemblies. These continuation committees held annual meetings which were Lausanne, Stockholm, or Jerusalem conferences in miniature. They drew leaders into fellowship and consultation. Major issues came under constant discussion. Arrival at important decisions was furthered by a steady process of education in one another's tenets. A Department of Study, established in Geneva, rendered a great contribution. The commission set up at Lausanne in order to study the doctrine of grace and the sacraments as well as the ministry of the church was also creative.

The primary goal of the ecumenical movement has not been to propose doctrinal compromises or to promote ecclesiastical mergers. The main goal was that hitherto estranged Christians and those indifferent toward one another should meet for the following reasons: to know one another, to take cognizance of what unites and what divides the churches, to study together the Biblical foundations of doctrine and of ecclesiastical institutions.

In a world, moreover, where peace hangs so delicately in the balance, where totalitarian trends are manifest, some attempt is necessary to discern the true mission of the church in every nation, in relation to the state, and in the world of nations. Such are some of the elements of the new climate in which all have to live, or to which they needed to be introduced by participation in the ecumenical movement.

[31] Cf. Marc Boegner, "Le mouvement oecuménique contemporaine et le problème de l'unité chrétienne," *Encyclopédie française,* Tome XIX, pp. 465–469.

It had been foreseen from the beginning that the conferences which gave birth to three branches of the movement would have a sequel. The year 1937 was chosen for an Oxford Conference on Life and Work [32] held July 12 to 20. In the same summer, the Second World Conference on Faith and Order, continuing the task of Lausanne, was held in Edinburgh.[33] In 1938, a universal conference on missions was to be held in the Far East.

A problem had meanwhile arisen in the course of discussions emanating from the Department of Study to which the Stockholm Conference had referred a project for investigation of perplexing ethical, social, and international issues. The problem revolved upon the growing conviction that it was both idle and vain to seek resolution of such matters until the role of the church in society and the nature of its function had been better determined and more clearly clarified.

A profound study of the church's relation to the state, and of the state's relation to the community was implicit. Hence the general theme chosen for the Oxford 1937 Conference: "Church, Community, and State." Hence, too, the central question raised prior to both the Oxford and Edinburgh conferences of that year: Is there not a way for elimination of such duality: Faith/Order and Life/Work, which the two principal branches of the ecumenical movement seem to imply?

Indeed when the Oxford and Edinburgh conferences opened, both bodies were seized of the request formulated by authorized representatives of the ecumenical movement. In effect, the request was that Stockholm and Lausanne be united more closely in an organic assembly of the churches, assuming the responsibility entrusted to the two branches of the ecumenical movement.

Subject to certain modifications proposed by the Second Edinburgh Conference, the plan of unification was approved and adopted. Each of the conferences, Oxford and Edinburgh, designated seven members charged with execution of that decision.

Deliberations of that "Committee of Fourteen" culminated in a

[32] *The Churches Survey Their Task* (George Allen & Unwin, Ltd., London, 1937), 7 vols.

[33] Leonard Hodgson, ed., *The Second World Conference on Faith and Order* (SCM Press Ltd., London, 1937).

conference at Utrecht in May, 1938. When the Continuation Committee of the Faith and Order branch met at Clarens, later in the year, it discussed a draft constitution of the World Council of Churches. It agreed that the World Conference on Faith and Order should become a part of such a World Council of Churches when organized. A new chapter was about to be written in the story of ecumenicity.

An etymological explanation of the word "ecumenical" might at this juncture serve the purpose. "Ecumenical" is a term derived from the Greek *oikos,* house. It designates the "inhabited world" as if it were one great "household." In this sense, *oikoumenē,* in the nominative case, occurs in many New Testament passages. "Ecumenical" and "Catholic" are virtually synonymous. The former bears an accent on universality, the latter on totality.

The ecumenical movement is an expression of the churches' longing to meet, study, act, and pray together. Those are churches that find it impossible any longer to hold that any particular church is in itself or by itself alone the one true church of Christ. Those are churches, moreover, that have discovered that every church has something to receive from others as well as something to impart. They are thus illumined by a vision of the church universal: calling upon all communions and denominations in their "togetherness" to offer a visible testimony to the reality of the *Una Sancta,* the One Holy Church.

Such a reality exists and nothing can annul it. "We cannot seek union unless we already possess unity," said William Temple at Edinburgh. Those were words that set the true significance of the ecumenical movement in proper light. They illumined the manner for posing the problem of church unity.

In May, 1938, the Utrecht Conference had drafted a constitution for the World Council of Churches. Headquarters were established in Geneva, Switzerland, and as of 1938, "The World Council of Churches in process of formation" began to function. It was admittedly provisional in character. Its resolutions were subject to ratification at the First General Assembly to be held in principle in the U.S.A. in 1941. War broke out in 1939, however, and delayed a formal opening of the organization.

It seemed advisable in the meantime to hold a meeting in January, 1939, at Saint-Germain-en-Laye. A decision was then reached to send a letter announcing the forthcoming establishment of the World Council of Churches to the Holy See. The letter recalled that earlier communications had convinced the senders that the Roman Catholic Church did not desire to be associated with the ecumenical movement and its efforts toward unity of the churches. Courtesy nevertheless required, the letter went on, that the Holy See be kept informed of what was being done. Hope was at the same time expressed that an occasion might sometime present itself for private contacts with Roman Catholic theologians. The response of the Vatican left the door for contacts but partly open.

The years of World War II were now upon mankind. It was a time when darkness covered a large part of the earth. From its very inception, albeit in provisional structure, the World Council of Churches was called upon to discharge heavy responsibilities. On the one hand, it had to maintain communion among Christians of warring states; on the other, it was constrained to take the initiative in mutual aid imposed on an accelerating scale by the tragic distresses of total war.

A vast inquiry was in the meantime carried out in Geneva under the Department of Study and in conjunction with the General Secretariat. That was an inquiry into the responsibility of the church in the international order. Involved was the function of the church in society.

Another organ was the Commission on Refugees, which wrestled with a situation destined to grow in complexity with the passing years. A kindred commission was, thirdly, set up to provide spiritual aid among prisoners of war. The personality of the ecumenical movement was more and more recognized, especially in countries where its ministries were authorized.

There was a fourth department, that of Reconstruction and Inter-Church Aid. The task assigned it was that of spiritual and material rehabilitation of churches and institutions imperiled by war. Fifthly, an Ecumenical Institute was formally inaugurated at the Château de Bossey, some twelve miles from Geneva. Its purpose was defined as the formation of an apostolic leadership. The Institute thus sought peaceful penetration of the community at various levels and in diverse areas of operation. New services for lay people were thereby opened up in many churches. Many in secular life were thus encouraged and trained to reach out in their chosen occupations as ambassadors of Christ and the church to a world of profound spiritual need and hunger.

Finally, a commission of the churches on International Affairs came into being in the summer of 1946. It was the outcome of a conference held in Cambridge, England, at the call of the then Federal Council of the Churches of Christ in the U.S.A., and notably at the initiative of Walter Van Kirk. This commission was conceived as an organ for study and witness in the field of international relations. Kenneth Grubb, of London, was appointed Director, and O. F. Nolde, of New York, Associate Director. It owed its origin to a joint understanding that brought the World Council of Churches and the International Missionary Council to effective partnership. The commission rendered highly significant service, particularly in the critical years 1946–1956.

At Geneva the total effort of the churches began to bear fruit. A body of highly qualified specialists took the lead. As a visible demonstration of the churches' ecumenicity, a cluster of departments and commissions arose around the General Secretariat. Those brought together a multiplicity of races and nations, of creeds and confessions, all within the household of faith.

Through arduous and tearful years, progress was slowly achieved. All hearts looked toward the day when the formative period would end and the Provisional Committee would remit its power to the First General Assembly of the World Council of Churches. That epoch-making event did take place at Amsterdam, August 22 to September 4, 1948.

The Amsterdam Assembly, which officially instituted the World Council of Churches, had for its theme: " Man's Disorder and God's Design." [34] In the history of the ecumenical movement it marked arrival and departure. It concluded a union on the basis of doughty effort. Intercession, faith, theological reflection, and above all, love, which could be stronger than all things that divide, had prospered the efforts. An exigency received from Christ himself had brought the union into being. At work was fidelity to the Truth whereby

[34] W. A. Visser 't Hooft, ed., *The Amsterdam Series* (SCM Press Ltd., London, 1949), 5 vols.

each Christian thinks his own particular church is the authentic witness.

Amsterdam was hailed as a momentous event of profound spiritual significance. It brought together hundreds of personalities drawn from all points of the compass. It attested before all eyes, and through them to mankind, that the Christian churches are ready to resume their march together. It was a march unhappily interrupted during years of agony. It was a march toward visible manifestation of the unity of the body of Christ.

It was on the second day of the Amsterdam Assembly that the World Council of Churches was declared constituted. At Amsterdam was thus achieved the purely constitutional phase of the ecumenical movement. Theological discussions of the central theme were to enrich Christian thought for a long time to come. Such discussions revolved upon four separate parts: The Universal Church in God's Design, The Church's Witness to God's Design, The Church and the Disorder of Society, and The Church and International Disorder.

Amsterdam furthermore marked a point of departure. It was not just a reunion of delegates from a hundred and fifty denominations. These denominations formally met together at Amsterdam. Before the gaze of Christianity, the exact role and position of the World Council of Churches was revealed. What the World Council of Churches was, what it was not, became a subject for long debate and serene inquiry. At the Second General Assembly held at Evanston, Illinois, 1954, these discussions were continued.

Obviously, the World Council of Churches is not a superchurch. It exercises no ecclesiastical authority. No church loses its autonomy in joining the world body. The World Council of Churches neither negotiates unions nor promotes mergers. However, it does offer a point of contact between churches contemplating union. In itself the Council does not represent a particular concept of the church. Upon joining the Council, no church need think of its own conception of the church as relative. Nor does such a church need to adopt a concept of church unity which happens to be that of the Council.

At its meeting in Toronto, held in July, 1950, the Central Committee of the World Council of Churches received and made response to the question: What is the World Council of Churches?

In accordance with the above document, the World Council of Churches is of the opinion that conversation among the churches, their cooperation in a common witness, are founded on a common faith that Christ is the divine Head of the church. It relies, therefore, on the teaching of Christ, and of the apostles, as contained in the New Testament, in affirming the unity of the church of Christ.

Common reflection on the relation of the churches to the holy and universal church, confessed in the ecumenical creed, was suggested as a further step to be taken in seeking an answer to the question raised. Emphasis was laid on the following. Membership in the World Council of Churches does not require a church to regard other churches as churches in the same meaning of the word. The direct opposite is what an Eastern Orthodox theologian maintained. Every church, he proposed, in faithfulness to what it regards as true ecumenicity of which it believes itself as holding the deposit, would regard other churches heretical as regards doctrines taught by the church itself.

Solidarity among the churches does imply, nevertheless, an obligation to cooperate in interchurch aid. They do commit themselves solemnly to refrain from any act incompatible with maintenance of fraternal relations. Such spiritual relations as they establish among themselves shall contribute to constant renewal of their life and the edification of the body of Christ in their being.

The Evanston Assembly[35] of 1954, Second World Council of Churches, completed the administrative organization of the ecumenical body. The Assembly was held under the Biblical and dogmatic theme: "Christ the Only Hope of the World." The several divisions and offices were placed under the jurisdiction of the General Secretariat in Geneva.

Those are the divisions directed by the General Secretary and Associate General Secretaries.

1. An Ecumenical Action Division with subsections including Youth, Laity, Men and Women, and an Ecumenical Institute.
2. A Study Division including Faith and Order, Church and Society, Missionary Studies, and Evangelism departments.
3. Inter-Church Aid and Service to Refugees.
4. Commission of the Churches on International Affairs with a

[35] W. A. Visser 't Hooft, *The Evanston Report* (SCM Press Ltd., London, 1955).

Director in London and an Associate Director in New York.

Since Evanston, 1954, the World Council Central Committee met at Switzerland, Hungary, the U.S.A., Denmark, and on the island of Rhodes. In 1960, on the fiftieth anniversary of the Edinburgh Conference, it appropriately met in Scotland. In 1956 and 1960, the small Executive Committee of twelve met in Australia and Argentina, respectively.

The Third Assembly of the World Council of Churches met at Vigyan Bhavan, New Delhi, India,[36] November 18 to December 6, 1961. The theme was "Jesus Christ — the Light of the World." Integration of the World Council of Churches and the International Missionary Council was the chief accomplishment of the assembly. The International Missionary Council was renamed the Commission on World Mission and Evangelism. It became a division of the World Council of Churches and had headquarters in Geneva with offices in London and New York. It continued to hold its own gatherings every few years. The first such postintegration meeting took place December 7 and 8 immediately after the New Delhi Assembly.

A new climate has gradually come to many churches of the world. It was signalized at New Delhi upon admission of the Russian Orthodox Church into the World Council of Churches. Nothing like this had ever happened before, not since the schisms that rocked Christendom in the eleventh and sixteenth centuries. In Western Christianity, the concept of the church — pivotal to any understanding — divides Roman Catholics and Protestants to a degree that they cannot recognize each other as one flock under one shepherd. They must leave in God's hand the question whether, and how far, they ought to be one.[37]

The Roman Catholic Church, as already intimated, from the very inception of the drive toward unity, affirmed and reaffirmed its own special doctrine of church unity. A growing number of its learned representatives, however, continued to show an interest in the World Council of Churches. On October 11, 1962, the Ecumenical (Second Vatican) Council of the Roman Catholic Church opened. In this and other moves, an apparent readiness to wrestle with ecumenical problems was exhibited.

36 *The New Delhi Report* (Association Press, 1962).

37 See Karl Barth, *Theology and Church: Shorter Writings, 1920–1928* (Harper & Row, Publishers, Inc., 1962), p. 273.

Whether they recognize it or not, all churches are drawn together by an irreversible trend. Today no church needs to stand alone. Those churches which have chosen to remain outside the ecumenical movement — be they the Roman Catholic, Orthodox, Ancient, Protestant, or sectarian — have a compelling sense of urgency to converge. All men and churches who sincerely confess Jesus Christ as Lord and Savior belong in the Christian *koinōnia* and share in common Christian history. For the present, a neat ecclesiological formulary is not to be expected.[38]

In short, the phenomenon of Christianity reveals that the churches are drawn together and impelled toward self-examination in depth and height. Their efforts to listen together to the revelation contained in the Scriptures are manifest as are their longings to grasp the mystery of the church and of its intrinsic unity. The churches await the day when all the redeemed shall be brought together as one. It will be a day when believers and churches, of every order and creed, shall accede to the plenitude of hope and grace.

The Phenomenon of Islam

Clear-cut and distinctive patterns of faith, thought, and life disclose the phenomenon of Islam, serving to differentiate its role in history. An apparent utter simplicity, bordering on formlessness of design and organization, ought not to turn our gaze from the splendor, robust character, and intricate making of this faith.

A pattern that hews closely to the line of Koranic doctrine is primary. Accent falls here upon God's sovereignty and omnipotence. Faith is acknowledged in a self-disclosing compassionate Allah. The intelligent Moslem encounters more than a fair share of contradiction between the Koran's theological decrees and modern scientific methodology as applied in the history of religions. In his study of the sacred text, he has not yet fully adjusted to such techniques as those of textual criticism. Although a battle has long raged between faith and reason, theology and science, the outcome is not yet clear, the issues remain in doubt.

Islam is heir to an impressive, medieval Arab culture. This is a heritage comprising humanist and scientific components of the highest order. It has served as a vehicle in the communication of the

[38] Albert C. Outler, *The Christian Tradition and the Unity We Seek* (Oxford University Press, London, 1957), pp. 147–148.

Koranic message. Few religions have been better served by their own Latin than Islam by Arabic. Arab culture performed a key role not only in the dissemination of Islam and edification of the Muslim. It rendered a contribution to world civilization: in astronomy and mathematics, in medicine and sociology, in art and architecture — to cite but a few notable areas. By virtue of these and a vigorous theology coupled with military might and economic wealth, the Caliphates moved from strength to strength.

A holy war, *jihad,* psychology, virtually outmoded, is yet hardly without echoes in contemporary Islamic consciousness. Essentially an attitude and temper, the " good fight " ideal is explicit in Islamic statecraft inherent in evolving social institutions.

Concrete yet quiet compensation for loss of empire came indirectly. It came in the expansion of a globe-encircling brotherhood of the believers; also more recently, in achievement of political freedom from foreign domination.

A direct and historic flair for law and jurisprudence is a pattern peculiarly Islamic. This is a pattern instinct with meaning. Sacred law has a way of permeating all that pertains to political organization, communal integrity, and the resurgence of new states. Such constitutional and juridical foundations are not detachable from theology: a theology that breathes worship of Allah, inculcates the message of the Arabian Prophet, and knits all believers in bonds of close fraternity and fellowship within the community of Allah.

In sum, a dynamic determination is the outcome of Islam's beliefs and institutions. Such a determination is sharpened in the name of an Islamic nation *ummah,* a community of solidarity and destiny. It is a determination annually confirmed on a universal plane at the time of the pilgrimage, *hajj.* There the Islamic community discovers itself afresh each passing year.

Quickened in a moment of exaltation and reawakening of godliness, the community spirit is fired with enthusiasm. As pilgrims from all over the world head toward Mecca, Islam's Holy Land in Saudi Arabia's Hijaz province becomes a rallying point, a source of renewal and strength.

Within the confines of such a community, the higher life consists in dignity, honor, and personal religion. Against individual and massive turpitude, against crass ignorance and unbelief, Islam summons the faithful to an exemplary pattern of living.

I

Islam is, above all else, a religion. It is a religion of absolute submission. Next to Christianity, Islam stands as numerically largest among world religions. Founded by the Prophet Mohammed (ca. A.D. 571–632), it carries recollections of seventh-century vestiges of Arabia's folk religion.

Against the polytheistic notions of his kinsmen Mohammed bravely elected to tread the dangerous grounds of theism. He unalterably committed himself to the doctrine of divine revelation. His was an austere and unequivocal view of revealed truth. Upon that central position, he wagered all. He lost little time in declaring for the sovereignty of Allah. He vehemently warned of an imminent judgment.

"Arise! Warn!"[1] may not have been his initially revealed utterance. Nonetheless, these two words do convey his sense of urgency if not his marching orders. Man lives in callous indifference, largely because of his fear of fate. Yet only God's judgments fashion his nature and shape his destiny. Hence a universal thirst for redemption. The genius of nascent Islam spells itself in an experience of God.

Experienced as sovereign, Allah is proclaimed as indeterminable will. Beside him there is no other God. There is no being independent of him. There is no law, be it moral or otherwise, which stands above the Godhead. Necessity prescribes that all persons and things be tributary to him.

As for this world's goods, power, and status, they are ultimate in neither form nor degree. The Almighty assigns a green pasture unto whomsoever he elects. Of his own unworthiness Mohammed himself had no illusions. Yet how gracious unto him Allah indeed was. To him the Lord revealed the miraculous chapters of a Holy Book. Such is the note of irrationality struck with incredible cadence and vivid imagery.

The God of Mohammed is a sovereign Lord. He is unpredictable,

[1] Koran 74:2. See Arthur Jeffery, ed., *Islam: Muhammad and His Religion* (The Liberal Arts Press, Inc., 1958), p. 6.

inscrutable. He is unknowable, inaccessible. Yet upon him all that have breath must inevitably depend. He created the world. By effective decree he governs all things. The creation is nevertheless predicated upon an immanent law. The certainty of divine intervention is proof positive Allah is accountable to no one.

Whosoever exists is under an inexorable natural law. As such it can be of but accidental concern to the Creator. Whatever has life, and whatever happens to exist, might at any moment lapse. It is snuffed off, rescinded, suspended, as the case might be. By divine fiat, all are in time cut off.

What the Eternal requires of man, the divine law stipulates. The universal character of Islamic legislation is explicit in its total all-embracing scope and dimension. It includes ordinances touching every aspect and sphere of existence. These ordinances are articulate wherever religion and society meet and interact. Everywhere they are vibrant, whether in the order of the sacred or that of the profane. Next to the religion of ancient Israel, Islam ranks as a religion of book and law. Under a single legal determination, the entire gamut of a believer's existence falls.

From those fundamental conceptions, two dispositions of human behavior derive their origin: an unpredictable, fully irrational sovereignty of divine will power imposes an unconditional and absolute surrender, *Islam*. True, such unintelligible and unexplainable incidents as do happen are governed by the mercy and compassion of Allah. Yet one looks in vain for an assurance "that all things work together for good to them that love God, to them who are the called according to his purpose" (Rom. 8:28).

Might such a will of the Eternal lead men astray? In the Koran,[2] one reads: "Whomsoever God desires to guide, He expands his breast to Islam; whomsoever He desires to lead astray, He makes his breast narrow, tight, as if he were climbing to heaven. So God lays abomination upon those who believe not." Yet, modern Islamic theology repudiates any suggestion of demonic features in the Koranic idea of God.

At his will and pleasure God is merciful. Surrender to him ought not, however, to be altogether understood as fatalism. This surrender,

[2] 6:125. See Arthur J. Arberry, *The Koran Interpreted* (George Allen & Unwin, Ltd., London, 1955), Vol. I, p. 164.

in its genuine form, consists in a religious disposition of the soul. Nor is surrender to God soundly understood as a diffuse and motionless passivity. Taken for what it is, true surrender of heart and mind must be evaluated in terms of religious essence: the total dependence of man and his destiny upon an irrational divine will.

The other disposition of the Muslim heart and personality follows in neat order. Molded as he is sustained by pragmatic unconditional surrender, the believer must live in absolute obedience to the law. Islam may be said to have scored its major victories as it regimented the lives of men and led them through to the fulfillment of doctrinal obligations.

As indicated above, such doctrinal obligations embraced the whole fabric of existence. Alongside the demands of the cultus stood the order of civil and penal law, forms of salutation, greetings, and address, as well as a protocol for dining, social intercourse, and dietary regulations.

Major doctrinal obligations are the so-called five " Pillars ": 1. The creedal confession, *shahadah:* " There is no other God than Allah." 2. Ritual prayer, *salah:* to be performed at five prescribed seasons daily, in a precise, well-defined posture, to the accompaniment of proper gestures. 3. Alms, *zakah,* charities to be levied on a fixed capital tax rate. 4. The Fast of the month of Ramadan: abstinence from food throughout the livelong day. 5. The pilgrimage, *hajj,* to Mecca and vicinity, at least once in a lifetime.

In a memorable passage, the Koran [3] crystallizes the ethos of the Islamic religion and defines the nature of its godliness: " It is not Godliness that ye turn your faces to the East and the West; but Godliness is he who believes in Allah and the last day and the angels and the Scripture and the Prophets; and gives his wealth for love of Him, to kinfolk and to orphans and the needy and the wayfarer and to those who ask, and to set slaves free; and observes proper worship and pays the poor-due. And those who keep their treaty when they make one and the patient in tribulation and adversity and time of stress. Such are they who are sincere. Such are the God-fearing."

[3] 2:172. Cf. Mohammed Marmaduke Pickthall, *The Meaning of the Glorious Koran* (The New American Library of World Literature, Inc., a Mentor Book, 1954), p. 48.

On the sociological side of things Islam disclosed itself as theocracy. One expects and finds that the divine legislation bears certain results. Islamic legislation is not in the last analysis merely concerned with rules and regulations for trade, business administration, personal status, and restraint of Allah's servants. Legislation extended its scope and operation to include family law, society in its private and public sectors, and above all, the duties and responsibilities of subjects in a theocratic state.[4]

One ventures this further observation on the relation between religion and state. Islam exhibits a reversal of common trends in folk religion. For in a folk religion, the vital community (or state) may be said to achieve status and dignity sanctioned by religion. In a world religion such as Islam, however, the interests of the religious community are tacitly at the mercy of those who hold the reins of political power. It is therefore clear why in Islam the religious community, *ummah,* must function as an arm of the secular order even though religious law forms the backbone of society.

Over non-Muslims, only Islamic sovereignty and military power prevailed. Non-Muslims did not come under sacred legislation, theological doctrine, or jurisprudence. Equally inaccurate historically is it to say that Islamic expansion took place through fire and sword. Military operations undertaken early by Mohammed had by the time of his death secured partial mastery of western Arabia. Those and subsequent Arab campaigns had for objective the creation of an Islamic state and not as a rule propagation of the Islamic religion.

II

Marxist materialism happens to be the world's greatest revolutionary phenomenon since the eruption of Islam. An idea of action and interaction between these two revolutions might illumine both and throw light on Islamic vigor today. Indeed, the struggle of Islamic peoples under the Soviet regime is revelatory of Islamic stamina no less than of the Communist attitude to nationalities in their society.

[4] Muhammad Abu Zahra, "Family Law," in *Law in the Middle East,* ed. by Majid Khadduri and Herbert J. Liebesny (The Middle East Institute, 1955), Vol. I, pp. 132–178.

The Islamic Turkic peoples of Russia greeted the fall of the Romanov dynasty in March, 1917, as dawn of freedom from centuries of enslavement: "The country which for a long time played the role of a cruel mother toward us, which daily oppressed our Muslim brethren, humbled, crushed, and wronged them, that selfsame country wherein Muslims rated as third-class citizens now becomes to us a fatherland and mother."[5]

A surge of enthusiasm ran high as congress followed congress. Each of these congresses was held under the theme: "Religion, Freedom, National Independence." In March, 1917, Muslim representatives in Parliament, *Duma,* conferred and organized for the May All-Russian Muslim Congress, in due course attended by eight hundred delegates.

In July, 1917, a Muslim All-Russian War council sat in Kazan, attended by religious dignitaries. Close in its wake, another All-Russian Muslim Congress was held. At that time the political autonomy of Muslims in Turkic-Tatar Inner Russia and Siberia was projected. In November of that year, Muslims met at Ufa for their first National Assembly. As capital of Bashkir in East European Russia, Ufa had a telling symbolic character.

The conclusion was inescapable that intermittent Islamic struggle had netted nothing less than an intense anti-Slav feeling. A more positive and constructive outlook did not seem forthcoming.[6] If a national unification of Russia's Muslims was impending, it showed few signs of concord between the Islamic theological formula and the Marxist idealogy of the Russian Revolution. To the average pious Muslim, the aims of Bolshevism were awfully ambiguous.

As early as June 20, 1917, the All-Russian Congress of the Soviets endorsed in behalf of national minorities the principle of self-determination, including the right of secession.[7] However, cultural autonomy of Muslims within a liberal Russian state might be tantamount to secession. Instead, a category of independent state within a unified system was projected. The plan proposed by Enver Pasha,

[5] Josef Glazik, *Die Islammission der Russisch-Orthodoxen Kirche* (Aschendorffsche Verlagsbuchhandlung, Münster, 1959), pp. 164–180, cites primary source material.

[6] Consult J. Benzing, "Die Türkvölker der Sowjetunion," in *Der Orient in deutscher Forschung* (Leipzig, 1944).

[7] Michael T. Florinsky, *Russia* (The Macmillan Company, 1953), Vol. II, p. 1427.

the Ottoman statesman, for a Muslim federation in Central Asia, a virtual protectorate of the Turkish sultanate, never was more than a dead letter.

What did happen is that population transfers were set in motion on a grand scale. Turkish Muslim peoples en masse, for instance, the Crimean Turks, were subjected to wholesale compulsory migration and have since disappeared from the map. The influx of Slavs, who already under the czars had penetrated regions occupied by Turks, was accelerated. In connection with the Five Year Plans, and of the later wartime administration, the Slav's displacement of the Turk became a gigantic operation. The population of Turkistan is already one-quarter Slav.[8]

As for Islamic self-determination, it was never implemented. Rather did the Soviet Union enforce its own Communist version of autonomy. This took the form of four Turkic Soviet Republics: Uzbekistan, Turkmenistan, Kazakhstan, and Kirghizistan. There was a fifth republic in Caucasia: Azerbaijan. There was also formed under the name of Turkistan a Soviet Republic consisting of Iran's former Tajik subjects. These six political entities rank as so-called Federal Republics of the Soviet Union. A peg lower is the autonomy granted the Tatars, Bashkirs, Crimean Turks, and certain other lesser Islamic communities. In a word, toward Russia's Muslims, Lenin's policy was applied. They were to be national in form, Communist in essence.[9]

The Bolshevik authorities fomented disunity among the Turkic peoples. As far back as 1917, the Party Congress had sought to resolve the problem of Russia's "nationalities." Plans were laid down but never carried out. Such plans, at any rate, were received by Muslims with ill grace and denounced as prejudicial to their welfare. Hence the determination of the Revolutionaries to reduce the Islamic bloc and to whittle down its solidarity through systematic polarization and fragmentation.

A look at those opening years of the Russian Revolution reveals the staunch character of the Russian Muslim. How unceasingly the

[8] F. W. Fernau, *Moslems on the March* (Alfred A. Knopf, Inc., 1954), pp. 251–252.

[9] Walter Kolarz, *Russia and Her Colonies* (George Philip & Son, Ltd., London, 1952), p. 258.

Muslim pressed to pry himself loose from the Revolutionary grip. In a Communist manifesto of November 20, 1917, one notes: To all Muslim workers of Russia and the East . . . from now on your customs and beliefs, your national and cultural institutions, are declared free and inviolable.

Nevertheless, in 1921 Stalin [10] spoke out openly on the question of the Islamic minority. Both his position and record lent weight to his words. For at one time Stalin was commissar for nationalities and signer of the "Declaration of the Rights of the Peoples of Russia," which proclaimed the "equality and sovereignty of all the peoples of Russia."

Upon that occasion, Stalin outlined under three points the nature of the campaign against Islam: 1. Dismemberment and expropriation of land estates. 2. Dissolution of Islamic bodies. 3. Breakup of pan-Turkic societies. In return Stalin vowed emancipation of women, erection of schools, introduction of the national language and restitution of land seized by Slav settlers. The application of such a program threatened to stifle pursuit of the classical Islamic heritage within the Soviet Union.

A struggle ensued which can be touched upon here but briefly. Soviet policy was governed by the principle of "Divide and Rule." In the Volga Basin the Tatar and Chuvash republics were carved out of Bashkir land.

Soon the exercise of unbridled power politics gave way to more subtle tactics of scientific repression. It was for the most part a language approach. The Arabic letters of the alphabet were first replaced by Roman. Those in turn were superseded by the Cyrillic Russian alphabet. Ostensibly a harmless measure to modernize Islamic education, the campaign to weed out Arabic and the Islamic vernacular languages was exceedingly ingenious. It aimed at nothing less than the elimination of Islamic culture and its intellectual vitality. Certain measures calculated to cripple the Islamic family and shatter community morale were taken. In this phase, too, the initial emphasis was upon a laudable goal, that of women's emancipation.

Already stabbed awake under the czars, the Muslims of Russia took strides toward feminine freedom. The voices of suffragettes

[10] P. Catrice, "L'Islam en Asie Centrale: Les Soviets contre l'Islam," *En terre d'Islam* (Nov.–Dec., 1933), pp. 381–396.

such as Shafika Gasprinska and Aisha Ishakov were heard. They demanded prohibition of polygamy, child marriage, and bride purchase. When the Revolution broke out, it incorporated such demands in its platform.

Those moves proved generally inadequate. The Islamic female population was still behind the times. The shackles of old customs had scarcely been broken. Throughout Central Asia and the Caucasus region, women bore the brunt of disabilities and social inertia. Keeping women as they were became the mark of *status quo* traditionalism.

The veil and black shawl were invariably worn by the women of Islam. Those had long been the sign and symbol of an immutable society faltering in its medievalism. Upon the veil Soviet propaganda delivered its mightiest barrage. In 1927 Turkistan witnessed the spectacle of a legal holiday commemorating progress in the field. Public unveiling of women was then inaugurated: while veils were committed to the flames, Muslim women stood at city squares for the first time garbed in modern styles.

In conservative eyes, relegation of the veil to oblivion loomed as nothing short of degradation of womanhood. The shock of it all threatened the unity of many a household. Few seemed quite ready for such a radical break with the past. The outcome of this premature reform was pervasive apathy. Husbands, one learns, shot wives dead. Brothers strangled sisters in utter dismay and outrage.

Till then official suppression of all religions, including Islam, was a formal state posture. Religions were denounced wholesale chiefly because they reflected upon public welfare and national interest. As early as 1917, the Mufti of Orenburg, upon his election by the Turkic Volga people, did not go so far as to justify Soviet antireligious policies. He did lend support, however, to the cause of Soviet propaganda abroad. In 1922 he came out openly for Soviet denunciation of British foreign policy. The Soviets authorized in 1923, on the strength of such favorable comments and attitudes of Muslim leaders, a joint Russian-Islamic congress in Ufa. In attendance at that meeting, other than the Mufti of Orenburg, were the Sunnite Muftis of Crimea and Caucasus, respectively.

That apparent harmony did not long endure. In the making was a radical change. From 1926 onward, Islam loomed as an enemy of the Revolution. It was represented as a superstition and branded as lamentably behind the times. Islam was ridiculed and despised as antinational. Mullahs and muezzins were persecuted as antisocial parasites. As unproductive members of society, they were summarily dismissed. Along with sanctuaries of other faiths, mosques were ordered closed in 1928.

On April 8, 1929, a decree was promulgated which restricted still further the practice of Islam. In effect, the decree provided that all sanctuaries already closed be forthwith converted to some useful purpose or else demolished. Numerous churches, synagogues, and mosques, across the Soviet Union were on the basis of this legislation either confiscated or transformed into Party centers. Others were razed.

What the legislation aimed at was substantially realized. As of May 1, 1937, no cult building in the entire country was any longer regarded as public. Not so readily achieved, however, as the census itself conceded, was the ultimate aim of the legislation. About 90 percent of the population were believers still. In the course of the third Five Year Plan a resolution was thus formulated. It specified that by 1942, all churches, mosques, and synagogues will have been demolished insofar as the security of the population was not jeopardized.

For Muslims, the assault on the mosque was a bitter pill to take. That is not to say, however, that the religious core of their society was thereby dissolved. An Islamic community is already there where three believers gather to repeat the prescribed confession: "There is no God but Allah and Mohammed is his Apostle." Neither did prohibition of religious assembly, without state or party approval, prove more effective. What gave them a reason to worry, however, was an order that made it illegal for Muslim children to receive religious nurture. To instruct adults in the articles of Islam was similarly proscribed. In the upshot the battle against Islam amounted to a battle against Islamic youth.[11]

As regards ritual observances, likewise banned, Islamic inventiveness could be relied upon to devise a substitute or contrive some makeshift arrangement. Take, for instance, the ban on circumcision.

[11] Bertold Spuler, "Wolga-Tataren und Baschkiren unter russischer Herrschaft," *Der Islam,* ed. by R. Strothmann and B. Spuler (Berlin, 1950), Vol. 29, pp. 142–216.

What could be more resourceful than to dodge the issue by construing the rite under the heading of hygiene? Doctors might be found who would perform a circumcision as a hygienic measure. In fact such an operation could be carried out to the accompaniment of sacred intonation and acts of worship.

In the case of funerals, this was a possible strategy. The Muslim divine, *mulla,* could arrange to send some harmless old gentlemen to the bereaved home. Carefully coached in advance, such unidentifiable persons accompanied the cortege to the cemetery. As acceptably as any divine these agents recited the customary invocations and pronounced the blessing.

Yet for that one aspect, alluded to above, there was no possible substitute. There was no known alternative to religious education. Children had to be grounded in the standards of the faith. At precisely that point Muslims felt humiliated and cheated. It was rank cruelty, in their judgment, to stamp out religious consciousness at the child's level. Here as nowhere else, the Islamic community felt threatened. How crushing the Islamic agony under Communist machination, an outsider will never know in detail. It may be partly surmised, however, from the nature of measures resorted to in order to foil the oppressor. A Muslim community must feel terribly distressed before it takes its case to the pope of Rome. That was precisely what happened, however, in 1930. Émigrés of Volga-Tatar origin dispatched an appeal to Pope Pius XI. In it they complained of an inordinately difficult predicament under the Kremlin.

Their coreligionists of the Volga and Crimea area, the communication protested, suffered persecution as did the Christians. Their mosques were demolished, their spiritual leaders jailed, and their faith proscribed. "Moscow is intent upon the annihilation of all religious practices. It militates against God. . . . We trust your Holiness will raise your voice in behalf of the Islamic world." [12]

The battle against Islam was inextricable from that waged against the nationality of Turkic peoples. Each blow taken against the faith was simultaneously a stroke against the community. Up to a point, the political and economic implementation of Soviet policy complied with the antireligious and anti-Islamic campaign. It fitted into the program of Party purges and mopping up operations. Such

[12] *Osservatore Romano* (Aug. 24, 1930).

was the real Red posture in Central Asia and the Caucasus region. It followed the schedule of forcible collectivization of farmlands. What religious vitality managed to persist under those circumstances, it is exceedingly difficult to ascertain.

Then came the year 1936. The battle against religion was temporarily relaxed. Stalin himself found it expedient to speak in terms of moderate persecution. At the tenth Komsomol (Communist youth) League, April, 1938, Stalin described the posture toward religion as a "fundamental and burning controversial issue." He found himself constrained to address the Komsomol thus: Why must strong words such as "resolute" and "relentless" be used? This is not the essential thing. We must emphasize to our silent and patient youth what a disadvantage religious prejudice is. For our youth we must win, Stalin declared, a materialist world outlook.[13] The new constitution, adopted under Stalin, December 5, 1936, in Article 124 marked a new deal for the church. The article reads: "In order to ensure to citizens freedom of conscience, the church in the U.S.S.R. is separated from the state, and the school from the church. Freedom of religious worship and freedom of antireligious propaganda is recognized for all citizens."[14]

But a really conciliatory note was not struck till World War II. In 1944, like the Orthodox Church, Islam regained some freedom of action. Everywhere and always, of course, compromises had to be made. Loyalty to the state was first and absolute. To be at all tolerated, public worship had to open and conclude with acknowledgment of the Soviet state. Muslims had no recourse but to affirm that "Soviet power is power from God." Also, that "whoever turns against Soviet power turns against Allah and his Prophet." But no sooner had the Nazi battalions departed than hostility to Islam and the campaign against religion reared its head again.

The Soviet Government, as stated above, embarked upon a massive transportation of the Crimean Tatars. A pretext for such deportation was found in the reconquest of the Crimean Peninsula in 1944. Such forced relocation is said to have deprived the Crimea of

[13] See G. Simon, *Islam und Bolschewismus* (Das Evangelium im Osten, Wernigerode, 1937), *passim*.

[14] Ivar Spector, *An Introduction to Russian History and Culture* (D. Van Nostrand Company, Inc., 1961), p. 486.

the entire Islamic element in the population. Reportedly some of these Muslim citizens were settled in the lowland region, oblast of Grodno in Belorussia. Others apparently were removed to Siberia. Many others must have perished. In all probability, the history of Crimea Tatar Islam as a nation had come to an end.[15]

In a fiery speech before the Party Congress on February 25, 1956, Nikita S. Khrushchev frankly admitted the fate of the nationalities. They had sought to free themselves from the Soviet yoke. They had therefore forfeited any real claim to protection. Entire races and nationalities were summarily expelled from home and farm. They had preferred assistance from German occupation forces. They had spurned enthusiastic Soviet friendship. The deportations and frontier adjustments that followed brought the Islamic peoples of the Soviet Union nothing but heartache and suffering.

Nor did the end of World War II bring a surcease to ideological discord. Moscow broadcasts informed the world that the Koran justified human exploitation. It held the ideas of the Prophet responsible for reaction. Islam was obsolete, a hindrance to the association of working masses. Islamic festivals were ridiculed. The broadcasts maintained that the Fast of the month of Ramadan interfered with agricultural productivity and retarded industry.

In Turkistan, a vigorous smear campaign was launched against Islam. Newspapers carried articles to show Islam was established by an Arab aristocracy in order to suppress the masses. Islam is today a servant of imperialism, it cried out. Soviet propaganda found Islam's religious message obnoxious. It contradicted the findings of science and lent little if any support at all to the cause of progress.

Islamic defiance, as might be expected, followed. An Islamic counteroffensive had a popular appeal among peasants and intellectuals. Youthful fury was enkindled. A variety of feelings for religion prevailed among the young Islamic elements. Hearing only mockery of their cherished religious tenets, bequeathed by their fathers and forefathers, the younger men of Islam began to rebel. They found that rugged loyalty to the Islamic tradition held them together. Their revulsion against Russianism was deepened, their wrath against an imperialist atheist propaganda awakened.

[15] Bertold Spuler, *The Muslim World: The Mongol Period,* tr. by F. R. C. Bagley (E. J. Brill, Leiden, 1960), Pt. II, p. 101.

What keeps the flames of Islam burning could possibly be the fear of ever-recurring purges. Against Moscow's intentions, an Asian Islamic suspicion has had a long memory. It is a consciousness of vigil and caution against an enmity of long standing. At any rate, statistics show a drop in Communist membership among Muslims. A reported estimate shows a total membership of 78 for 1953 as compared with 600 for 1952.

The inescapable conclusion is that Soviet measures against the Turkic-Tatar folk was an outcome of impatience with Islam. Certain observers persist in seeing only the pleasant side of the picture: the Kremlin's exceedingly friendly attitude toward Islam and generous as well as cordial relations with Islamic countries and peoples.[16]

Indeed the Soviet Union does see in its Central Asian possessions a golden opportunity for the extension of its influence across Asian horizons. Those are regions that make Russia an immediate neighbor to China, India, Iran, and Afghanistan. The classic words of Peter the Great were never taken more seriously than they are today: whoever owns Turkistan holds hegemony over Asia. No less revelatory was the advice of Stalin: in Samarkand and Bukhara a lighthouse arises which will beam Soviet radiance in the entire Orient.

In short, an incompatibility, radical in the extreme, exists between communism and Islam. In more recent acts, the Soviet Union has sought, nevertheless, to create an image of itself as benefactor of Muslims: Islamic faith and Arab culture were the light of medieval history. Time has run a full circle, and in the modern world, Marxist socialism in its new interpretation is the bearer of light to mankind.

Soviet Muslims will therefore travel to Mecca, pilgrims in the rank of first-class citizens. The airplanes which they fly are met by Soviet embassy and consular officials. Yet across the world of Islam few informed persons see a close philosophic affinity between Islam and communism. Nor are such distinguished Soviet passengers as go on the pilgrimage free from suspicion as agents of the Kremlin. In the

[16] See, for example, N. Bassiches, "Moscow et l'Islam," *Vie Intellectuelle* (1926), Vol. 22, pp. 15–31. Cf. Serge A. Zenkosky, *Pan-Turkism and Islam in Russia* (Harvard University Press, 1960), pp. 268–282.

U.S.S.R., the Muslim reform movement "Jadidism" is itself an expression of growing national self-consciousness.

III

Godliness is an unmistakable manifestation of the Islamic religious phenomenon. It is by no means limited to those in minority status, such as the Turkic-Tatar Muslims of the Soviet Union. Nor is godliness the monopoly of the Sunnite majority of Muslim believers. The Shiite Muslims have a godliness that merits careful consideration.

This section represents an attempt to document very briefly three major areas where this Islamic godliness exhibits itself. There is, first, a community spirit and piety which in a worldwide distribution of Islamic societies comes to the forefront in personal commitment and prayer, in the festivals, as well as in the Friday worship service and in the pilgrimage to Mecca, Arafat, and Mina. A second form of godliness springs from imitation of the example set by the prophet. Thirdly, there are those standards of godliness which Koranic interpretation discloses.

[A] From the Volga to Cape Town and from Fez to Mindanao, godliness, on the basis of generally accepted creedal principles holds some three hundred and forty million Muslims [17] together. Well did Rudolf Strothmann [18] (1877–1960), of the University of Hamburg, remind his students: Islam is in the first instance a religion. To it belong a certain cultus, worship, prayer life, and sacred festivals. Those are essential elements of any religion, and apart from them Islam, no less than any other faith, can hardly be understood.

If under this central theme of godliness a given Islamic unity is envisaged, historical, political, and sociological varieties must not be forgotten.[19] Yet essentially Islam is here seen in the perspective of faith and theology. One need not follow the late Prof. Rudolf Strothmann all the way especially where he failed to discover much gen-

[17] W. Schneefuss in Franz König, ed., *Religionswissenschaftliches Wörterbuch* (Verlag Herder, Freiburg, 1959), pp. 753–754.

[18] See Bertold Spuler, "Rudolf Strothmann," *Der Islam* (October, 1960), Vol. 36, Nos. 1–2, pp. 1–3.

[19] Gustave E. Von Grunebaum, ed., *Unity and Variety in Muslim Civilization* (The University of Chicago Press, 1955).

uine Islamic piety among the Sunnites. Strothmann was eminently justified, however, in his evaluation of Sunnite Islam. This majority body of the believers do tend to permit worldly ambition and political crises to obscure the scope of godliness. Yet neither the Shiite nor the Sunnite holds any monopoly on the essence of Islamic faith and experience.

Something is surely to be gained if in the development of a fuller comprehension of modern Islam, the smaller confessions, particularly those supposedly tinged with the charge of " heresy," were featured. The Zaidis of Yemen, the Twelvers of Iran, Pakistan, and India, as well as the Nusairis of northern Syria and the Druze people of the Eastern Mediterranean, are relatively smaller Islamic enclaves. Yet without due regard for these communities' forms of godliness, the larger picture of the Islamic religion must remain incomplete.

Within this Shiite family (to which the aforementioned sects belong or from which they historically sprang) self-sufficient societies have emerged. A peculiar type of religious affiliation is encountered here. It seeks to hold secularism at bay. It resists the temptations of worldly power. To say, however, that the Shiite sects spell nothing but remorseless and downright superstition is quite inaccurate. Beliefs are faithfully espoused. Steering clear of skeptical rationalism, the Shiites abide constant in allegiance to their own norms of righteousness and creedal convictions.

Equally illuminating is the Islamic pattern of godliness in modern westernizing states such as India, Ceylon, Thailand, and Lebanon. In those countries, Muslims find themselves in minority status within a free, democratic, and relatively open society. In every state of this type, the goals of a particularist nationalism run counter to the vested interests and outlooks of an Islamic segment of the citizenry.

In those circumstances, a confessional godliness comes to the Muslim's rescue. Such a godliness is the heartbeat of Islamic minorities, a way of life, and a refuge from strangeness and insecurity. For instance, in the secular republic of India, Muslims enjoy full citizenship. The Islamic community has, nevertheless, developed its own spiritual, cultural, and at times, political attitudes. In Lebanon, violent discord between Christian and Muslim does flare up. Yet for the most part such discord dissolves in an underlying if mixed allegiance to Arab culture.

In Ceylon four communities are recognized: the Buddhists, the (mostly Roman Catholic) Christians, the Hindus, and the Muslims. Taking Ceylon as a case in point, the status of its Islamic citizens sheds light on the subject.[20] An equal partner in the British Commonwealth of Nations since 1947, Ceylon is a democratic state. On the island four distinct communities are recognized. They do not form a single linguistic order as Christians and Muslims do in the Republic of Lebanon. Buddhists, constituting the majority, and the Christians are Singhalese in speech. The Hindus and Muslims speak Tamil.

The Muslims of Ceylon are, moreover, open to influx of men and ideas from both Arab and non-Arab points of Islamic radiation. A question that only the future will answer is this: Will an Islamic minority of this type, holding a form of godliness at variance with the total human milieu, ever discover its position in the national structure?

In tropical Africa, Islamic minorities were at work long before European penetration. There the cause of Islamic godliness has tended to consolidate and extend its hold. Elsewhere the same sociological factors have drawn Christianity to fill the vacuum.[21] A further factor in certain localities operates in Islam's favor: Islam is regarded as offering the attractions of a comparatively lofty theology and worldwide brotherhood. Again Islam is recommended by a less exacting morality and freedom from European associations.[22] Such African conditions set the stage for a thriving Islamic godliness.

That an Islamic community finds godliness in individual and corporate experience without religious observance is unthinkable. In imitation of, and in contrast to, the Jewish and Christian Sabbath, Mohammed designated Friday as the day of community worship. On that day of the week, a congregational assembly replaces the regular noontime worship.[23] But Friday is not a Muslim day of rest. Business is suspended for duration of the worship period only.

[20] Gustave E. Von Grunebaum, "Ceylon und seine Muslimische Minderheit," *Der Islam* (1960), Vol. 36, Pts. 1–2, pp. 122–127.

[21] Cf. R. Oliver, *The Missionary Factor in East Africa* (Longmans, Green & Co., Ltd., London, 1952), pp. 202–207.

[22] J. N. D. Anderson, "Tropical Africa: Infiltration and Expanding Horizons," in *Unity and Variety in Muslim Civilization,* ed. by Von Grunebaum, p. 283 n 66.

[23] Koran 62:9–10.

The Friday service consists of kneelings, *rak'as,* and is enlivened by an address or sermon, *khutbah.* Such a sermon has for content, the praise of God and a blessing upon the Prophet. Additionally, it consists in a prayer for the Islamic community, a recitation from the Koran, and an admonition of the congregation, urging godliness. God's blessing is invoked, furthermore, upon the head of the state.[24]

Only upon fulfilling his ritual obligations is a believer entitled to utter a personal invocation, *du'a.* Prayer is valid only when performed in a state of ritual purity. It must be preceded, therefore, by ablution, *wudu.* It is this duty of ablution which accounts for the availability of fountains in mosque courts.

The great theologian al-Ghazzali (+1111) said in an explanation of kneeling, prostration, and bowing in prayer: "Next you bend down for the prostration, which is the highest degree of submission, for the dearest of your members, which is your face, gets hold of the humblest thing, which is the dust. . . . Wherever you place yourself in the place of lowliness know that you have placed it in its proper place and have returned the branch to the trunk, for of the dust were you formed and to it you return." [25]

Koranic, canonical, and ritualistic regulations institute the norms of godliness during the performance of the pilgrimage. Mecca must be entered in a state of consecration, *ihram.* Like prayer, the pilgrimage is to be undertaken only in a state of purity. Upon assumption of the state of consecration, the intention, *niya* is to be declared. The official rites of the pilgrimage start on the eighth of Dhu-al-Hijjah, the last month of the Muslim year. On the seventh, the pilgrims hear an address delivered at al-Kaaba. It describes the ceremonies about to begin.[26]

The two universal Muslim festivals are of immense religious as well as sociological import. The Great Festival, *Id al-Adha,* falls upon conclusion of the pilgrimage. It is universally observed across the world of Islam. Pilgrims, as well as the millions they left behind, unite in a global sacrificial slaughtering of animals. The Little Fes-

[24] G. E. Von Grunebaum, *Muhammedan Festivals* (Henry Schuman, Inc., 1951), pp. 10–11.

[25] E. E. Calverley, *Worship in Islam* (The Christian Literature Society for India, Madras, 1925), p. 118.

[26] Cf. Evelyn Cobbold, *Pilgrimage to Mecca* (John Murray, Publishers, Ltd., London, 1934), pp. 237–238.

tival, *Id al-Fitr,* marks the termination of the Ramadan Fast.

Although known popularly as the Little Festival, the latter holiday is an occasion for even greater rejoicing and gaiety than the former. The faithful by it signalize the closing of a month-long period of austerity and vigil. Whether it be prayer on Friday or any other day, performance of the pilgrimage, or celebration of the stated festival, Islam ardently exults at those seasons of refreshment and relaxation. A characteristically Islamic experience of godliness therefore pervades the community of believers.

For the Shiites, the principal and most impressive festival commemorates the death of Husain on the tenth of Muharram, A.H. 61 (October 10, 680). On that day, Husain, son of Ali and Fatimah and grandson of the Prophet, fell victim in a skirmish between Umayyad government troops and his own small band of supporters who had escorted him from Medina to Kufa in Iraq. Bruised and decapitated, Husain's remains were buried not far from the field of battle. His final resting place lay at a distance of some sixty miles from the future site of Baghdad.

Shiite devotion and godliness come to focus during the opening days of Muharram, first month of the Muslim year. The tenth day, *Ashura,* marks the inception of the Shiite tradition. It combines elements of passion and lamentation, or worship and holiness, together with certain demonic motifs. Overtones of shock, agony, and anger over the death of Husain are attestable. Dogmatic affirmations of soteriology, incarnation, and eschatology are the more profoundly religious attributes of this Shiite godliness.

On a lower level are orgies of self-flagellation and dreadful anathemas against the adversary. The shedding of Husain's innocent blood and the Passion Play, *ta' ziyah,* which mark it as an annual day of mourning, have perpetuated his mediatorial role, in the words of an early mourner, as "the bond of reconciliation with God on the Day of Judgment." [27]

[B] The example and message of Mohammed make him the chief model of godliness among Muslims of whatever race or sect. Other than the Koran and tradition, four canonical schools formulate the systematic Sunnite expression of Islam. Practical religion, *deen,* is

[27] Rudolf Strothmann, "Ta 'ziya," *Encyclopedia of Islam* (E. J. Brill, Leiden, 1913–1938), Vol. IV, p. 712.

crystallized under the above-noted Five Pillars. But Islam consists also of faith, *iman,* under six articles: Faith in Allah, His Angels, His Books, His Prophets, the Last Day, and Predestination of Good and Evil.

Theology gave rise to two unforgettable schools: that of al-Ash'ari (+955) and that of al-Maturidi (+944). Together with the five pillars, the six articles of faith provide an objective view of the phenomenon of Islam. As a groundwork for Islamic theology these, along with the way of life inspired by the godliness of the Prophet's personal example, prove indispensable.[28]

Such was Mohammed's impress upon mankind and his own people that both the historical drama he authored and the originality he displayed are indisputable. As a man he symbolized the Arabs most admirably. As founder of Islam, he won the believers' encomium for all time. His was an intellect both vigorous and poetic. He communed intensely with nature. He evidently held eventful converse with the invisible reality beyond all things. In his acts and decisions are reflected both the anomalies and fantasies of nature as are its neat and faultless dispositions.[29]

In personal and daily conduct, Mohammed practiced magnanimity and virtue, tenderness and charity, as well as forgiveness of injury. According to authentic records, he appears as a product of his time and environment. In his frailties, he was fully human. He was capable of violent outbursts of emotion, even acts of ferocity. With all such mortal imperfections, however, he was thoroughly dissatisfied. In all his undertakings, he invoked God's mighty support.

Although Mohammed was a formidable mystic, the divine presence did not abandon him to solitude. From protracted contemplation he arose unto gigantic feats of chastened character, under the power of sustaining revelation. Though not a theologian, the Prophet possessed superior intelligence and exceptional faculties of discernment. In all his prophetic career, and as a ruler, Mohammed believed God's hand lay upon him. Whatever the political imponderables that taxed his imagination and tested his sagacity, he knew his dependence on divine providence would carry him through. Thus in laying

[28] See Jeffery, *op. cit.,* pp. xi–xiv.

[29] Cf. Maurice Gaudefroy-Demombynes, *Mahomet* (Michel, Paris, 1957), pp. 659–660.

the foundation of a new Islamic state, no less than in shaping the contours of a world religion, with all the logical sequels of a drastic social reformation, his allegiance to the Almighty neither wavered nor waned.

The Arab nation that Mohammed put together does not weary of recalling his leadership. Ahmad al-Shaybani,[30] a citizen of Syria, in a book on the revolutionary foundations of Arab nationalism, wrote:

"The world is in desperate need today for spiritual leadership, a leadership capable of organizing the vast resources of mankind and directing their employment toward human welfare. Such leadership is not born at all unless love be its father and mother. We Arabs are ready to assume responsibility for such leadership. The annals of our civilization illustrate our qualifications to ensure realization of such an ideal. I am confident that the peoples of the world will welcome us and assign us such a task of leadership. That will come to pass when we convince those peoples that Arab nationalism in all its episodes indeed emanated from the wellsprings of love. That has been true from the time of its first national hero, the Prophet Mohammed, till this very moment. It is a love devoid of ulterior motives and stripped of selfish interest. For such love, Arab nationalism lives, and by it, it grows and flourishes."

[C] An indisputable index of Islamic godliness arises in the direction taken by Koranic interpretation. Since the Koran itself is the fundamental document for the religion of Islam, and is regarded by the faithful as the holy, revealed, and eternal Word of God, it is not strange that its exposition and exegesis should direct the bent and chart the course of godliness and piety. In his work dealing with the above theme, Ignaz Goldziher (1850–1921) noted, in the first instance, the primitive rung in the ladder of Koran interpretation.

Goldziher further explored the traditional and dogmatic patterns of exegesis. He went on to formulate a judgment on Islamic mysticism. Incidentally, this is the medievally extensive and by no means negligible modern form of Islamic godliness, better known as Sufism. Extramural insofar as Sunnite and Shiite doctrine are concerned, Sufism is, nevertheless, an expression of piety, thought, and devotional experience. The sectarian exposition of the Koran was the

30 *Al-Usus al-Thawrawiyah li-al-Qawmiyah al-Arabiyah* (Dar al-Yaqzah, Damascus, 1958), pp. 81–82.

final phase of the subject in Goldziher's treatment. It presaged his last chapter: "Islamic Modernism and Its Koranic Interpretation."[31]

What the Koran means for Islamic godliness today is disclosed in individual careers as well as in current literary landmarks. Taking two key Islamic culture areas, Urdu and Arabic, the Indo-Pakistan subcontinent and the Arab world, certain developments in recent Koran interpretations might be delineated.

Within the Arab orbit, an Egyptian Mohammed Abdu (1849–1905) made a diligent attempt to arrive at a new evaluation of Islamic principles. Unlike his Indian counterpart Ahmad Khan (1817–1898), Abdu did not start with composing a Koran commentary, *tafsir*. Instead he composed in 1897, an Epistle on the Divine Unity, *Risalat al-Tawhid*.

It was obvious why an Arab Muslim scholar such as Abdu chose to begin with a work on theology. There was a readiness for such a venture in an environment where the full gamut of sacred Islamic writings were accessible in the mother tongue. Abdu's contemporary Ahmad Khan happened to belong in a society where another challenge evoked a different response. Descendant of an aristocratic family closely associated with the Mogul court, Ahmad Khan grew up where Persian culture and refinement held sway. His was not the kind of theological training requisite for an evaluation of Islamic faith and doctrine.

In 1880 appeared Ahmad Khan's six-volume Koran commentary. Lacking Abdu's theological acumen and Arabic competence, Ahmad Khan produced, nevertheless, a remarkable interpretation of the first seventeen chapters of the Koran. It was a first step in the direction of modern Koranic study by a Muslim scholar.

Abdu finally yielded to pressure, largely exerted by his pupil Mohammed Rashid Rida, to produce a Koran commentary. He proved incapable, however, of any major deviation from the established norms of orthodoxy. He missed hardly any opportunity at all to flavor his commentary with homiletical material wherever the text permitted. In contrast, Ahmad Khan embarked upon his task with a due sense of responsibility. Apprehension lest Islam become obsolete led him to study the Koran with great expectancy. He came to the

[31] Ignaz Goldziher, *Die Richtungen der Islamischen Koransauslegung* (E. J. Brill, Leiden, 1920).

Book, firm in the conviction it contained the truth. Here was a truth fully applicable at the present time.

Another Indian Muslim who rendered a contribution in this field was Abu-al-Kalam Azad (1888–1958). Azad was born to Indian parents in Mecca. At the age of ten he was brought back to India and settled with his family in Calcutta. Azad strove for Islamic-Hindu reconciliation. He served as Gandhi's adviser on Islamic affairs. He spent years as political prisoner at Fort Ahmednagar Jail. In free India, he became Minister of Education from 1947 till his death.

Azad, too, wrote a commentary on the Koran. His purpose was to show the brilliance of the one, universal truth. It was a truth mankind desperately needed. On this truth, there was a chief document available, the Koran. From his intellectual and spiritual quest, Azad drew these insights: that truth is won by conquest of doubt, the doubt that science and religion can coexist. Above all, he maintained, the discovery of a universal religion was prefigured in the Koran.[32]

A third reflective Muslim of non-Arab stock is Ghulam Ahmad Parwez (1903–   ) of Pakistan. A research center he founded in Karachi goes by the name, Rise of Islam, *Tulu Islam*. Its purpose is to achieve better understanding of the Koran in the light of modern sophistication. Rejection of the Tradition, however, has made the institute notorious. No Muslim well aware of the problems involved would concede that Tradition is irrelevant today to Koran interpretation. Tradition, *Hadith,* is the practice of the Prophet and his companions. As such it can only be ignored at grave risk. The four volumes of Parwez on Koranic knowledge, *Maarif al-Quran* (1941–1949), are no conventional commentary. It is more accurate to say that they constitute a Koranic theology. Evaluations of basic doctrines are therein provided.

Parwez leads off with the Koranic doctrine of God. His creation, power, providence, grace, wrath, knowledge, wisdom, dominion, will, and other attributes noted in the Koran are enunciated. The author then takes up the doctrine of man: his relation to Satan, *Iblis,* and to angels, as well as his relation to the other world.

Under the caption of revelation and prophecy, Parwez reviews,

[32] For Azad's Commentary on the Koran, *Tarjuman al-Quran* (1930), see J. M. S. Baljon, "A Modern Urdu Tafsir," *The World of Islam* (1952), Vol. II, No. 2, pp. 95 ff.

among other things, the subject of divine messengers. This leads to a survey of the principal non-Muslim religions: Judaism, Christianity, Hinduism, Chinese and Japanese faiths. Strangely, his dogmatics omit mention of eschatology, essential as it is to any Islamic theology.

Such silence on eschatology, the doctrine of the final issue of things, seems characteristic of Islamic modernism in its most recent expression. Rather than dwell on eschatology, his last chapter devotes attention to the new world. It is to be ushered in by the revolutionary thrust of the Koran.

Seminal within the Arab Islamic orbit and beyond, Egyptian modernism shows marked disengagement from the conservatism of the Abdu school. A departure from the beaten track comes to light in the methodology of Tantawi Jawhari (+1940). Ornamented with Koranic proof texts, his commentary, *Jewels, Jawahir,* is in reality a manual offered the general reader on biology and other sciences. For example, the Koranic subject of hell affords the author an opportunity to describe the earth as a fiery globe and among other things, to discern Mt. Etna's volcanic eruptions.[33]

Koranic research in Egypt has produced also Mohammed Ahmad Khalaf-Allah. His best-known work is "Narrative Artistry of the Holy Koran" (*al-Fann al-Qasasi fi-al-Quran al-Karim,* 1950–1951). Another versatile Egyptian writer is Mohammed Kamil Husain. His major contributions lie in the realm of Biblical topics. His dramatized account of *Good Friday*[34] reflects the impression the crucifixion left on three distinct groups: Jews, Romans, and the disciples. It is in the form of long dialogues with a minimum of action. Egyptian scholarship is bound to effect significant transformations in the field of Koranic studies.

Modernist Islamic theology inveighs against the slightest suggestion of demonism in the concept of Allah. Characteristic are its attempts to expunge the Koranic interpretation of any such demonic feature. The craft, *makr,* of Allah[35] is explained away as God's

[33] Tantawi Jawhari, *al-Jawahir,* Vol. II, pp. 163 ff. See J. M. S. Baljon, *Modern Muslim Koran Interpretation,* 1880–1960 (E. J. Brill, Leiden, 1961), pp. 5–6.

[34] *Qarya Zalimah.* Eng. tr., Kenneth Cragg, *City of Wrong* (Djambatan, Amsterdam, 1958).

[35] Koran 7:97–99. See Baljon, *op. cit.,* p. 58.

concealed decree. The divine name Tyrant, *Jabbar,* is said to mean wisdom and sound policy with no taint of suppression or despotism.

The Islam communicated by Mohammed is nothing, hence, if not an eternal religion in its final form. It is an extension of a message and covenant which God revealed to the first men. In it is found the confluence of the Old Testament, the New Testament, and the Last Testament which is the Koran.[36] Fear of God, *taqwa,* is the essence of godliness. It is what Sayyid Qutb describes in commenting on a pertinent Koranic text [37] as "that very specific notion of God's paternal care and of his being closer to man than man is to himself." [38]

IV

The phenomenon of Islam unavoidably means doctrinal structures and dogmatics. To these a simple approach is afforded by the rise of sects and deviations. The problem of the essence of the Koran leads to the heart of Islamic dogmatics. The first problem to agitate the believers had to do with controversy over the nature of Islam: What is the nature of an Islam adequate to meet the complex of religious and political issues? In other words, what kind of Islam would be sound enough to pass the test of orthodoxy? What kind of Islam would simultaneously prove fit to satisfy the exigencies of everyday living?

[A] Siffin is the name of a battle that brought these problems to a head. On the one side were Ali and his Iraqi cohorts. On the other, was a Syrian army, led by the provincial governor, Muawiyah. Fighting began on July 26, 657. In order to spare Muslim lives hostilities were halted, however, in response to a call for arbitration. Such arbitration was to be conducted "according to the will of Allah." It was thus agreed to take the issue out of the clash between personalities so that the merits of the case might be assayed.

The burning issue at the moment was that of the precise relation between faith and work.[39] The Seceders, Kharijites, turned against

[36] Sayyid Qutb, *Fi Zilal al-Qur'an* (Dar al-Maarif, Cairo, 1945), Vol. I, pp. 36 ff.

[37] Koran 4:130–131.

[38] Qutb, *op. cit.,* Vol. V, p. 79.

[39] See Annemarie Schimmel, "Der Islam," Friedrich Heiler, *Die Religionen der Menschheit* (Reclam-Verlag, Stuttgart, 1959), pp. 828, 841–847.

Ali on the grounds that he did not literally seek the decisive verdict of the Koran. They insisted that only through exclusive surrender to the judgment of Allah will one ever find out what the right ethics of a given situation ought to be. They further maintained: there can be no faith without work to confirm it. For faith is known by good works done. Worship performances are not only to follow a form of outer purity, they must flow out of a pure conscience.

Otherwise, so the Kharijite argument continued, one is guilty of capital sin and is no more a Muslim at all. He is in fact worthy of infernal damnation. Among the most heinous sins already reckoned were idolatry, sorcery, murder, defrauding of orphans, usury, desertion from the army, violation of believing women. But the greatest of these was failure to make the Koran decisive in everything.

Those seceding Kharijites were Islam's first sect. They diverged from the Sunnite majority on the issue of both faith and practice.[40] Mainly nomads and seminomads of Iraq and the fringes of Arabia, the Kharijites have survived in certain small and little-known Islamic communities — in southern Algeria, Oman, and Zanzibar. Whereas the bulk of Muslims have rejected the doctrine of religious fanaticism, the Kharijites (and their spiritual offspring) insist on this: it is the duty of every Muslim to carry out the letter as well as the intent of the Koran.[41]

Important schools of doctrine were thus of first Islamic century vintage. A close kinship arises between Kharijite fanaticism and eighteenth-century Wahhabism. The Wahhabis (dynamic in Saudi Arabia and beyond), not unlike the Kharijites, experience rejection at the hands of a Sunnite majority conscious of the utter futility of fanaticism.

The classical antagonists of the Kharijites were the political conformists, Murjites. They were standpatters who suspended all radical decisions and favored a middle-of-the-road horse sense. Far more important as a school were the rationalists, Mutazilites. They bequeathed an imperishable legacy: moderation coupled with strict faithful "works," intelligent imagination wedded to inquiry and re-

[40] On Sunnite Islam, recognized earlier in this chapter, see Bertold Spuler, "Der Islam (Sunniten)," in Gustav Mensching, ed., *Handbuch der Religionswissenschaft* (Wissenschaftliche Editionsgesellschaft MBH, Berlin, 1948), pp. 73–94.

[41] H. A. R. Gibb, *Mohammedanism* (Oxford University Press, London, 1949), p. 119.

search. Their balanced judgment remains a bastion of modern Islamic thought.

[B] The partisans, Shiites, of Ali constitute a mighty minority in the world of Islam. Actually, they are a cluster of sects at variance with the main Sunnite orthodoxy. Doctrine, history, survival of faith, and ideals tend to divide Shiite from Sunnite. Common to both Sunnite and Shiite wings are belief in God, Mohammed and his message, and the revealed Koran. To these, the Shiites add faith in a legitimate Imam: chief of the believers and veritable interpreter of the Koran.

According to Shiite theology shortly before his death, Mohammed initiated Ali, his cousin and son-in-law, into the divine mysteries. A further tenet of the Shiites is that Ali's charismatic gifts were bequeathed to a line of succession in his family. Such an introduction of the Imams to divine mystery became the hallmark of Shiite Islam. It found expression in a variety of ways.

These varieties are important. They serve to distinguish the Shiite sects the one from the other. Thus Yemen's Zaidis affirm a divine preference for Ali and his heirs. Extremists, *ghulah,* among Shiite sects will go as far as to see in these holy personages not just a divine illumination but an actual incarnation of Deity.

Tradition has it that Ali was an early disciple of Mohammed. Nothing satisfied Ali more than a religious way of life. Orthodoxy concurs in stamping him out as veritable saint and valiant soldier. Popular fancy went on to depict this Companion of the Prophet as maker of a thousand wonders. The sun was once made to stop for him. To him innumerable sayings as well as mighty deeds were ascribed. He was a Friend of God, *Wali-Allah,* just as Mohammed was the Apostle of God, *Rasul-Allah.* Added to the title of Mohammed, that of Ali gives the Shiites dual allegiance to the two founders of their faith.

The already mentioned death of Husain, younger son of Ali, and Fatimah, at Karbala, Iraq, on the tenth of Muharram, A.H. 61 (October 10, 680) imparted to Shiite Islam a singular sense of tragedy and passion " motif." Lamentation over the cruel fate of the Prophet's grandson became an annual observance. It was a bereavement compounded with the sorrowful episodes of other Shiite Imams who fell at enemy hands. Such a record of sacred recollections was enshrined in poetry and prose. Its dark overtones sharpen the sense of desolation in Shiite faith and religious experience.

1. The first distinctly Shiite doctrine did not, however, concern the personality of Ali. Nor did it project the profiles of his two sons, Hasan and Husain, grandsons of the Prophet. It had, rather, to do with a third son of Ali, Mohammed ibn-al-Hanafiyah. His mother was not Fatimah, the Prophet's daughter, but another wife of Ali. Regarding this third son, a disciple named Mukhtar advanced an amazing report: it was to the effect that Mohammed ibn-al-Hanafiyah, who died in 684, was still alive. As Mahdi, he shall return in the last day to fill the earth with righteousness as it is now filled with corruption.

This parousia, " second coming," was applicable to other scions of the House of Ali. The Mahdi who shall return might be the Fifth, Seventh, or Twelfth Imam. They had all suffered tragic death. The choice of Imam was a confessional matter for Shiites, and the Imam regarded as Mahdi varied from sect to sect.

Following the death of Husain, Shiite attention centered in the problem of his legitimate heir.[42] He had left behind one son, Zain-al-Abidin (+ ca. 712), who in turn was father of Zaid (+ ca. 740). After the latter, Zaid, the Zaidis of Yemen are named. Of all Shiite forms, the Zaidiyah is nearest to Sunnite orthodoxy. Zaidi theology recognizes five Imams: Ali, Hasan, Husain, Zain-al-Abidin, and Zaid, to the exclusion of all others. Zaid is their fifth and last Imam.

2. Opposed to recognition of Zaid, the bulk of the world's Shiites looked to other Imams as they took their several ways. Noteworthy are the Twelvers and Seveners. The Twelvers revere Mohammed al-Muntazar, " the Expected " (+878), as twelfth Imam and Mahdi. The Seveners look to Ismail (+760) as final heir of Ali and the Prophet. All in all the Shiite minority does not constitute over 12 percent of the world's total Muslim population. They number about twenty-eight million souls.

The Twelvers, *Ithna Ashariyah,* constitute the central Shiite corps. They occupy a middle-of-the-road position, between the Extremists, *ghulah,* and the tolerant Zaidis. In the historical evolution of the Islamic community theirs has been a relatively significant role. As

[42] See Alid Genealogical Tree, Philip K. Hitti, *History of the Arabs* (Macmillan & Co., Ltd., London, 1940), p. 442.

a despised minority under both the Umayyad and Abbasid caliphates, they endured medieval persecution. In 1502, the Twelver faith was established, under Safawid rule, as Iran's state religion.

Two dogmas are distinctively Shiite. The first inculcates, particularly under adverse circumstances, a form of casuistry or dissimulation, *taqiyah.* This provides for an overt denial of one's religious affiliation and conviction while inwardly conforming to the religious dictates of conscience. The other dogma ordains that the Imam who presides over the religious community enjoys a divine luminosity. He wields a charismatic power to disclose the hidden meaning of religious truth.

Such an Imam in his role as interpreter of the law is regarded as infallible, even impeccable. The last such Imam being Hidden, he will someday return as Mahdi, "a person divinely led." He will then restore Islam, bring in the millennium, and witness the end of the world. Meanwhile the Shah of Iran is his *locum tenens,* aided by the corps of learned theologians.

The Twelvers theologically lean toward a Mutazilite rationalist position. Their scholarly authorities excel in Arabic language and literature. They rank as masters of the custom, *sunnah,* the customary way of acting, particularly that of the Prophet. This is especially true where the Alid expression of Islam is involved. They can be and are as rigorous as any Sunnite divine in debate over issues of faith and doctrine. As a rule they do not lag behind in fanaticism. Infidels are looked upon as unclean. A variety of temporary marriage, *mut'ah,* is authorized. The tombs of Imams at Karbala, Najaf, and Qum attract multitudes of pilgrims. Exceedingly coveted by the faithful are those graveyards as final resting places.

3. Shiites of the Ismaili Sevener persuasion developed revolutionary theories and practices. They shook then established Near East regimes to their foundations. Within the entire region, from the tenth to the eleventh centuries they acquired a reputation for sowing seeds of discord.

Among such seditionist Shiite elements none surpassed the Qarmatians. They owed their name to the initiator of the sect, Hamdan Qarmat. The Qarmatians became the most malignant growth on the Islamic body politic; their particular religious attachment centered in a prophet of their own, Mohammed, son of the seventh Imam

Ismail. Him they elevated to the rank of legislating divine, *natiq,* and passionately revered.

Already in the ninth century, Qarmatian propaganda had promoted a branch of religious "communism." Those Islamic Bolsheviks devised a theology which went so far as to countenance community of wives and property. Their stronghold in Iraq was Kufa, later transferred to Ahsa, a wasteland on the western shores of the Persian Gulf. There in 899, they built an independent state. The Qarmatians carried off in 930 the Black Stone from the Kaaba. Thereafter, for twenty-two years, till its return, the pilgrim traffic was interrupted.

In educational philosophy, too, the Qarmatians differed. They set up a curriculum of their own, based on an ascending scale for acquisition of religious knowledge. Grounding in divine truth was geared to a step-by-step approach to eternal verities. A syncretism was evolved. It drew together both basic Islamic concepts and ideas derived from Neoplatonic as well as Gnostic sources.

Their doctrines included a formulation akin to the evolutionary hypothesis on the origin of species. Western scholars attest that the formation of European guilds as well as Freemasonry owe something to the Brethren of Purity (or Sincerity), a Qarmatian eclectic school of popular philosophy. Man was conceived as a microcosm derived from divine essence along a descending order. His intelligence and "light of mystery" arose from a universal mind, *aql,* and a world soul, *nafs.*

In an ultimate state, Qarmatian theology inferred, man, eternally loosed from the influences of nature and the world, shall stand beyond the burdens of earthly change. The good shall then dwell in an abode of purity and bliss. The evil shall be consigned to a life of heedless wandering below the nether region of the moon.

It is self-evident that a Qarmatian theology so heretical could scarcely abide by a liberal interpretation of the Koran. Indeed, this schismatic faction held an esoteric, *batini,* epistemology with its own peculiar view of inner meaning. Its complex methodology introduced a system of degrees whereby the adept progressed in the deeper and inner knowledge of the Holy Book.

An eminent propagandist of this fringe movement was a celebrated traveler, the Persian Nasir-i-Khusraw (+ ca. 1074). He elegantly depicted its esoteric trend along the following lines: The outward meaning of prayer, *salah,* is visible in kneeling and bowing, in invocations and petitions, by use of the physical body oriented toward the Holy Land, as one's voice intones the proper words and as he faces in the direction of the Kaaba which lies in the Holy City and is the noblest of sanctuaries. But an invisible spiritual exposition of the inner meaning of prayer is something else. It comes into being when God is sought, with the thinking soul acquired by man himself from knowledge of the Holy Book and of Divine Law. The aim of such spiritual prayer is to bring the worshiper into the House of God, any house where divine discernment dwells. There it is that the Imam of Truth presides, upon him be peace.

Another phase of the Ismaili current shaped up the Fatimid movement. It broke into the open in North Africa at the beginning of the tenth century. In 969, it overran Egypt and produced a political state that lasted some two centuries. Most noteworthy Fatimid sovereign was al-Hakim (996–1021), a sufferer evidently from mental illness. One day he mysteriously vanished, in all probability murdered. His demise might have occurred at the instigation of his sister, Sitt-al-Muluk, whom he had accused of unchastity. According to his admirers, al-Hakim had declared himself in 1017 an incarnation of Deity. Other than the intrepid Persian Hamza, among al-Hakim's devotees none surpassed Ismail al-Darazi (+1019).

It is after this al-Darazi that the Druzes of Lebanon, and of Hawran in Syria, are named. They subscribe to belief in the return of divinized caliph al-Hakim. In line with the above-noted doctrine of dissimulation, *taqiyah,* the Druzes own to whatever religious form they deem it prudent to recognize. Concealment of one's convictions under adverse circumstances is a known oddity of Shiite faith and ethics.

At any rate, the Fatimid dynastic line came to an impasse upon the death of Caliph al-Muntasir in 1094. The rightful heir to the throne, Nizar, fled the country in the face of Egyptian preference for his brother, al-Mustali (1094–1101).

Nizar was accorded asylum at the Assassins' mountain retreat, Alamut, in Iran, by the celebrated al-Hasan ibn-al-Sabbah (+1124). A Persian who claimed Arab descent, al-Sabbah inaugurated the Assassin movement. In dedicated fealty to their Master, members of this secret order had a reputation for being as fearless of death as they were reckless in inflicting it.

The term "Assassin" is recognizable in the Arabic plural *Hasshashun.* In the original, it denotes those addicted to use of the narcotic *hashish,* a stupefying hemp. During the crusades, the Assassins exercised a highly notorious role. Their dread autocrat, the Old Man of the Mountain, from a hideout nestled in the fastnesses of North Syria instigated intrigues. He cut the figure of a fearful and dangerous outlaw. His agents were at large both within and beyond the overriding conflict raging between Arab and Frank. He could always count upon his daring men: a band of rough-and-ready, self-forgetful young killers, poised to descend upon any foe.

Eventually, the death-dealing secret order was liquidated in two stages. First, in 1256, by order of Mongol Hulagu, who wrecked the Abbasid Caliphate of Baghdad. He destroyed Alamut, Assassin fortress in the east. A later stage was reached in 1272. Baybars, the Mamluk Sultan of Egypt, then dealt the Assassins' western stronghold, in the Syrian heights, its coup de grace.

Around the Fatimid royalty sheltered by Hasan ibn-al-Sabbah an Ismaili community sprang. For a period of time, it was known as Nizari. In due course, the Nizaris migrated to India where they formed a sect. Their titular head is now addressed as Agha Khan. With headquarters in Bombay, this principal figure of the Ismailis claims descent from Ismail, seventh Shiite Imam.

Such sectarian cleavages as arise among the Shiites serve as a counterpoise to the relatively more classic forms and institutions of Sunnite orthodoxy. Reaction against Koranic transcendentalism also engendered the spiritual vitality of the mystical Sufi orders. To the intellectual and devotional, ethical and theological facets of Islam, the Sufis rendered a substantial and enriching contribution. In the overall phenomenon of Islam, Sunnite, Shiite, and Sufi strands were of necessity interlocked.

In a volume of popularized scholarship, Mohammed Kamil,[43] of the United Arab Republic, refers to sectarianism as a major factor in the fragmentation of Arab society. The first Arab cultural con-

[43] *Al-Dawlah al-Arabiyah al-Kubra* (Dar al-Maarif, Cairo, 1958), pp. 163–197, 564.

gress, held in Lebanon, September 2 to 10, 1947, and attended by delegates of the League of Arab States, went on record as saying: "Arabness was not in the past, nor is now, confined to any particular sect or religion." The Arabs were torn asunder, the document went on, for the most part through a religious fanaticism engendered under foreign rule. "The world as it evolves advances toward unification and solidarity. In itself, the League of Arab States is an expression of such evolution."

Arabness is thus quickened as emblem of manhood and citizenship. It is an attribute of cultural stature and national maturity. It distinguishes the Arabs as persons and citizens regardless of religious affiliation. Side by side with Arabness, a deepened Islamic consciousness gains ascendancy. The two need not be contradictory as the curriculum reforms and statistics of Cairo's (university-mosque) al-Azhar disclose.[44] A nation might be politically free and sovereign; yet apart from religion and faith, it will not long endure. A nation's primary armor is its commitment to what is true and ultimate, under the dictates of conscience alone. Such a phenomenon of Islam exhibits itself not as an adjunct of communism nor of Western democracy but as a third force on the world stage.

[44] See Bayard Dodge, *Al-Azhar: A Millennium of Muslim Learning* (The Middle East Institute, 1961), pp. 125–221.

CHAPTER

7

MODERN RIVALS OF LIVING FAITH

THE RELEVANCE of religious phenomenology to the world's religions may now be read in reverse, that is, in such challenges to living faith as certain mighty rivals present. The burden of this chapter is not so much to sketch the dimension of the subject in all its vastness as it is to indicate in modest terms instances of this rivalry to religion that arise in our era. It is quite a simple matter to see how both the scope and relevance of the book's central theme are involved here.

A startling realignment of the living religions seems to be in progress. The primary focus of tension tends to shift steadily. Such tension is apparently less between Christianity and its historic Eastern competitors. The lines of a more devastating rivalry loom on the horizon. This seems to exhibit itself between the classic religions of the modern world, on the one hand, and, on the other, the seductive options of scientism and nationalism, of secularism, historicism, and communism.

I

The first area of rivalry matures via indifference and is represented by both *scientism* and *humanism*. Science as such acquires a certain mystical quality whence the poses of scientism derive. This is because the mind grows fond of scientific revelations; it looks for an unending stream of positive answers from those engaged in research and experimentation. Science may thus become symbolic of certitude, the certitude of a knowledge that will both promise and fulfill. Mesmerized by hypnotic scientific marvels, man develops an indifference to living faith which fixes attention on the infinite, eternal, and ultimate. Such an indifference offers consistent rivalry to the pursuit of religious truth through living faith.

Man stands in awe before science. He is spellbound by its twofold divisions: an organized knowledge of nature, and by extension, an organized science of man in all the intricacies of his being.

Why must any rivalry arise between science and religion? An adequate reply will recognize the unity in a common ground of life with which the two major viewpoints of science and religion deal. Science is a study of life, nature, and man. Religion gives priority to the realm of the spirit, yet nothing can disqualify a living faith as disengagement from nature, life, and man.

[A] In the study of nature, the accent of science necessarily falls on *physics* and *biology*. Applied to man and life generally, the concerns of science find an expression in biology as well as the more strictly man-centered fields of psychology and sociology. It is now an open secret that the growth of these sciences has not followed a similar course. The historical as well as the validational integrity and security of one differs from those of another. One assumes that owing to their relatively recent origin, psychology and sociology in whole areas are built on foundations of sand; Freudian psychoanalysis and the analytical psychology of Jung have added to our stock of ideas, but their scientific validation is little more respectable than astrology or alchemy.[1] Physics, biology, and allied fields have steadily advanced. They have established new standards and methods involving a theory of knowledge, an epistemology articulate in creative thought. Positive results have justified confidence in the efficacy of experimentation.

These scientific clusters — physics, biology, psychology, and sociology — have produced an impact at times disproportionate to their areas of specialty.[2] The laws of physics, for example, have had a value and significance in the general structure of knowledge. It will not be proper or indeed possible to attempt here a formulation of all such values even in broad outline. A number of them, however, are easily recalled and may be stated in simple language.

For one thing, we have learned from the laws of physics that physical determinations are far more extensive than the ancients

[1] Cf. William F. Albright, "Return to Biblical Theology," in *The Christian Century* (Nov. 19, 1958), p. 1328.

[2] Brillant and Aigrain, *Histoire des Religions,* Vol. I, pp. 38–42.

supposed. For another, life has been identified with matter; yet in tracing continuity from one life to another, that is, from one individual to another, a certain personal distinctiveness and finality seems to persist. In the development of the race, moreover, an incontestable evolutionary process seems to be at work although precise causality remains unknown. Thirdly, psychology concedes that to the domain of consciousness, an object of intense interest and research in a former generation, certain prolongations belong which rest partly in the conscious and partly in the unconscious. Fourthly, in the orbit of social studies we have increasingly learned that sociology is basically rooted in the principles of psychology. That is to say, an actual person is almost inexplicable apart from ecology and heredity; he cannot be isolated from either of them.

If only because it led to materialism and naturalism, such an extension of scientific implication could not fail to produce a rivalry to living faith. Such an extension has been in process of acceleration during the last forty years. Nor is it deniable that religion had long pushed its frontiers over terrain that did not properly fall within its jurisdiction. That arrogation of authority was partly a response to the clamor of believers who looked to religious mentors for guidance in the fields of wisdom, knowledge, and understanding. Did not the stars constitute a unified order where the gods ruled and overruled? How could they manifest sovereignty if not through signs of the zodiac and eclipses?

After centuries, yea millennia, of tension science eventually came to its own. It took over realms of scientific and technical exploration ordained for it from the beginning. Once set in motion, this process could prove the undoing of much so-called religion. If step by step one sphere of knowledge after another were removed from idealistic control, religion, some feared, would end up in atrophy. The issue was not that simple. Competition between traditional religion and the combined forces of science and humanism has done some good. Only when indifferentism bred by science neglects the aspirations of man and threatens the spiritual core of his being does rivalry to living faith result.

It is vital that such a rivalry be from the outset properly appraised as an outgrowth of indifference. In reality, the theories and postulates of science could cause religion little if any distress. Surely

Galileo upset comfortable religious beliefs in 1632 when his *Dialogues Concerning the Two Chief Systems of the World* was published. Therein he supported, presumably contrary to an established Biblical injunction, the system of Copernicus which held the sun to be the central body and the earth a planet revolving with other planets around the sun. He was tried before the Inquisition. His scientific and philosophical views, however, did little or no harm to the cause of true religion.

Insofar as science retained a practical, laboratory character it had hardly any opportunity to jostle religion or arouse the ire of those who served as its stewards. Not until recently did physics acquire a pretentious role and devise its own speculative metaphysics. Take the case of radiation as an illustration. First, radiation was construed as the emission of energy by matter and its transfer through space. Next, radiation came to be viewed both as visible and invisible light. Although tests proved such invisible radiation to be classifiable as energy, empirically it was outside the realm of experience and of sense perception. Such radiation as is invisible and untouchable can only be accepted on trust.

Certain theories and propositions in physical science have of late resembled a house of cards. The French physicist Fresnel advanced a wave theory of light wherein the concept of transverse vibrations supplanted Newton's theory of emissions. Contemporaneously, however, the conquest of space dominates the thought and activity of physicists. A breakthrough in the theory of nuclear processes seems imminent as immense amounts of detailed information pile up without any theory adequate to set them in orderly relationship to each other. Meanwhile, objective reality remains conspicuously masked and every approach thereto seems merely symbolic.

Other feats of science have evoked their own problems. Such valuable accomplishments as telephone and airplane are by no means isolated cases. Even symbols disclose a phase or aspect of reality. In this vast world of marvels and wonders, which science creates, one question remains unresolved. What part of a given wonder comes from matter and what part comes from the intangible self which is in man? Neither philosophers of science nor critics of culture, much less their peers in learning and reflection, have as yet produced a persuasive answer.

Meanwhile, the indifference of science toward Ultimate Reality has increased directly with the common man's reverence for science as a source of power. Despite failure to give adequate response to the above question masses of mankind have put their trust in the technician. Without much relish for mathematical insight or deep reflection, they have hailed each law of physics as a solid formulation excelling any other law or prophet. Since physics has offered an open sesame to what is widely regarded as the good life, its flaws have been ignored. Nothing is detected in its revelations save an objectivity and an industry capable of providing greater ease and comfort and of adding to daily living a new dimension of beauty. Indeed, the pronouncements of physicists begin to elicit the kind of response due to political opinion, artistic taste, and religious doctrine. At times they bear a striking resemblance to the attributes of the collective conscious.

Certain scientific observations sound obvious in a given historical era. That is largely because they happen to agree with the status of human knowledge and techniques. There was a time, for instance, when nothing was known to move faster than a cannonball or, say, the rotation of the earth around its orbit. That happened to be in the eighteenth century when Lavoisier, the French chemist and experimenter, thought in terms of the conservation of matter. But things looked different when Sir Isaac Newton proposed a corpuscular or emission theory of light traveling through space at a fantastic velocity. In order then was a quantum theory that conceived of light in the form of radiant energy moving at a rate of 186,000 miles per second. Under a changed scientific climate, nothing seemed more likely than to suppose that matter itself incurred change through velocity. All of which must mean that a constant relationship exists between collective conscious and scientific ideas.

Both the collective conscious and its reflection in science are evidently sensitive to the stimuli from the economic and political fields. Now, the saying that science knows no homeland is a commonplace; even less than art, we are told, it is bound up with a given land. Yet, how universal has science really been? Lavoisier might indeed proclaim the conservation of matter. But what did his law mean to the Asia and Africa of those days? Mastered by the formula, Europe even went as far as to generalize it in the dogma that matter is eternal. That was indubitably in keeping with the spirit of an age that took the machine for symbol and found far more delight in material than spiritual things.

From Lavoisier the mind turns to Darwin and his hypothesis. There is a close parallel between the fundamental assumption of Marxism that the history of all hitherto existing society is the record of class struggle, on the one hand, and on the other, Darwin's theory of natural selection. If one rejects what the Communist texts teach about the struggle taking place between the oppressing and the oppressed, can he simultaneously give credence to Darwin's hypothesis of struggle for existence and survival of the fittest? The latter hypothesis gained currency in a Great Britain on which the nineteenth century had bestowed world power. From an island home, England ruled a far-flung empire over which the sun never set. As democracy's schoolteacher, purveyor of justice and fair play, and defender of freedom of the seas, Britain fully earned the praise of mankind. Essentially, however, it was Britannia's rule of the waves that counted most. And the timely biology of Darwin neatly fitted into all that.

More recently the Marxists have reproached the Western world on the grounds that Mendel's laws and their application to genetics and heredity are essentially bourgeoisie laws. That was not an entirely false accusation. Mendel's laws have impressed critics as a justification of Europe's long inertia in the field of agriculture. Now that the reproach has been sustained, Europeans have finally renewed their ambition to adopt improved methods not merely in horticulture but in animal husbandry and the farming industry in general.

Enough has been said to show that the influence of the physical sciences is preponderant, their indifference to living faith disquieting. They do not thrive only in schoolroom and laboratory. To their formulas a romantic aura attaches. Inducing popular attitudes and emotions, theirs is a penetrability not unlike that of religious beliefs which invade the whole fabric of existence. Happily, however, these two major arenas, physics and living faith, do not involve identical concerns, and the chances of direct collision between them are slim. But our problem grows more complex as we take up the scrutiny of discoveries in the fields of biology and the humanities.

[B] Three sciences, *biology, psychology,* and *sociology,* may be looked at together. Two of their characteristics are somewhat relevant to our theme. One is that their norms being less precise than those of physics, their expression in language is often short on clarity, relies rather unduly on intuition, and tends to treat things of a proximate or immediate nature; how painfully akin their methods are to those of the religionist who sets out matters logically, arranges the corollaries, and makes a nice dogmatic lesson of it. The other sparkling characteristic of these sciences is that a primary object of their common concerns happens to center in life and thought as such; and these are areas far excelling the material and physical realms in their hospitality to religion.

These three sciences indeed came to birth on soil where religion had long been stationed. This surely is the case in all that pertains to man. Across dreary stages of his wanderings in quest of subsistence, it was religion that sought to tell him what he was. Most religions held that man consisted of body plus soul. Such a soul survived death for a time or for ever. Certain beliefs maintained that the souls, prior to arrival at Nirvana, after death, became incarnate in human or animal bodies. The assumption is that all psychology had its inception in religion.

Ignored by religion was sociology. Too great an emphasis on man's destiny left hardly any room for concern with the group as a whole. In fact, thoughtful concern of any kind could scarcely arise at a time when man was immersed in the mass. When at last a deeper thought on major issues of existence did begin to appear, man's lot was by now cast not in the shadow of a nation but of an empire presumably ruled by a prince. Nor were societies as institutions too conspicuous in an environment where population distribution was relatively thin.

Similar factors conspired to remove the idea of evolution, whether human or animal, from religious concern. Paleography and history were not cultivated till later. For if living beings were created by the gods, the latter from the beginning must have ordained destiny. Few dared doubt the immutability of such a creation. In other words, religious speculation did not just ignore sociology and evolution, it flatly rejected their validity.

The indifference that science, psychology included, breeds toward religion does occasionally erupt into open revolt. Indeed it is a rivalry that engenders inner conflicts and disharmonies. If evolution postulates man's descent from the ape, how do we conceive of him as a being set apart, possessing an immortal soul, and capable of religious faith? If sociology leads us to think of the individual as a component of society, it should follow then that to society and not the individual destiny belongs. In that event, the individual will not count save as a function of society. That the very hairs of his head are numbered would be strange indeed. Stranger still that serious thought be given to a hereafter. What matters most is not the survival of a mere person but of nation and party.

Psychology in its modern assumptions sets up its own special rivalry to living faith. That was practically inevitable since the great living religions offered such concepts as those of soul, intelligence, and responsibility which psychology meant to reduce. Psychology takes little stock in an old-fashioned dichotomy of body-soul formation of personality. Nor is it inclined to assign intelligence sole authority in the conduct of personal existence. Existence as such is subject to an overriding ensemble whereby along with intelligence two other faculties, namely, activity and effectiveness, figure although they are irreducible to notional perception. As for responsibility its place seemed assured when psychology amounted to a science of the conscious. But since the subconscious has turned up as a major concern, emphasis on responsibility has progressively receded.

One further step and we shall see that modern psychology is not content over its own prospects as a speculative science. Its real ambition is to know man and to operate on him. Presumably through orientation tests it desires to discover more about us in order to settle us in society where we best fit in and where we can develop most. Having worked out a balance sheet of our capabilities, it will counsel us in the management of our lives. Then we shall know how to function at top efficiency.

Psychology will next move along to provide healing and by psychoanalytic therapy to offer salvation from uprootedness and anguish. In due course, man begins to feel equal to mastery over his fate. Armed with these new resources, he will imagine himself strong enough to lay piety aside and to neglect the practice of prayer. What peace he needs, he thinks he can draw out of his own depths. Such a concentration on the human may be understood as an aspect of the universal longing for freedom. This generation has been caught up with a consuming desire to escape all shackles and those of religion are no exception.

Emphasis on the human has not limited itself, however, to rejection of the material impediments of freedom. It has rebelled against the divine. Hence the tragedy of a generation more skeptical than ever where the fidelities of living faith are concerned. Pivotal areas properly held by genuine faith do not yield to scientific treatment. Doubt, that probing, questing uncertainty which acts as a cathartic, can also degenerate into a fearful symptom of loneliness, a bankruptcy brought about by rejection of hope and the forfeiture of meaning and joy.

II

Other than physics, biology, sociology, and psychology — representative sciences that rival religion — a second rivalry manifests itself where *nationalism* and *collective powers* are in full control. This is a rivalry of channeling that tends to utilize faith as a means or so to condition human life and institutions as to render the spiritual way of life obsolete.

[A] What we have hitherto known as a *community* is in a state of flux. Unforeseen technological domination is changing the relation of the individual to the community. An unfathomable past, a unique heritage transmitted along peculiarly ethnic lines, and a heritage unpredictable historically, these are a community's traditional attributes. But the old community is passing. What was depicted in literature, morality, mores, and manners is giving way to something new. A transitoriness, a surprise element, and a consolidation have transformed the old community or scattered its members. A technological collective has emerged. In contrast to the former community this is a *Gesellschaft,* a society.[3] It is capable of appearing and disappearing quickly. Planned down to infinite details it spreads into suburbia, into rebuilt slum areas, and out of a blueprint into a Levittown.

The exercise of collective power through such a mass society is

[3] Karl Jaspers, "The Individual and Mass Society," in Walter Leibrecht, ed., *Religion and Culture: Essays in Honor of Paul Tillich,* pp. 37–43.

capable of channeling even religion in the service of community interests. A mythical domination of this type might pose a staunch rivalry to living faith in a manner unfamiliar to pretechnological history.

In a classical Chinese setting, for instance, man considered himself to be one with the eternal Tao order. All irregularity was but a passing phase, a disturbance in the ordinary rhythm of existence which eternally identical reality sooner or later repaired. In his own inimitable way, Plato conceived of a world where ideas were set in a permanent configuration. In that social structure relationships were deemed stable, their stability beyond the strain and stress of contingencies. Stoicism projected an order of reason to which it looked with dazzled admiration as the eternally requisite fount of security.

For the Christian, there is an order of serenity and joy. A state of dedication extends from creation through the Fall, unto death, the resurrection, and the life everlasting. All holy living is summed up in the Kingdom of God. This implies life on a plane of meaningful and edifying faith. Today all these schemes of existence, whether classical Chinese, philosophical Greek, Biblical, or other, are under fire. To many, they seem naïve, exceedingly fanciful, and shaky. Science and technics have revolutionized the world. New economics and power politics have redefined society. While this vast reorganization is in process, the relation of man to his neighbors has altered. He and they are exposed to new pressures, as a relentless program of channeling spares no one.

We are not saying that individuality has fallen by the wayside. Where collective power and nationalism have silenced the individual and reduced man to a functional stature, democracy and culture have sought to redeem him. Education, the arts, and a tempered variety of nationalism still exist. They, too, seek to offset the ravages of extreme collectivism. Even where the cause of liberty is in eclipse, the love of freedom is not altogether lost. Yet an overshadowing fear of total extinction threatens. Beside it every other problem, even that of submerged individuality, pales into relative inferiority.

[B] *Nationalism* itself neither delivers man from the crisis of anxiety nor fills him with lasting inspiration in the midst of personal and social calamity. In fact, volatile nationalism, and the myth of power whereon it feeds, depraves man. The extent of such depravity varies with the degree to which nationalist emotionalism subordinates reason to the dictates of an irrational will. Hence a shortness of breath pervades nationalist movements, an immorality attaches to the state, and both originate in a tragic sense of collective power.

To be more specific, the tragedy of the state lies in the fact that it is ever tempted to sin. It is tragically driven toward immorality by a sheer struggle for self-preservation and the service of selfish national interests. For the state to follow the voice of conscience and morality is to court disaster if not to commit national suicide.[4] From Aristotle down, philosophers have conceded that the principle of necessity is fundamental to the existence of the state. To Bishop Berggrav of Norway, who knew Nazi tyranny at first hand, we owe a formulation of the first commandment in the catechism of the state: "Thou shalt not be concerned with anything but that which is necessary for thine own welfare. Above all else thou shalt serve and obey thine own interests."[5]

Nationalism and the state therefore tend to utilize religion as a device to serve political goals. And that is the core of rivalry to religious faith via channeling. Such channeling gives rise to an almost tragicomical situation. What else is there to expect, seeing that the profound regenerative powers in any society lie outside the scope of statesmanship? Driven by sheer necessity, politics, nationalism, and the state turn to expedient, extraordinary, temporary, and at times, violent measures in order to achieve their purposes. Napoleon, de Robespierre, and their ilk look upon terror as a temporary measure. "Wait till the revolution is ended," they delude their followers. "Paradise will then begin." What a revolution actually devours are its own children. Crooked means which devious statesmanship employs tend to corrupt its better ends.

Even laws codified in the national interest do not as a rule represent the higher tradition of a given culture. For as nations admittedly act out of necessity, security, or force, all higher motives are set aside. It will be just a matter of time before such considerations sap the vitality of law. Neither Hitler nor Mussolini invented the

[4] Eivind Berggrav, *Man and State,* tr. by George Aus (Muhlenberg Press, 1951), p. 31.

[5] *Ibid.*

slogan that might makes right; it was a natural corollary to Machiavelli's political thinking and thrives in the climate of all unrestrained nationalisms. Early in the seventeenth century Hugo Grotius introduced the concept of *jus gentium,* international law. Underlying his juridical view were principles of law, later designated as "human rights," which were as old as the gospel, even older in substance. But such foundations as he posited are virtually nullified where the particular interests of a nation constitute the sovereign lawgiving authority.

National interests and collective power wielded by statesmen and autocrats are not, however, the only instances of rivalry to living faith, a rivalry that channels and utilizes religion. Great literature and the masterpieces of inspired artists may produce the same effect. No less a student of Russia than Thomas G. Masaryk [6] depicted Dostoevsky as the most representative Russian and his ideas as the key to the understanding of the Russian Revolution and the Slavic soul. Two of Dostoevsky's greatest novels, *The Possessed* and *The Brothers Karamazov,* the journals he edited, and his famous lecture on Pushkin were devoted to what he regarded as burden and message of his career: to shepherd the Russian intellectuals back to the true tradition of the Russian folk and soil, and thus to save Russia and the world.

Taking the nineteenth century as a whole, and with the literary flowering of the period fully in mind, Dostoevsky's perception as novelist and psychologist leaves him virtually peerless in his generation. His sentiment of extreme nationalism is voiced by Shatov, a character in *The Possessed.* As a man of the people, Shatov inquires, "Do you know who are the only god-fearing people on earth, destined to regenerate and save the world in the name of a new God and to whom are given the keys of life and of the new world?" The answer is obvious: the Russian nation and its God form an inseparable unit. Dostoevsky asserts that an atheist cannot be a Russian. He means that no one can be who does not believe in the Russian God, which is none other than the Russian nation.[7] In the

[6] *Russland und Europa: Studien über die geistigen Strömungen in Russland* (Diederichs, Jena, 1913), 2 vols.; tr. *The Spirit of Russia* (George Allen & Unwin, Ltd., London, 1919).

[7] Hans Kohn, *Prophets and Peoples* (The Macmillan Company, 1946), p. 148.

great literary, and possibly religious, texts of other peoples, the reader will note similar passages charged with ultranationalism.

Where vigorous, irrational nationalism and collective power are concerned, rivalry to religion will channel personal faith in subtle and cynical patterns.

III

[A] Beyond science and humanism, and beside collective power and nationalism, there is a third rivalry to living faith. It proceeds via displacement and usurpation. That *secularism* and *atheism* threaten religion has been a common theme of the century. As far back as 1928, the eminent Quaker thinker, Rufus M. Jones,[8] issued a solemn warning on this score. It was addressed to the Protestant ecumenical world then struggling to be born. The real rival of Christianity, he advised, was not Buddhism, Islam, or any other higher religion. It was secularism. His understanding of secularism was rather broad and inclusive. It was " a way of life and an interpretation of life that include only the natural order of things and that do not find God, or a realm of spiritual reality, essential for life and thought."

Rufus Jones went on to set forth the causes of such secularism. They included Renaissance humanism and modern nationalism. Among them were the breakdown of Protestant unity in the Reformation and its mutually hostile sects. Other contributing factors were the rise of science, rationalism, and nationalism, as well as the historical criticism of the Bible, also, the Industrial Revolution, with its loss of contact with nature, its slums and depressed conditions as well as its intense economic competition and excessive materialism.

With the rising tide of secularism, its rivalry to religion was to deepen and intensify. From the Protestant conference at Jerusalem in 1928 to the Second Universal Christian Conference held in 1937 at Oxford, the secular forces had had a spectacular growth.

That latter year (1937) witnessed a bitter assault on European Christendom delivered in Alfred Rosenberg's *The Myth of the Twentieth Century*. The secular challenge was already beginning

[8] *Reports of the Jerusalem Meeting of the International Missionary Council* (8 vols., Oxford University Press, London, 1928), Vol. I, pp. 230–273.

to be felt among Christian scholars. Karl Barth had fashioned a tentative yet vibrant theology, initially mediated to an American audience in a translation (1928) by Douglas Horton, entitled *The Word of God and the Word of Man*. In 1935, H. Richard Niebuhr, Wilhelm Pauck, and Francis P. Miller jointly addressed themselves to the same problem in a volume, *The Church Against the World*. At the aforenamed Oxford conference, secularism was sharply rebuked as "deification of political and cultural ideas." [9]

At any rate, essential secularism is not a derivative from science, technology, nationalism, or concern with social affairs. Technological inventions have been known to engender deeper reverence before the Creator. Neither modern physics nor technology is the original cause of secularism rightly so-called. Discoverers of the physical conception of the cosmos and of causal calculability, as Karl Heim reminds us, were for the most part believers. Such giants as Kepler, Galileo, Descartes, and Newton were not secular men. They did regard mathematical laws as basic formulas of the world process. But these laws did not lead them astray. On the contrary, mathematically expressible natural laws tended to reveal the mystery of the universe to them.[10] Descartes himself, let it be said, was a man of deep convictions, member of the religious circle of Port-Royal. Did he not convert to the Catholic faith Queen Christina of Sweden while giving her instruction in philosophy and mathematics?

[B] What, then, is this phenomenon of secularism in the unalloyed state? One thing is clear, it antedates modern physics. Such men of ancient Greece as Democritus (ca. 460–ca. 370 B.C.) and Epicurus (342?–270 B.C.) were its champions. Mechanism as to motion, atomism as to structure, materialism as to substance, that is the whole system of Democritus. Epicurus departed from the reserve of Socrates, and looking for a material philosophy that might support his ethics,

[9] Cf. Edwin E. Aubrey, *Secularism a Myth* (Harper & Brothers, 1954). Aubrey criticized current attacks on secularism, acknowledged the debt of Christianity to secular quarters, and warned that dissociation from secular culture would prove fatal to development of Christianity. He was sound in making secularism a bogey but not in making a myth of it. True, every secularist is not a communist, but a true communist must be a secularist and his secularism is no myth.

[10] Johann Kepler, *Harmonices mundi,* liber V (Lincii, Austriae, 1619); Karl Heim, "Christian Faith and the Growing Power of Secularism," in Walter Leibrecht, *loc. cit.,* pp. 181–195.

found the system of Democritus most congenial.[11]

And who will not be struck by that provocative passage of Lucretius (+55 B.C.) which so fascinated Goethe? It occurs in an encyclopedic Latin defense of Epicurus, a philosophical poem, *De rerum natura*.[12] How the lines breathe an enmity to religion, a consummate this-worldliness. "When the life of man lay foul to see and groveling upon the earth, crushed by the weight of religion, which showed her face from the realms of heaven, lowering upon mortals with dreadful mein," mused Lucretius, "'twas a man of Greece," Epicurus, of course, "who dared first to raise his mortal eyes to meet her, and first to stand forth to meet her: him neither the stories of the gods nor thunderbolts checked, nor the sky with its revengeful roar, but all the more spurred the eager daring of his mind to yearn to be the first to burst through the close-set bolts upon doors of nature."

It is one thing to take secularism for what it really is and to judge the degree of displacement and usurpation whereby it effects its rivalry to living faith. Quite another it is to follow in the wake of those who like Oswald Spengler misread its place in the history of civilization. To him, secularism was nothing but a phantom of old age, a sign of atrophy in the late autumn of a culture intimating that the end is near. Only in a civilization grown hoary with age and decrepit, he maintained, does man's spirit lack power to hold and to keep faith and causality together in a single unity of being.

Greek secularism indeed marked the last polytheistic era extending approximately from Democritus down. Yet in its characteristic manifestation, secularism is a phenomenon of the Western world that throve on so-called Christian soil. The problems it evoked were hardly germane elsewhere. Other noteworthy cultural configurations achieved ascendancy through symbiosis between religion and culture. Such was the case in ancient Egypt, Vedic India, and Confucianist China. If that symbiosis collapsed, the days of an Oriental civilization became numbered and it swiftly moved toward dissolution.

11 George Santayana, *Three Philosophical Poets: Lucretius, Dante, and Goethe* (Doubleday & Company, Inc., 1953), pp. 32, 35.

12 *Lucretius on the Nature of Things,* tr. by Cyril Bailey (Clarendon Press, Oxford, 1955), p. 29.

Whereas in the non-Western world, a wedlock-bound religion and culture, Biblical religion challenged any such association. While such an association is not entirely foreign to the West, it tends to face a constant tension between church and state. The Judeo-Christian tradition and Islam conceived only of the Divine as eternal and totally other. Apart from him, they took the material world to be impermanent and without eternity. Such a cosmic merger of deity and matter as the non-Occidental world indicates obviously left little reason for the kind of secularism we know to arise. A doctrine, however, that saw the whole creation as subject to corruption and thought of man as living, moving, and having a being only in God, was bound to elicit dissent. Secularism is the most impressive such dissent. It sought to free man from the shackles of religion. For this world of matter it coveted nothing more than an eternity apart from God.

Endemic in the West, secularism claims an eternal character for two main things, self and nature. In other words, a finality attaches to both consciousness and the world of objects. In its Platonic form, the secularism of self or ego culminated in the belief in individual immortality. Against such an immortality of the soul the early church preached personal resurrection as a creative act of God. Although formally superseded, Plato's idea of immortality is by no means defunct. It corresponds with much of man's belief in a hereafter, the kind of deathless, albeit godless, hope that men rarely succeed in shaking off.

The other basic secularism is rooted in eternizing nature, that is, the world we live in. Abreast with the march of science and the broadening sphere of knowledge, this is a secularism of the deepest order. It is as old as Democritus and Epicurus. Their conjecture was that nothing existed save atoms and the void. All else was illusory. The world process accordingly comprised a perpetual mingling of small indestructible particles. Hence its eternity. What eternity religion saw in God, the materialists identified with matter. Confronted with this eternization of the world, Immanuel Kant described it in *Critique of Pure Reason* as the hallmark of man's desperate yearning for an enduring principle in a changing world.

No such eternization could outlast the nineteenth century. Unimpressed with arguments for the eternity of matter, brilliant minds turned to energy. Since energy was constantly passing to a wasteland of dissipation, a quantum theory gained wide acceptance. Unalterably it led to a secular eschatology that commensurately with the ultimate exhaustibility of energy postulated a similar dead end for all life and movement. A metaphysics of matter and energy had to crystallize. Among its German propounders were eminent scientists such as the biologist Ernst Heinrich Haeckel (1834–1919) and the chemist Wilhelm Ostwald (1853–1932). The former wrote *The Riddle of the Universe* and the latter is famed for work on the philosophy of nature. Both fostered a theory of the relatively unconscious life which gave currency to popular secularism. Just such a popular secularism, espoused to the religious passion of the Russian soul, appears in Communist atheism.

Again in Germany the voice of a philosopher was joined to those of the biologist and chemist. The philosopher happened to be Friedrich Karl Christian Ludwig Büchner (1824–1899). His work, *Power and Matter,* reenforced the secularist cause and presaged its worldwide dissemination. Awakening cultures in Asia and Africa were shaken to the rouse of a causal-mechanical world view and technology. Primitive mythological faiths suffered eclipse and gradually faded into something else. Displacement and usurpation were the order of the day. Soon modernity's own springtime would break. Whatever else it meant, popular secularism had to follow in its trail.

The process of displacement gained momentum. New misgivings disturbed the Western tradition. A Western culture that had accepted self-surrender to secularism was sorely disillusioned. The very criteria of physics and matter were in jeopardy. The quanta and standards once held as absolute were being relativized. Relativity as a theory attained its point of culmination in Albert Einstein. Constant body and constant energy quantum were shelved. Absolute space and absolute time, presupposed by Newton, became relative constructs.

What else was there to recognize as self-sustaining and self-subsistent? When the whole story of secularism is reviewed in its relation to matter and energy, the mind is thrown back upon that ground of our being which living faith acknowledges as God. Far from being destructive to living faith, relativity, having tempered the conceits of the secularist and the absolutism of science, leaves open the road to spiritual pilgrimage.

IV

A fourth rivalry to religion is identifiable as *historicism*. Declaring religion to be dead, history as such poses as a formidable foe of living faith. In that sense, history ranks along with science and humanism, nationalism, and secularism, as an alternative way of life.

[A] Has history a broad structure, a background against which its developments may be in their fullness grasped? Hundreds of thousands of years conceal prehistory from the great civilizations of antiquity that began millennia before the Christian dawn. Historical phenomena at last took on monumental form in creative arts and crafts. River valleys became the scenes of historical activity and vitality: along the banks of the Tigris and Euphrates, the Nile, the Indus, and the Hwang-ho.

In an ever-changing panorama, the unfolding drama of history draws upon the resources of geography, race, and epoch. Geography stands out as one great sweep of mainland. It stretches from the western shores of Europe and Africa to the farthest eastern coastlines of America, that is, from the European-African side of the Atlantic and back again. Within that environment, the uttermost reaches of north and south in Asia, Europe, Africa, and America witnessed at the dawn of history little development that was significant to the ancient spirit and mind. Instead displaced populations there displayed what man could improvise under pressure. For early civilization's fertile landscapes one must look elsewhere: to river valleys and Mediterranean shorelines, to ocean borders, archipelagos, plains, steppes, and the deserts.

History's supporting cast was made up of four races. Until fairly recent times, each race was restricted to its own habitation and that was a closed region as a rule. Intermingling and intermarriage did not occur on a large scale save at peripheral and transition points. Negroes, Mongols, Caucasians, and Amerinds, those were the four great racial groupings. Immigration from Asia into what we call the New World began at a rather recent age and followed a north-south route. Accordingly the Amerinds do not constitute a separate race but simply an offshoot from the Mongol, and the original races of mankind can only be three.

The epochs of history vary considerably in output and human ingenuity. They may be said to follow no predictable order. Time is erratic and in the occurrence of decisive moments it divulges little hint or indication of uniformity. Humanly viewed, phenomena such as cultural effervescences, golden ages, and political heydays, as well as religious enlightenments, come as they may and scarcely fit into any handy or neat pattern. In fact, the earliest spiritual awakenings of the world arose in three parallel though strictly independent centers of diffusion: China, India, and the West. The Western cluster represented an original bifurcation into a set of two polarized pulsations, the ancient Orient and occidental Greece.

Within the three orbits of ancient civilization, the sixth pre-Christian century was a time of unprecedented flowering. It set a high record of cultural growth and spiritual productivity. A radiant era, it was anticipated by no less than two centuries of preparation. It was followed by four more centuries of unabated glow. An epoch six hundred years in duration thus witnessed keener self-comprehension and more fabulous wealth of ideas than the world had ever known. It has been called an "axial period" (800–200 B.C.),[13] for in it so much of the intellectual and moral foundations of subsequent times was laid.

An idea of what was accomplished in this era, "the axis of world history,"[14] may be barely introduced. In China, Confucius and Lao-tse foreshadowed the fuller glow of philosophy and of contributions by such sages as Moti, Chuang-tse, and Lieh-tse. India produced the Upanishads and the Buddha, and like China, provided a groundwork for then unborn schools of philosophy ranging all the way from skepticism to nihilism. Iran sired Zarathustra. His world view, centered in the conflict between good and evil, was reflected in much of later religious history. Major and minor prophets arose in Judah and Israel. Heard were the elevating voices of Amos, Habakkuk, Micah, Elijah, Isaiah, Jeremiah, and Second Isaiah. Greece was immortalized by many: Homer, Herodotus, and the philosophers

[13] See above, p. 90.

[14] Karl Jaspers, *The Origin and Goal of History* (Yale University Press, 1953), p. 1.

Socrates, Plato, and Aristotle, as well as by the tragedians, also, Thucydides and Archimedes. Despite virtual isolation one from another, these three cradles nurtured men whose minds were stirred up as never before. Being as a whole and mortal limitations were in the foreground of consciousness. Face to face with the void, man began to prize freedom and sought more knowledge about himself.

On his arduous journey across the ages, opportunity came knocking on man's door four times and beckoned him to make a fresh start. The first was when in a Promethean epoch speech, tools, and fire made a genesis, though but faintly discernible to us, which must have revolutionized life and elevated man's visions. No one can properly gauge those early discoveries or define their role as a landmark of manhood. There was, secondly, the already mentioned "axial period" with its breath of fresh air and exciting challenge to mind and spirit. Thirdly, in the fullness of time, history was split and the Logos became flesh; a new yet ancient light shone in the darkness as that divine Figure bestowed life and immortality upon those who believed, and gave faith, hope, and love in a manner which the world has never forgotten. Fourthly, an epoch of dynamism in science, philosophy, and the arts began to unfold. The revelations of the modern world occurred when many of nature's hidden secrets were marvelously unlocked and technology wrought her astounding wonders.

[B] Such is the drama of history, but what of its meaning? The schema of history might support a historicism that defies faith and imprisons the spirit in earthbound concerns and idolatries.

It is at this point that we need to cast a glance at the various world views contending for a role in historical criticism. Discordant world views masquerade behind a variety of symbols. These symbols depict the origin, articulation, and goal that are the everlasting realm of the spirit. A diversity of cultural backgrounds, moreover, conditions the nature of world views. Wilhelm Dilthey[15] (1833–1911), the German philosopher of history, attributed such disparities in structure and type of world views to whether they spring from the religious, artistic, or metaphysical disposition. Religious world views, he conjectured, derive from man's unique life relationships. Within

[15] See William Kluback and Martin Weinbaum, *Dilthey's Philosophy of Existence* (Columbia University Press, 1957), pp. 31, *passim.*

a given religious relationship, he contended, tradition tends to take on an aura of power and to emerge as a determining factor in the organizations of religious life. Such a tradition in its multiple proliferations sets the norm for all further growth and development. In the earlier stages of a religion's history, the collective mind might conceivably exercise an active role. A religious genius could actually effect progress and introduce higher phases in mystery, rite, and interpretation: prophets might flourish. But a consolidated tradition puts an end to all that.

In order to resolve the riddle of an ingrown tradition, historicism might appeal to metaphysics — this in the hope of breaking the deadlock between history and faith in anticipation, one may infer, of a more rational world view. The word "metaphysics" suggests philosophical concern with being, an examination of causality in a spirit of openness to the possibility that a supersensible determination of reality exists. To such an intellectual orientation, the higher religions might lend initial support. Certainly the religious structures of China and India have not been immune or inimical to metaphysics.

Hinduism has evolved a monumental heritage of pantheistic speculation. Hindu reflection on the All-One together with Greek mystery and gnosis produced each its own peculiar brand of world outlook. From these beginnings in metaphysics the road led to the Neoplatonists, Spinoza, and Schopenhauer. Metaphysical reckoning with history and the problem of ultimacy owes something to Jewish, Christian, and Islamic thinkers. Theistic emphasis on metaphysics was brought under heavy debt by Descartes, Kant, and philosophers of the early nineteenth-century reactionary period. Yet a purely religious world view alive to a sacramental universe, to a world created by God and inhabited by men, whose souls bear the image of the Eternal, is practically irreducible to metaphysical categories. Religions thrive best on rite and faith, community fellowship, and association with the sacred and divine.

Historicism does not, however, totally rely on metaphysics in its rivalry with living faith. It can toll the knell of religion. That is precisely what Arnold Toynbee[16] did despite his well-known

[16] *An Historian's Approach to Religion* (Oxford University Press, London, 1956), p. 215.

enthusiasm for the creative role of religion in civilization. "As the traditional ecumenical institutions of Western Christendom were liquidated or rejected, one after another, a post-Christian Western society began to feel the painfulness and dangerousness of the vacuum," he declared, "and it deliberately set itself to fill the gap with new ecumenical institutions of its own creation."

How historicism tries to seize the initiative is seen from one of the normative assumptions underlying its study methods. Essentially this consists in the contention that the methods of natural science do not apply to the study of human society and culture. Since the latter constitutes a different range of subjects, they do call for special treatment and analysis.[17] Rather than uphold the typical enlightenment belief in a natural law of causation Wilhelm Dilthey[18] argued that the free will of the individual, a unique national heritage, and the specific historical situation afford an adequate explanation of human affairs.

Historicism took as its starting point the unalterable necessity of establishing the facts in a given case. Leopold von Ranke (1795–1886), historian of Europe and the popes, stipulated that the foundation of historical knowledge rested in the first instance upon accuracy in investigating the facts in their proper setting. A second requirement of historical investigation related to individuals and their impress upon the course of history.

The role of individuals in the shaping of history may be illustrated from von Ranke's own treatment of two key figures of whom the first was involved in the Diet of Worms in 1495. These were Emperor Maximilian I and Pope Pius V. Of Maximilian I, the historian wrote that the emperor's restless energy was spent in securing and enlarging the Hapsburg family domain; von Ranke spoke of the emperor's shrewdness and secretiveness in the pursuit of such plans, and of his ire when he believed his schemes had been discovered. The characterization of Pope Pius V is in a similar if more incisive vein. "Such a pious man, naïve as a child, and yet the strictest inquisitor and persecutor of the Protestants," writes von Ranke, "who, as re-

[17] Joachim Wach, *Das Verstehen: Grundzüge einer Geschichte der hermeneutischen Theorie im 19 Jahrhundert,* 3 vols. (Mohr, Tübingen, 1926–1929), Vol. I, p. 187.

[18] *Gesammelte Schriften,* 12 vols. (B. G. Teubner, Leipzig and Berlin, 1914–1936), Vol. III, p. 145.

gards the essence of his convictions, so closely agreed with them. That shows how much man is subject to error, how weak morally, a fool — and in his weakness great, at times noble even when he is most repulsive." [19]

With a remarkable consistency historicism betrays, whether facts are established or personalities characterized, a strong penchant for a natural interpretation of historical happenings and phenomena. Inferentially at least, it pronounces living faith dead and proposes a moratorium on the apocalyptic character of history.

At a third level of investigation, historicism probes the influence of leading ideas.[20] By empirical study, an understanding of creative ideas and their concrete manifestations in large scale movements is sought. Ideas are thus held to exert a formative influence on persons, nations, epochs, and works of art. Although free to act as he desires, man is at the same time subject to the impact of ideas. The superior forces of ideas are ever ready to show the individual and the group what his and their proper place and role are in universal history. Thus in commenting on the end of Pope Paul III (pontiff, 1534–1549), von Ranke said: "How impotent, how insignificant does even the most exalted of mortals appear when placed in contrast with the grand and ceaseless course of events. . . . He departs, but the destinies of humanity make no pause; they move on to their completion." [21]

German culture itself sheds light on the part played by historicism. As an example, we might mention the nineteenth-century phenomenon of Volksgeist, the idea of the nation and its organic growth.[22] The jurist Friedrich von Savigny (1779–1861) and his school propounded the theory that the intelligible social unit was not a group of people who made a contract but rather that group which had grown up historically and which had evolved the same cultural traditions, laws, and ideals. Barthold Niebuhr (1776–1831) had created a new national history of Rome. Philipp Bockh (1785–1867), philologist and antiquary, showed the unity of life in ancient Greece.

[19] Theodore H. Von Laue, *Leopold Ranke: The Formative Years* (Princeton University Press, 1950), p. 134.

[20] William Kluback, *Wilhelm Dilthey's Philosophy of History* (Columbia University Press, 1956), pp. 232 ff.

[21] Von Laue, *op. cit.*, p. 136.

[22] Kluback, *op. cit.*, p. 24.

Leopold von Ranke maintained that the spirit of each nation determined the course of its juridical and international involvement. Meanwhile the acute philologist Jacob Grimm (1785–1863) projected a comprehensive outline of life in German antiquity. His methodology was utilized by Wilhelm Dilthey, who otherwise espoused the viewpoint of the Heidelberg and Prussian schools, namely, that history was the educator of national morale. It is to Dilthey's credit, moreover, that he proclaimed the independence of the spiritual sciences as distinct from the natural.

What a formidable rivalry to living faith had thus been effected by a historicism that tended to jam the voice of religion and offer for perennial mysteries answers of its own making.

V

A fifth and last rivalry, communism, shares certain features with the other four. It offers an optional dynamism and operates against religion on the basis of an outright repudiation. It comes to the forefront in a Marxist ideology, realized in an evolving social structure. It stiffens by way of a radical cultural rejection of traditional faith.

In our fraction of the millennium an ordeal of force seems irrevocably to favor unbelievers or rather antibelievers. Totalitarian states, Hitler's once and more intently the Soviet, have waged war against organized religion, particularly Christianity. This is not the kind of terror that makes martyrs. Rather, it is a choking of spiritual life that leaves youth defenseless. A state thus claiming the right to govern the totality of human existence constitutes a church, atheist undoubtedly, nevertheless a church.[23]

A critical situation is thereby created for Christian churches regardless of creed or structure. Attuned to relative separation between the temporal authority and the spiritual, these churches have ordinarily more to hope for under a liberal political regime. Christians have survived through fire and sword, but that is not an experience to be coveted. Those under Communist tyranny might see deliverance in the eventual collapse of that totalitarian order. How well aware one must remain, however, that the great technological and demographic movements of our time have not generally fostered liberalism.

[23] Joseph Wilbois, in Brillant and Aigrain, *Histoire des Religions,* Vol. I, p. 81.

Focal issues are pending. It would seem that Slavic atheism cares less for religious matters than emotional. If its concern for human welfare is nothing short of natural, its response to overtures of love, extended by a concerned world Christianity, may not be lacking. Where totalitarianism bars interference by an ecclesiastical supranationalism, it might permit a national church loosely federated with an international religious organization. This hope is realized as Russian Orthodoxy participates in the World Council of Churches. The road ahead is not altogether blocked. But for the church of Christ there is no substitute for the way of the cross.

How do we track down such an authoritarianism and what of its wedlock with atheism? Precisely in what historical setting did its repudiation of religion materialize? Marx and Engels spelled out in *The Communist Manifesto* [24] their considered judgment on the Christian religion. " When the classical world was in its decline, the old religions were conquered by Christianity," they observed. They further remarked that " when Christian ideas were put to flight by eighteenth-century rationalism, it was at the time when feudal society was fighting for very existence against the bourgeoisie, which was then the revolutionary class. The abstract ideas termed ' freedom of conscience ' and ' religious liberty ' were but the expression of the supremacy of free competition within the realm of knowledge." So Christianity was an interim movement, an ally of the middle class, and an enemy of reason.

Karl Marx (1818–1883) is conveniently designated a primary exponent of such an attack on living faith. Prof. Sidney Hook [25] has shown, however, that in 1841–1844, crucial in Marx's career, he was a follower of the sensationalist German philosopher Ludwig Feuerbach [26] (1804–1872). It was from the latter, we are reminded, that Marx derived that " real humanism " on which he wrote *Die heilige Familie*.

Like Feuerbach, Karl Marx called for a reconstructed philosophy as a method of approaching man's practical problems. Like him, he

[24] Alfred Zimmern, *Modern Political Doctrines* (Oxford University Press, London, 1939), p. 72.

[25] *From Hegel to Marx: Studies in Karl Marx* (Humanities Press, Inc., 1950), pp. 272–293.

[26] See Foreword by H. Richard Niebuhr, in Ludwig Feuerbach, *The Essence of Christianity,* tr. by George Eliot (Marian Evans) (Harper & Brothers, 1957), pp. vii–ix.

regarded human beings in their empirical, social contexts as carriers of the social process. Also like him, he explained the false traditional concepts of the world in terms of a fetish, an expression of activities unconsciously engaged in at different times and places. What distinguishes Marx from Feuerbach is his historical approach and concrete analysis of those factors of social life which in Feuerbach appear only as abstractions.

As an illustration of the break with living faith championed by Marx and bequeathed to his successors, further comparison with Feuerbach might prove suggestive. Where Feuerbach claimed he discovered the secret of theology in anthropology, Marx sought to transform anthropology into realistic sociology. Feuerbach tried to prove the religious world illusory; Marx inquired instead, "How does it come about that the illusions arise?"[27]

Neither Marx nor any of his orthodox followers worked out a detailed analysis of the great religions from the standpoint of dialectical materialism. That task was left to such men as the German Social Democratic leader and author, Eduard Bernstein (1850–1932), the sociologist Max Weber (1846–1920), and the English economist Richard Henry Tawney[28] (1880–). Along with others, these endeavored to uncover the social contradictions that they thought were detectable at the basis of religious constructions. Unfortunately, none of them was specially equipped to undertake investigations along religious lines.

"Religion is the opium of the people"—that casual sentence of Marx, dating from 1843 and his association with Feuerbach, has been considered revelatory of his philosophy of religion. Upon the mind of friend and foe the words have indeed had the effect of a narcotic. Those have been words repeated by many who believed them an aphorism of what Marx had to say on the subject.

If religion were the opium of the people, a necessary precondition to all criticism would be the awakening of the people from drugged lethargy. That was precisely the position Marx criticized. When he argued against men such as Bruno Bauer (1809–1882), theologian

[27] Karl Marx and Friedrich Engels, *Historisch-kritische Gesamtausgabe* (Marx-Engels Archiv, Frankfurt, 1927), Vol. I, Bd. 5, p. 215.

[28] See his *Religion and the Rise of Capitalism* (A Mentor Book, The New American Library, 1926).

and Biblical critic, and Max Stirner (1806–1856), the individualist, as well as against Feuerbach, his position was clear. He held that political and social movements of the working class must not be explicitly or programmatically antireligious. According to him, the working-class movement must be directed in the first instance against the environment and its decadence which breeds religion. It is there, he thought, that social antagonisms were eased through the social opium dispensed by the ruling classes which control the means of production, education, and communication.

Marx did provoke, however, an open repudiation of religion. His *Das Kapital* has exercised an incalculable influence comparable to that of the New Testament or the Koran, or of Newton's *Principia*. Virtually all modern socialist and Communist thought is directly based on Marxism. Though primarily an economic, political doctrine, Marxism is the result of a method, dialectical materialism. This is applicable to any problem of human thought. In its fullest application it probably has had a wider impact on the development of society than any other doctrine since the advent of Islam.

Nowhere was the hostility of Marx to religion more clearly set forth than in his formulation of a new philosophy of history.[29] "The standpoint with which one satisfies himself in such histories of the spirit," he wrote, "is itself religious, for in it one is content to stop short with Religion, to conceive Religion as a cause of itself. This is done instead of explaining religion in terms of material conditions; showing how certain determinate industrial and commercial relations are necessarily bound up with certain social forms, how these are themselves bound up with certain forms of the state and therewith with a certain form of religious consciousness."[30]

Marxism is not simply Leninism or Stalinism or Marxism after Marx. It covers all these and more. At the deepest level, as Paul Tillich[31] has expressed it, it is the genuine impulses in the thought and action of Karl Marx himself. If opposition between Marxism and religion, however, is read into the titanic struggle between Communist Russia and the Western world, then what Marx posited about the origin of religion might not prove so false.

[29] See Hook, *op. cit.*, p. 180.

[30] Marx and Engels, *op. cit.*, Vol. I, Bd. 5, pp. 134–135.

[31] *Theology of Culture* (Oxford University Press, London, 1959), p. 183.

The contemporary phenomenon of communism represents an adaptation of Marxism, interwoven with the indigenous Russian revolutionary movement.[32] Such an adaptation involves the Marxist philosophy of history and the theory of society — historical materialism and the class struggle — as well as the vision of a worldwide proletarian revolution.

However, communism is not a monolith. It is a spectrum.[33] At one end of the spectrum lies China — messianic, austere, deeply fanatic. At the other end, are Poland and Yugoslavia — countries whose species of communism generally confound the Western observer. In between lies the U.S.S.R., the most powerful Communist nation — a singular mixture of excessive confidence and insecurity.

The essential drive of Communism continues to be inimical to all religion. Engels, following Hegel, defined freedom as "the recognition of necessity." Although the status of the churches in the Soviet Union is shrouded in ambiguity, religion does persist, the vitality of Russian Christianity is real. A new "Communist Manifesto," issued in October, 1961, indicated the degree of change effected.[34] The document spoke of the transformation of capitalism into socialism, and of the building of Communism on a world scale. It maintained, nevertheless, that peaceful coexistence is the basis for competition between socialism and capitalism.

[32] F. Ernest Johnson, *A Vital Encounter: Christianity and Communism* (Abingdon Press, 1962), pp. 36, 40–41, 110, 114.

[33] Arthur Schlesinger, Jr., "The Many Faces of Communism," in *Harper's Magazine* (Jan., 1960), p. 52.

[34] Cf. "Text of the Soviet Party's Draft Program," in *The New York Times* (Aug. 1, 1961).

POSTSCRIPT

ONLY TIME will tell whether conclusions surmised in this investigation are sound and realistic. A century has now elapsed since the structure of religious societies came under scientific study from several angles. It was a study conducted with whatever dexterity and precision philosophers, philologists, and historians could muster. Thanks to such pioneer efforts, the structures of Christianity and the other religions of the world are more readily perceived.

The causes behind the expansion of such faiths are significantly clarified. The cultural factors that underlie retreat and decline are also ascertained. The roles of politics, economics, geography, and societal change lead to deeper insights. The outcomes of contact and interaction are easier to detect.

An attempt was thus made at more rational classification and elucidation of religious types. Occasionally, a pattern of successive phenomena suggested the possibility of a sequence where frequent occurrences indicated constancy. The balanced outlook of Wilhelm Dilthey on systems of culture stimulated vigorous historical criticism of religious societies and their foundations.

As in other departments of scholarship, criteria and statistics are taken seriously, but not without a degree of reserve verging on caution. Cause and effect come under a discriminatory glance. Abandonment of formerly held positions unalterably draws false alarms. Let it. What a small price for precious certainty: that the mind need not surrender to capricious judgments which once made cannot be altered.

It is a healthy thing, moreover, that foundations should shake:

for instance, when the door is left open to interaction between the two orders of society, the secular and the religious. As elsewhere in the humanities, personality needs to be assured its right to freedom and conviction.

I

The foregoing chapters culminate in an awareness: epistemology raises no insuperable obstacle to study of religion as a phenomenon. Nor does it reject a sociology that approaches religion as a whole. Religious sociology indeed is a science normally constituted and full of promise. Yet one must hasten to remind himself that this sociology is still in its infancy. Many a problem has not as yet been fully probed. Methods require further testing. Verdicts await experimentation which is either in progress or not yet begun. Highly commendable, at any rate, is the exciting nature of a science that does not begin from a partisan contention. It is commendable because it does not hesitate to render honest service but tends to strengthen men of action and adds to dedication a new dimension.

Nothing is illusory that offered diverse religions a solid design for self-knowledge. Nor is it an unfounded fantasy to effect better articulation of religious faith. In its three classical traditions, Christianity stands in need of better visible organization. Orthodoxy, Catholicism, and Protestantism have by no means exhausted possibilities of methodology and strategy. Improvements are desirable even in areas such as those of administration and liturgy. As for missionary statecraft, it is ever in need of radical reform and rethinking.

Such a religious sociology undoubtedly elicits suspicion. In certain quarters, distressed supernaturalists, disturbed clergy, and highly imaginative individualists might register a vote of no confidence. A polite polemic against social studies might be intensified into a violent outburst against religious sociology. Recognition that findings in the truth can pose no substantial threat will dissipate such qualms. Whether in Christianity, Islam, or any other religion, sociology unveils the contours of new knowledge. Its results are based on observation and objectivity. They open new frontiers and offer religion an opportunity to deepen faith and communicate witness more meaningfully.

Governments have demonstrated a readiness to utilize the services of religious sociology. Foreign and national policies are rendered more effective when the scope of religious forces in society is taken into account, as for instance in North Africa where the problem of coexistence between Muslims and Christians arises. Such a religious sociology is not, however, the one and only source of knowledge available to a state. An alert political party or government is ever in intimate touch with the diverse segments of society. How unavoidably true that is in a democracy. Contact is maintained with religious bodies and institutions as well as with officials and representatives. Tradition and necessity ordain such a common practice.

II

This volume applauds the effort toward better communication and cooperation among world religions. Hope for the success of such an effort rests less in sociology and more in religious vitality. There are in different parts of the world social architects intent upon a common goal. Certain of these find their lot cast in organizations of their own religious communities. Their primary commitment is naturally formed under the cause to which they belong.

Other social architects are concerned with a broader range and outlook. With or without confessional presuppositions, they tend to envisage the sociology of religion in its overall character. With serenity and dedication they compare structures of faith and orders of organization. Transcending a personal attachment to this or that religion, they seek better comprehension. They may happen to be Hindus or Buddhists, Muslims, Jews, or Christians. Yet in sociology, they find an avenue to deeper understanding of other faiths even though their personal loyalty might be to one or none.

Hence, on the one hand, there is a religious sociology pursued from a denominational confessional background and intention. It presupposes adherence to one faith in all strictness. On the other, there is a sociology inspired by scientific curiosity and concerned to encompass the various faiths. In both categories, the common goal of social architects is integrity in examination of all data, a relentless appraisal of the phenomenon of religion. Of course there are certain sociologists of religion who simultaneously belong to the two schools.

What in the upshot gains favor is a disposition toward tolerance, possibly a meeting of minds. From a fellowship of learning, little less than dialogue is expected. Also some restraint on the excesses of diversity is hoped for. This tends to temper a far-reaching variability, product of discordant notes and settings.

III

A consistent and well-defined terminology delivers thought from many a pitfall. Awaiting precise definition is a vast repertoire of criteria, yardsticks, methodologies, and patterns. Scholars have not been unmindful of religious types. The three orders of primitive, folk, and world (or universal) religions are tolerably well explored and classified. Relatively small in personnel is the cadre of competent scholars in positions of responsibility capable of dealing with this colossal body of knowledge.

Those are the comparative specialists. According to the caliber of their versatility, they are occupied in study of structures. With unremitting effort, they endeavor to gauge religious forces in a given situation. Only such a comparative religion, concordant with modern thought, is adequate to cooperate fruitfully with religious sociology. Semantics and terminology figure at the core of such a comparative approach. Serious reflection on the essence of religion is inescapable.

It is a safe assumption that the relation of one religion to another hinges on such an essence as well as on the relation of religion to sociology. When we try to learn how a living religion adds up, when we seek to discover the particular genius of a given faith, we are inevitably thrown back upon a basic question: How are all religions interlinked, if they are, at their deepest essence?

From the very beginning of our inquiry we have been confronted with the problem of religious essence. In the science of religion, the conceptional determination of religion has received many formulations. These do not need to detain us here. In such formulations and determinations the disposition and bent of a given outlook tends to play a role more effective than the object defined.

When Kant, for example, defined religion as recognition of all our duties as divine commandments, he disclosed the bent of his own mind. His views on the subject were not so much on the essence of religion as they were on an entirely different and more personal problem: that is, on Kant's own rationalist philosophy, and his views on religion as an entirely moral theonomy.

We may in like manner understand Schleiermacher, conqueror of the Enlightenment. He came closer, however, to the generic essence of religion. He perceived religion neither in thought nor in action. Instead it was an intuition and feeling for the universe. He duly coined a celebrated definition of religion as "the feeling of absolute dependence."

IV

When we consider the dialectical theology of Karl Barth, we find a position steeped in the Scriptural principle of the Reformers. Barth has propounded a profound absolutist Christian theology. Whereas much of this doctrinal emphasis is sound and invigorating, it leaves out an important facet. Barth is apparently reluctant to take stock of one thing vital to the theme of this book: the crisis precipitated by the fact of world religions.

For any definition must prove inadequate that condemns the religions of mankind right out of hand. Any theology is deficient at the core that regards the religions as man's wasted effort and lets the matter go at that. To fail in discovering any truth whatever outside Christianity is a theological blind spot that cries out for a remedy.

There is a minimal requirement instituted by the science of religion. Without it, little service can be rendered in this field. This is a requirement which maintains that within the confines of all high religions a certain wrestling with the idea of the holy does occur.

Indeed such a significance attaches to all phenomena here brought under critical review. Beyond all varieties of religious experience, there is a revulsion against what is a merely abstract conception of the holy. Hence the essential characteristic of all religious phenomena: an experience of an encounter with the holy, and correspondingly a response from the holy received in faith.

Such a conclusion is unthinkable unless a similar approach is made to all religious phenomena. This is the crux of a comparative religion geared to the historical and behavioral method of study and evaluation. Hence an expanding horizon of our faith illumined by the phenomenon of religion as it touches man's total existence.

INDEX